Associations and Democracy

The Real Utopias Project

Series editor: Erik Olin Wright

The Real Utopias Project embraces a tension between dreams and practice. It is founded on the belief that what is pragmatically possible is not fixed independently of our imaginations, but is itself shaped by our visions. The fulfillment of such a belief involves 'real utopias': utopian ideals that are grounded in the real potentials for redesigning social institutions.

In its attempt at sustaining and deepening serious discussion of radical alternatives to existing social practices, the Real Utopias Project examines various basic institutions – property rights and the market, secondary associations, the family, the welfare state, among others – and focuses on specific proposals for their fundamental redesign. The books in the series are the result of workshop conferences, at which groups of scholars are invited to respond to provocative manuscripts.

Associations and Democracy

The Real Utopias Project
Volume I

◆

JOSHUA COHEN and JOEL ROGERS

with contributions by

Paul Q. Hirst, Ellen M. Immergut,
Ira Katznelson, Heinz Klug, Andrew Levine,
Jane Mansbridge, Claus Offe,
Philippe C. Schmitter, Wolfgang Streeck,
Andrew Szasz, Iris Marion Young

Edited by Erik Olin Wright

VERSO

London • New York

First published by Verso 1995
© this collection Verso 1995
© in individual contributions the contributors
All rights reserved

Verso
UK: 6 Meard Street, London W1V 3HR
USA: 180 Varick Street, New York NY 10014–4606

Verso is the imprint of New Left Books

ISBN 1–85984–928–8
ISBN 1–85984–048–5 (pbk)

British Library Cataloguing in Publication Data
A catalogue record for this book is available from the British Library

Library of Congress Cataloging-in-Publication Data
Associations and democracy / edited by Joshua Cohen and Joel Rogers.
p.   cm. — (The Real Utopias Project ; v. 1)
Edited papers from a conference held at the Havens Center for the Study of Social
Structure and Social Change, University of Wisconsin, in January 1992, as part of
the Real Utopias Project.
Includes bibliographical references and index.
ISBN 1–85984–928–8 (hbk.). — ISBN 1–85984–048–5 (pbk.)
1. Democracy—Congresses. 2. Associations, institutions, etc.—Congresses.
3. Voluntarism—Congresses. I. Cohen, Joshua, 1951– . II. Rogers, Joel, 1952– .
III. A.E. Havens Center for the Study of Social Structure and Social Change.
IV. Real Utopias Project. V. Series: Real Utopias Project (Series) ; v. 1.
JC423.A817 1995
321.8—dc20   95–31510
CIP

Typeset by Keystroke, Jacaranda Lodge, Wolverhampton
Printed in Great Britain by Biddles Ltd, Guildford and King's Lynn

Contents

CONTENTS

Acknowledgments

We would gratefully like to thank the Wisconsin Alumni Research Foundation and the Anonymous Fund of the University of Wisconsin for providing generous funding for the conference that led to this volume. We would also like to thank the A. E. Havens Center for covering many of the incidental costs involved in turning the conference papers into a book and the staff of the Center for making the practical arrangements for the conference.

A number of the papers included in this volume were previously published in a special issue of *Politics and Society*, © Sage Publications, Inc. 1992, and are reproduced here with permission. They are:

Chapter 1: Joshua Cohen and Joel Rogers, 'Secondary Associations and Democratic Governance', *Politics and Society* 20 (4) (December 1992), pp. 393–472.

Chapter 4: Jane Mansbridge, 'A Deliberative Perspective on Neocorporatism', ibid., pp. 493–505.

Chapter 5: Andrew Szasz, 'Progress through Mischief: The Social Movement Alternative to Secondary Associations', ibid., pp. 521–8.

Chapter 8: Wolfgang Streeck, 'Inclusion and Secession: Questions on the Boundaries of Associative Democracy', ibid., pp. 513–20.

Chapter 10: Ellen M. Immergut, 'An Institutional Critique of Associative Democracy', ibid., pp. 481–6.

Chapter 11: Iris Marion Young, 'Social Groups in Associative Democracy', ibid., pp. 529–34.

Preface
The Real Utopias Project
Erik Olin Wright

'Real Utopias' seems like a contradiction in terms. Utopias are fantasies, morally inspired designs for social life unconstrained by realistic considerations of human psychology and social feasibility. Realists eschew such fantasies. What is needed are hard-nosed proposals for pragmatically improving our institutions. Instead of indulging in utopian dreams we must accommodate to practical realities.

The Real Utopias Project embraces this tension between dreams and practice. It is founded on the belief that what is pragmatically possible is not fixed independently of our imaginations, but is itself shaped by our visions. Self-fulfilling prophecies are powerful forces in history, and while it may be Polyannaish to say 'Where there is a will there is a way', it is certainly true that without 'will' many 'ways' become impossible. Nurturing clear-sighted understandings of what it would take to create social institutions free of oppression is part of creating a political will for radical social changes to reduce oppression. A vital belief in a utopian ideal may be necessary to motivate people to leave on the journey from the status quo in the first place, even though the most likely destination may fall short of the utopian ideal. Yet, vague utopian fantasies may lead us astray, encouraging us to embark on trips that have no real destinations at all, or worse still, that lead us toward an unforeseen abyss. Along with 'where there is a will there is a way', the human struggle for emancipation confronts 'the road to hell is paved with good intentions'. What we need, then, are 'real utopias': utopian ideals that are grounded in the real potentials of humanity, utopian destinations that have accessible waystations, utopian designs of institutions which can inform our practical tasks of muddling through in a world of imperfect conditions for social change. These are the goals of the Real Utopias Project.

The idea that social institutions can be rationally transformed in ways that enhance human well-being and happiness has a long and controversial history. On the one hand, radicals of diverse stripes have argued that social arrangements inherited from the past are not immutable facts of nature, but transformable human creations. Social institutions can be designed in ways that eliminate forms of oppression that thwart human aspirations for fulfilling and meaningful lives. The central task of emancipatory politics is to create such institutions. On the other hand, conservatives have generally argued that grand designs for social reconstruction are nearly always disasters. While contemporary social institutions may be far from perfect, they are generally serviceable. At least, it is argued, they provide the minimal conditions for social order and stable interactions. These institutions have evolved through a process of slow, incremental modification as people adapt social rules and practices to changing circumstances. The process is driven by trial and error much more than by conscious design, and by and large those institutions that have endured have done so because they have enduring virtues. This does not preclude institutional change, even deliberate institutional change, but it means that such change should be piecemeal, not a wholesale rupture with existing arrangements.

At the heart of these various perspectives is a disagreement about the relationship between the intended and unintended consequences of deliberate efforts at social change. The conservative critique of radical projects is not mainly that the emancipatory goals of radicals are morally indefensible – although some conservatives criticize the underlying values of such projects as well – but that the uncontrollable, and usually negative, unintended consequences of these efforts at massive social change inevitably swamp the intended consequences. Radicals and revolutionaries suffer from what Frederick Hayek termed the 'fatal conceit' – the belief that through rational calculation and political will, society can be designed in ways that will significantly improve the human condition. Incremental tinkering may not be inspiring, but it is the best we can do.

Of course, one can point out that many reforms favored by conservatives also have massive, destructive, unintended consequences. The havoc created in many poor countries by World Bank structural adjustment programs is such an example. And furthermore, under certain circumstances, conservatives themselves argue for radical, society-wide projects of institutional design, as in the proposals for 'shock therapy' as a way of transforming command economies into free-market capitalism. Nevertheless, there is a certain apparent plausibility to the general claim made by conservatives that the bigger the scale and scope of conscious projects of social change, the less likely it is that we shall be able to predict ahead of time all the ramifications of those changes.

Radicals on the Left have generally rejected this pessimistic vision of human possibility. Particularly in the Marxist tradition, radical intellectuals have insisted that wholesale redesign of social institutions is within our grasp. This does not mean, as Marx emphasized, that detailed institutional 'blueprints' can be devised in advance of the opportunity to create an alternative. What can be worked out are the core organizing principles of alternatives to existing institutions, the principles that would guide the pragmatic trial-and-error task of institution-building. Of course, there will be unintended consequences of various sorts, but these can be dealt with as they arrive, 'after the revolution'. The crucial point is that unintended consequences need not pose a fatal threat to the emancipatory projects themselves.

Regardless of which of these stances seems more plausible, the *belief* in the possibility of radical alternatives to existing institutions has played an important role in contemporary political life. A good argument can be made that the political space for social democratic reforms was, at least in part, opened up because more radical ruptures with capitalism were seen as possible, and that possibility in turn depended crucially on many people believing that radical ruptures were workable. The belief in the viability of revolutionary socialism, especially when backed by the grand historical experiments in the USSR and elsewhere, enhanced the viability of reformist social democracy as a form of class compromise. The political conditions for progressive tinkering with social arrangements, therefore, may depend in significant ways on the presence of more radical visions of possible transformations. This does not mean, of course, that false beliefs are to be supported simply because they are thought to have desirable consequences, but it does suggest that it is important to seek firm foundations for plausible visions of radical alternatives.

We now live in a world in which these radical visions are mocked rather than taken seriously. Along with the postmodernist rejection of 'grand narratives', there is an ideological rejection of grand designs, even by those still on the left of the political spectrum. This need not mean an abandonment of deeply egalitarian emancipatory values, but it does reflect a cynicism about the human capacity to realize those values on a substantial scale. This cynicism, in turn, weakens progressive political forces in general.

The Real Utopias Project is an attempt at countering this cynicism by sustaining and deepening serious discussion of radical alternatives to existing institutions. The objective is to focus on specific proposals for the fundamental redesign of basic social institutions rather than on either general, abstract formulations of grand designs, or on small reforms of existing practices. This is a tricky kind of discussion to pursue rigorously. It is much easier to talk about concrete ways of tinkering with existing arrangements than it is to formulate plausible radical reconstructions. Marx was right that detailed blueprints of alternative designs are often futile exercises in fantasy. What we want to achieve is a clear elaboration of the *institutional principles* that inform radical alternatives to the existing world. This falls between a general discussion of the moral values that motivate the enterprise and the fine-grained details of institutional characteristics.

In practical terms, the Real Utopias Project is built around a series of workshop conferences sponsored by the A. E. Havens Center for the Study of Social Structure and Social Change at the University of Wisconsin. The general format of these conferences consists of selecting a provocative manuscript which lays out the basic outlines of a radical institutional proposal and then inviting fifteen to twenty scholars to write essays which in one way or another address this paper. These essays have ranged from short, point-by-point critiques of specific arguments to longer papers developing one or more of the themes of the focal manuscript. The papers are then circulated to all participants well in advance of the conference so that the discussions of each paper are informed by the arguments raised by the entire group. After the workshop, participants have an opportunity to revise their papers before they are published as a collection in the Real Utopias Project series. All royalties from the Real Utopias Project books go into a fund to support future conferences and books.

As of 1994, three conferences have been organized on this format:

1. *Basic Income Grants* (1991), organized around a manuscript by Philippe van Parijs. This conference explored the proposal that all income transfer programs of the welfare state be replaced by a simple, universal, unconditional income grant system. The papers from this conference were not published as a collection, although the themes are presented in a volume edited by van Parijs under the title *Arguing for Basic Income*, Verso, London 1993.

2. *Secondary Associations and Democratic Governance* (1992), organized around a manuscript by Joshua Cohen and Joel Rogers. The central issue of discussion was the potential for enhancing both the effectiveness and the democracy of democratic capitalism by institutionalizing a pervasive governance role for nonstate, quasi-voluntary

secondary associations. Some of the papers from this conference were published in a special issue of *Politics & Society* (December 1992). The entire set of papers appears as the first volume of Verso's Real Utopias Project series.

3. *Rethinking Socialism* (1994), organized around John Roemer's book, *A Future for Socialism*, Harvard University Press, Cambridge, MA 1994. This conference explored Roemer's proposal to create a form of market socialism in which there were two kinds of money – dollars for the purchase of commodities and coupons for the purchase of shares in firms. The core of the proposal is that (a) these coupons initially are equally distributed to all adults and then used to buy shares, which are subsequently traded on a coupon-share market; (b) coupons cannot be sold for dollars, so that dollar wealth cannot be converted into coupon wealth, and coupon wealth cannot be directly converted into dollar wealth; and (c) share ownership, denominated in coupon values, gives people property rights in the dollar profits of firms in the form of dividends. A subset of the papers appears in *Politics & Society* (December 1994), and the entire set as the second volume of Verso's Real Utopias Project series.

The specific plans for future conferences and volumes in the Real Utopias Project will depend in significant ways on the availability of the critical, focal manuscripts on specific topics. Currently we would like to organize future conferences on the following general themes:

1. *Efficient Redistribution in Advanced Capitalism.* This conference will be based on an essay written by Sam Bowles and Herb Gintis, which argues that in order to revitalize an economic strategy on the Left, the Left needs to focus on the redistribution of a wide variety of assets rather than on state provision of services and redistribution of income. Such asset-based redistribution, they argue, can form the core of a politics of decentralized, enhanced democratic reforms. Such an approach requires dropping the traditional left-wing aversion to using the market and institutions of private property in the service of democracy.

2. *Reconstructing Gender and the Family.* Feminist theoretical discussions generally have not systematically engaged the problem of institutional design for realizing emancipatory values. At this conference we hope to explore the range of institutional proposals that have been formulated by different traditions of feminism and subject them to the same kind of scrutiny accorded proposals for feasible socialism.

3. *Institutions for a Sustainable Environment.* Radical environmental discussions typically focus on how people should behave and on what norms should govern human engagement with the environment, but not on the institutional designs which would encourage such behavior or sustain such norms. However, the environmental movement, just as much as the movement for radical democracy and economic equality, needs an understanding of how institutions would have to be organized in order to accomplish a sustainable environment.

4. *Redesigning the Welfare State.* This conference would return to the issues explored in the earlier conference on basic income, but expand its institutional scope by including discussion of other issues in a reconstructed, progressive welfare state.

5. *Institutions for Global Equality.* This conference would examine the kinds of international trade and investment institutions that could function practically to reduce global inequality. This would be a kind of radical design alternative to such arrangements as GATT and NAFTA.

6. *Reconstructing Universalism in a World of Fragmented Identities.* Classical Marxism, following themes of the Enlightenment, argued that the working class embodied the universal interests of humanity. Ultimately, then, the identity of the working class was not just another particularism, but the core of a universal, human identity. Postmodernists argue that identities are irredeemably fragmented and plural. There are no privileged agents of history, no privileged identities. All there is are particularisms, which are historically articulated in specific ways. We would like to hold a conference that poses the problem of the institutional conditions for renewing more universalistic identities, since some kind of universalism arguably is critical for egalitarian, emancipatory politics.

Introduction
Erik Olin Wright

Few issues occupy a more central place on the political agenda around the world than democracy. In Latin America, military dictatorships have abandoned the direct levers of power in favor of more or less open, liberal democratic regimes. In South Africa, the anti-democratic apparatuses of apartheid have been replaced. In Eastern Europe and the former Soviet Union, Communist regimes have collapsed, to be replaced with the conventional institutions of democratic representation. And while democratic breakthroughs still seem remote in some parts of the world – in China, in the Middle East, in much of Africa – it is clear that in most of these places pressures for democratic politics are likely to increase in years to come.

This upsurge in democratic impulses in those parts of the world in which democratic institutions have previously either been absent or crippled has not been matched by impulses for a revitalization of democratic forms in the developed, capitalist democracies. Throughout the West the past decade has witnessed an erosion of belief in the capacity of democratic institutions to intervene effectively in shaping social and economic life and help solve our most pressing problems. A common refrain is that government is part of the problem, not the solution. Rather than seeking to deepen the democratic character of politics, the thrust of much political energy in the developed industrial democracies in recent years has been to reduce the role of politics altogether. Deregulation, privatization, reduction of social services, curtailments of state spending – these have been the watchwords, rather than participation, greater responsiveness and more creative and effective forms of democratic state intervention.

In the context of these global political developments, rethinking a wide range of questions about democratic institutions is a matter of urgency. This is as important for the future of those countries embarking on the transition to democracy as it is for those countries with established democratic institutions. In particular it is important to rethink the problem of the institutional forms through which democratic ideals are realized. As the tasks of the state become more complex and the size of polities larger, the institutional forms of liberal democracy developed in the nineteenth century seem increasingly ill-suited to the novel problems we face in the twenty-first century. 'Democracy' as a way of organizing the state has come to be narrowly identified with territorially-based competitive elections of political leadership for legislative and executive office. Yet increasingly, this mechanism of political representation seems ineffective in accomplishing the central ideals of democratic politics: active political involvement of the citizenry, forging political consensus through dialogue, participation, responsiveness to changing needs, and effective forms of state policies.

Perhaps this erosion of democratic vitality is an inevitable result of complexity and size. Perhaps the most we can hope for is to have some kind of limited popular constraint on the activities of government through regular, weakly competitive elections. Perhaps the era of the 'affirmative democratic state' – the state that plays a creative and active role in solving problems in response to popular demands – is at an end, and a retreat to privatism and political passivity is unavoidable. But perhaps the problem has more to do with the specific design of our political institutions than with the tasks they face as such.

This book revolves around a specific institutional proposal elaborated by Joshua Cohen and Joel Rogers for deepening and extending the democratic state. At its heart, the proposal involves invigorating secondary associations in ways which enable them to be, on the one hand, effective vehicles for the representation and formulation of the interests of citizens, and on the other, to be directly involved in the implementation and execution of state policies. Secondary associations include unions, works councils, neighborhood associations, parent-teacher organizations, environmental groups, women's associations, and so on. They are characterized by their organizational autonomy from the state on the one hand, and their role in politically representing and shaping the interests of individuals on the other. The Cohen-Rogers proposal, then, is to enhance democracy by transforming the ways in which such associations mediate between citizens and states. This poses a range of difficult issues: enhancing the political role for such associations risks undermining their autonomy from the state and turning them into tools of social control rather than vehicles of democratic participation; secondary associations often claim illegitimately a monopoly of interest representation for specific constituencies and any formal role in democratic governance risks consolidating such monopolistic claims; the shift from a primary emphasis on territorial representation to functional representation risks strengthening tendencies toward particularistic identities, thus further fragmenting the polity. These and many other issues are discussed at length in the papers that follow.

The book begins with Cohen and Rogers's extended presentation of this model of democratic governance. This is followed by a number of wide-ranging commentaries by the participants in a workshop conference held at the Havens Center for the Study of Social Structure and Social Change at the University of Wisconsin in January 1992.

A Proposal for Reconstructing Democratic Institutions

Secondary Associations and Democratic Governance

Joshua Cohen and Joel Rogers

Prominent among the problems of democratic theory and practice are the 'mischiefs of faction'[1] produced in mass democracies by 'secondary associations' – the wide range of nonfamilial organizations intermediate between individuals or firms and the institutions of the state and formal electoral system.[2] Such associations play a central role in the politics of modern democratic societies. They help to set the political agenda, to determine choices from that agenda, to implement (or to thwart the implementation of) those choices and to shape the beliefs, preferences, self-understandings and habits of thought and action that individuals bring to more encompassing political arenas. Stated abstractly, the problem of faction consists in the potential of secondary associations to deploy their powers in ways that undermine the conditions of well-ordered democracy.

This potential has always been a special preoccupation in US politics. Curbing the 'mischiefs of faction' was announced by James Madison as the core problem of US constitutional design. Ever since modern political science rediscovered the 'group basis' of politics, secondary associations and attendant problems of faction have dominated the discipline's most serious efforts at democratic theory.

Recent discussion of American solutions to the problem of faction has featured more skepticism than celebration. Concerns about the bias of the 'interest group system' in favor of wealthier citizens[3] and about the 'feudalization' of the administrative state through the capture of its agencies by organized interests[4] have been restated and supplemented by three major strands of contemporary constitutional-political argument, each addressed, inter alia, to the sources of faction and prospects for its cure: (1) a *neoliberal constitutionalism* which traces the proliferation of organized groups and their destructive 'rent-seeking behavior' to the powers of the state to confer such rents, and so proposes to address tendencies to faction by setting clear constitutional limits on those powers; (2) a latter-day *civic republicanism* which seeks to preserve an autonomous realm of deliberative politics devoted to discerning and pursuing the common good, and argues that that preservation requires the insulation of an activist state from the maneuvering of particularistic groups; and (3) an *egalitarian pluralism* which seeks to accommodate the inevitable importance of group activity to modern democratic politics while limiting the distortions that organized groups produce in democratic politics by securing greater equality in the conditions of group organization and facilitating group access to legislative and administrative arenas.

These diverse proposals for addressing contemporary problems of faction resonate with more general doubts about the structure of the US political system and its capacity to address issues of broad national importance. These are fueled by two decades of weak economic performance and failed adjustment, sharp dissensus on the appropriate form and powers of the US welfare state, and the growth of a 'single-issue' politics, which defies conventional political management. In all these areas, the power of secondary associations to thwart fair and constructive policy is commonly alleged to be a major part of the problem, if not its principal source.

But whereas observers of the US system have rediscovered the pervasiveness of faction, students of comparative politics have pointed to an approximately opposite result: that certain forms of group organization play a central role in resolving problems of successful governance, not in causing them. In the 1970s, another 'rediscovery' of groups, this time of 'societal corporatist' (or 'liberal corporatist') systems of interest representation in Northern European democracies, argued that gains in economic performance and state efficiency were consequent on the incorporation of diverse, organized interests into policy formation within densely organized systems of peak bargaining and sectoral governance.[5] More recent discussions, even as they have dissented from claims made about corporatism, or paused to note its devolution or collapse, have also stressed the importance of associative activity to economic performance. Students of the successful alternatives to mass production that are marked, simultaneously, by high wages, skills, productivity and competitiveness have argued that this success requires a dense social infrastructure of secondary association and coordination. This organizational infrastructure provides the basis for cooperation between management and labor, among firms, and between firms and the government on issues of work organization, training, technology diffusion, research and development, and new product ventures. And that cooperation, it is argued, is essential to ensuring economic adjustment that is both rapid and fair.[6]

Apart from simply noting the positive contributions of associations, this comparative work suggests as well that certain 'qualitative' features of groups and systems of group representation – for example, differences in the encompassingness of groups or in the scope of their powers – and not simply the sheer 'quantity of associability', provide a key to explaining that contribution.[7] This work is not without its own concern about faction – specifically, about the compatibility of the forms of group organization and representation that contribute to favorable economic performance and state efficiency with democratic ideals of popular sovereignty and political equality. Still, the contention that certain qualitative features of groups account for their favorable contribution to certain specific areas of governance implicitly suggests a *general strategy* for curbing the mischiefs of faction, namely, explicit efforts to encourage forms of group representation that stand less sharply in tension with the norms of democratic governance.

In this essay, we pursue this suggestion. Emphasizing both qualitative variations among groups and the 'artifactual' aspect of associations, we suggest that the range of cures for the mischiefs of faction is commonly understood too narrowly. The potential cures are not limited to the options of imposing stringent constitutional limits on the affirmative state, accommodating groups while seeking to ensure equality in the 'pluralist bazaar', or constructing cloistered deliberative arenas alongside that bazaar. In addition to these strategies, and in many respects preferable to them, is the cure of using public powers to encourage less factionalizing forms of secondary association – engaging in an artful democratic politics of secondary association. More positively stated, the same deliberate politics of association can harness group contributions to democratic order. By altering the terms, conditions and public status of groups, we believe, it can improve economic performance and government efficiency and advance egalitarian-democratic norms of popular sovereignty, political equality, distributive equity and civic consciousness (discussed later in this essay). This deliberate politics of associations and the view of contemporary democratic governance that embraces it as essential to such governance we call 'associative democracy'.[8]

We would recommend an associative democratic strategy in a wide range of administrative and property regimes. Here, however, we assume the context of modern capitalism, where markets are the primary mechanism of resource allocation and private individual decisions are the central determinant of investment. Admitting the limits which this context places on the satisfaction of egalitarian-democratic norms, our argument is that associative democracy can improve the practical approximation to those norms.

Before presenting that argument, we conclude our introductory remarks by noting two broader aims of the effort.

First, we wish to advance discussion of the more institutional aspects of egalitarian-democratic political philosophy. Since the publication of John Rawls's *A Theory of Justice*, normative democratic theory has focused principally on three tasks: refining principles of justice, clarifying the nature of political justification, and exploring the public policies required to ensure a just distribution of education, health care and other basic resources. Much less attention has been devoted to examining the political institutions and social arrangements that might plausibly implement reasonable political principles.[9] Moreover, the amount of attention paid to issues of organizational and institutional implementation has varied sharply across the different species of normative theory. Neoliberal theorists concerned chiefly with protecting liberty by taming power, and essentially hostile to the affirmative state, have been far more sensitive to such issues than egalitarian-democratic theorists, who simultaneously embrace classically liberal concerns with choice, egalitarian concerns with the distribution of resources and a republican emphasis on the values of citizen participation and public debate. Neglect of how such values might be implemented has deepened the vulnerability of egalitarian-democratic views to the charge of being unrealistic: 'good in theory but not so good in practice'. This essay is motivated in part by an interest in addressing this vulnerability by examining the constructive role that secondary associations can play in a democracy.

Second, and more practically, we wish to join and advance, from the point of view of democratic ideals, current discussion about the shape of a reasonable alternative to the political-economic arrangements that have characterized the United States and other, more developed welfare states since the end of World War II. Over the past generation, owing principally to shifts in the underlying conditions of economic ordering – intensified international competition and integration, rapid technological change, and a growing dispersion of labor market positions defined increasingly by endowments of human capital – the central governing institutions and practices characteristic of the post-war 'Keynesian welfare state' have been subjected to sharp challenge. Together, these changes have served to weaken the force of national regulatory institutions. Whatever the ultimate assessment of their past achievement, those institutions seem clearly less suited than they once were to ensuring a reasonable and fair society.

The second aim of our argument, then, is to respond to these circumstances with some suggestions for institutional reform. Using the problem of faction to focus our discussion, we outline certain elements of a scheme of association which we believe to be more democratic and better suited to promoting the general welfare than present institutional arrangements. According secondary groups an extensive and explicitly public role, the proposed scheme represents an elaboration of the implications of the idea of associative democracy in light of present circumstances. In general terms, it would preserve a social-democratic emphasis on generic social regulation defined and enforced through national institutions, while linking it with classical liberal and republican emphases on decentralized coordination and administration through local jurisdictions or secondary organizations. This elaboration of associative democracy is intended not only to clarify that conception further, however, but to show how it may be used to address a range of pressing problems of contemporary states.

We make the argument for associative democracy in four steps. Section 1 provides a critical assessment of neoliberal constitutionalist, civic republican and egalitarian pluralist approaches to the problem of faction, to which associative democracy stands in contrast. Section 2 gives a positive characterization of the associative view. We describe basic egalitarian-democratic norms, indicate some of the ways that secondary associations can help to satisfy them, and begin exploring the possibility of netting this contribution, while reducing faction, through a more deliberate politics of groups. Section 3 illustrates this strategy by showing how it might be applied to a wide range of practical problems of democratic governance and what effect such application would have on the various norms of democratic association identified earlier. Section 4 rounds out the discussion with some suggestions for associative reform in the United States, offered in light of the previous analysis.

1. Three Cures for the Mischiefs of Faction

Three views dominate current debate about the relation between democracy and groups. We refer to them, respectively, as neoliberal constitutionalism, civic republicanism and egalitarian pluralism. In this section, we provide a critical assessment of these views, examining their normative underpinnings, their analyses of group contribution and faction, and their proposals for reconciling associations and democracy. While our discussion focuses on these views themselves, our principal aims are to clarify and to motivate the idea of associative democracy by indicating how it emerges naturally from reflection on the strengths and deficiencies of the main alternatives.

Strategies of Limitation: Neoliberal Constitutionalism[10]

Neoliberal constitutionalism is perhaps the most influential contemporary approach to reconciling democracy and group practice, and the one most ascendant in recent discussions of the problem. For these reasons, we consider it at some length.

Background View

Neoliberal constitutionalism is a contemporary descendant of the liberalisms of John Locke and Adam Smith.[11] Drawing on those strands of classical liberal political theory, neoliberal constitutionalism advances the normative ideal of an efficient 'constitution of liberty', a set of social and political arrangements that simultaneously protects a fundamental *right to liberty* and advances the *general welfare*. The fundamental right to liberty is understood to imply that, as a general rule (excepting, for example, children and adults with severe mental handicaps), it is permissible for the state to restrain individual choice only where the restraints are necessary to protect choice itself, that 'liberty should only be restrained for the sake of liberty'. So, for example, restrictions on the liberty of contracting parties are legitimate only in so far as those restrictions are themselves necessary to preserve the institution of free contracting, as is the case, for example, with prohibitions on unilateral amendment of contract terms. The idea of the general welfare is typically interpreted in terms of the requirement of Pareto efficiency. Thus social arrangements (set within a framework of liberty) promote the general welfare if and only if any rearrangement of them would decrease the satisfaction of at least one person's preferences.

Given their emphasis on the values of choice and efficiency, neoliberal constitutionalists are strong proponents of competitive markets. These provide a mechanism of social coordination based in individual choice that also, under certain conditions, generates Pareto-efficient allocations of resources. Commitments to choice and efficiency also lead neoliberals to be deeply wary of concentrations of power, which can be used to restrict choice or hinder allocative efficiency. Here, too, there are advantages to competitive markets, as the possibility of exit from unsatisfactory commercial relations that markets provide limits the abuse of power. Indeed, if power is defined as the ability to impose uncompensated costs on others, then perfectly competitive markets abolish power.[12]

Neoliberal views on the appropriate functions of the state follow from these perceptions and commitments. As a general matter, a sharply 'limited' state is desired. Because markets honor choice and can produce efficient resource allocations, the central role of the state is typically defined as one of defending the legal framework of formal liberty itself and securing the prerequisites of competitive market operation. To play this role, the state does need to regulate and restrict choice, but these activities are justified by reference to the contention that they protect choice itself. So, for example, the state can legitimately regulate and restrict choice in order to protect property, enforce contracts, secure a stable money supply, curb anti-competitive behavior, mandate that property be relinquished when market power is unduly concentrated, and raise the taxes required to pay for each of these functions – because all these are necessary to securing a competitive market order that respects choice.

Of course, economic coordination through existing markets does not always result in allocatively efficient outcomes. Even under perfectly competitive conditions, 'market failures' may occur, generated in particular by the effects of economic transactions on third parties. Because the state cannot always promote the general welfare simply by protecting choice in markets, it will sometimes need to supplement the market by, for example, providing public goods undersupplied on it, raising the revenue for such goods through taxation. Because of difficulties in determining the extent and sources of market failure and in assessing the likelihood that state action will remedy it,[13] particular proposals for such supplementary state action will often be controversial. And because choice remains a fundamental value and the taxation to support state action is mandatory and thus abridges choice, neoliberalism endorses a strong presumption against any affirmative state action. But that presumption is rebuttable if the regulatory means are minimally restrictive of choice, and if they can reasonably be expected to work a substantial improvement in the general welfare.

Finally, although neoliberal constitutionalism endorses the legitimacy of state action that regulates individual choice in order to protect liberty and to secure the general welfare, it denies the legitimacy of restrictions and regulations of conduct designed to assure equality.

In competitive markets, inequalities in the lifetime expectations of different citizens arise from differences in their inherited resources, their native endowments, their individual tastes and values (reflected for example in their preferences about work and leisure) and their good and bad fortune. Because neoliberalism supposes that the protection of competitive markets is required to assure the right to liberty, it holds that inequalities of each of these kinds are the more or less inevitable price to be paid for securing that right. Regulating inequalities resulting from differences in inherited resource endowments, for example, would require significant restrictions on parental choice about the transmission of wealth to children. For neoliberal constitutionalists, such a restriction on individual liberty is unacceptable. Rights to liberty remain 'core' and cannot be abridged by egalitarian concerns.

As a matter of the design of public institutions, neoliberalism proposes to meet these commitments to choice and the general welfare through a variety of checks on the concentration of public power. Markets themselves are seen as one such check. A system of vigorous electoral competition is another. And within the state itself, constitutional limits on the state's plenary powers, an independent judiciary with powers to review and invalidate legislation, and a separation and federalism of powers to assure competition in the authorship of policy are others. In combination, market-ordered civil society, party competition and limited and divided government help to secure the blessings of a 'constitution of liberty', while disabling its opponents.

The Neoliberal Approach to Groups

Neoliberals respect the right of association and recognize the value that can come from exercising it. If associations are wholly voluntary and do not impede market efficiency or burden the fundamental liberties of non-members, they are tolerated, or more, in the neoliberal scheme.[14] Neoliberals recognize that some sorts of associative activity can even produce efficiency gains and an expansion of choice by their role in ordering markets, as in privately ordered product standard-setting secured through a trade association. In so far as they perform educative and coordinating functions without drawing down the public purse, all manner of groups can promote the meaningful exercise of liberty, in ways consistent with a commitment to a minimal state, while contributing to the common advantage. Although they do not contribute to efficiency, charitable organizations and private welfare efforts find particular favor, as these 'thousand points of light' relieve pressures for expansion of the welfare state. Thus neoliberals are enthusiastic about the proliferation of brotherhoods and sisterhoods, community organizations and gun clubs, chambers of commerce and parent-teacher associations, and menageries of Elks, Moose, Odd-fellows and Zor Shriners exercising their associational rights.

What neoliberals object to are organizations that are not wholly voluntary or that in some way impede market operation or otherwise infringe economic efficiency and choice. Trade unions are a favorite target, as these are seen to combine restrictions on the liberty of members and of employers with economic inefficiency. Business associations engaging in restrictive market practices are another. With Adam Smith, the neoliberals deplore the fact that 'people of the same trade seldom meet together, even for merriment and diversion, but the conversation ends in a conspiracy against the public, or in some contrivance to raise prices.'[15]

What gives neoliberal constitutionalism a distinctive contemporary identity is its particular concern that such obnoxious group practices are tolerated, encouraged and lent sanction by the affirmative state. Indeed, the core of the neoliberal view of faction is that the problem arises not so much from groups themselves as from the way in which that state has corrupted the environment of voluntary association by providing countless opportunities for returns to political bargaining.

In modern administrative states, government action ranges far more widely than the protection of choice and the promotion of allocative efficiency. The burden that must be met to justify state action in the name of the general welfare has been substantially reduced.[16] Administrative agencies, with powers to act in particular markets and arenas of social policy, are principal instruments of state action. And agency action is not, as a general matter, limited by precise rules or standards of either a procedural or substantive kind. In brief, liberty is threatened by a substantially 'untamed' power.

The way that faction arises from such affirmative state capacities was suggested in Smith's critique of mercantilism. Smith argued for limited government in part because he thought the more extensive state associated with mercantilist regulations of trade would inevitably be captured by merchants and manufacturers. Inspired by the 'spirit of monopoly' and facing relatively few obstacles to common action, they would use the powers of the state to protect their positions in particular markets. By thus securing special advantages for themselves, they would limit the choices of others and in so doing would reduce the wealth of the nation.[17]

Neoliberals essentially transpose Smith's quarrel with the mercantilists to the context of mass democracy. There, they argue, undue restrictions on choice and departures from efficiency are introduced by the combination of associational rights, an affirmative state with the power to confer benefits on discrete groups, and the need by those with power to secure electoral support in order to retain that power. Rights of association enable groups to form. Incentives to group formation are then provided by the state's ability to provide benefits to select populations that are paid for by all – as in, for example, a tariff or subsidy for a particular industry that benefits members of that industry while imposing the costs of higher prices on everyone else. Such situations are ripe for political exploitation, because the clear incentives for groups to demand such benefits are typically not matched by public concerns to limit them. While the benefits are concentrated, the costs – even if they are in the aggregate greater than the benefits – are dispersed across an accordingly demobilized citizenry. Moreover, political officials need to bid for political support. So, they rationally seek to supply benefits to groups that demand them in exchange for such support, with little fear of sanction from an exploited but inactive public. Group exploitation of these opportunities, finally, is exacerbated by the access of groups to private information, difficulties in legislative monitoring of agency performance and the increased chances for group 'capture' of agencies that result, and the capture of relevant legislative committees by organized interests. Gradually, state policies come to be defined by the agendas of different groups.

The result, as Hayek puts it, is the 'domination of government by coalitions of organized interests' – by 'an enormous and exceedingly wasteful apparatus of para-government . . . [that] has arisen *only in response to (or partly as defense against being disadvantaged in) the increasing necessity of an all-mighty majority government maintaining its majority by buying the support of particular small groups*'. While such factional domination may appear to be the product of corruption and vice, its roots go deeper and are in fact 'the inescapable result of a system in which government has unlimited powers to take whatever measures are required to satisfy the wishes of those on whose support it relies'.[18]

Both the reduction of politics to group bargaining and the policies that result from that bargaining are sources of inefficiency and restrictions on choice. The processes of group organization and political bargaining themselves produce inefficiencies because they divert the energy of citizens away from economically productive contributions into political activity. The legislative and administrative results of the process (e.g. licensing arrangements, entry restrictions, price supports and redistributive tax-and-transfer schemes) restrict choice itself while producing further inefficiencies – for example, artificial scarcities that produce a divergence of market prices from true opportunity costs, incentives to substitute leisure for labor that follow from rewards paid to nonproductive action, and incentives to engage unproductive acts of appropriation through the state.

The neoliberal constitutionalist institutional program follows fairly straightforwardly from this analysis. Since advantage-seeking groups will inevitably form in response to the opportunities for private benefit at general expense created by an affirmative state, and since their actions will result in efficiency losses and unjustified restrictions on choice, there are only two possible cures for faction: either limit associational liberties or limit the affirmative state. Since the curtailment of associational liberties is ruled out as a matter of principle and would restrict desirable as well as undesirable associative activity, the second strategy is mandated. Specifically, then, the program is to eliminate, at the level of basic constitutional principle and design, the 'affirmative' aspects of the modern state. By staunching the flow of discrete benefits from the state, such constitutional reform limits the key incentive to advantage-seeking, namely, the availability of returns to political action. It thus discourages the formation of destructive groups and the pathologies of 'bargaining democracy' associated with them.[19]

Analysis and Criticism

Parts of the neoliberal constitutionalist view are correct and important, and we will wish to take them over in elaborating our own view of associative democracy.

As a normative matter, individual choice and allocative efficiency are important social values, as is government competence and efficiency. These concerns must be ingredients in any working conception of democratic order. Furthermore, constitutional limits on state power seem essential to securing the conditions of a democratic order worthy of support. Even if constitutional design were not the only way to limit the state, the express statement of limitations at law would remain desirable because it makes manifest the terms and conditions of citizenship, a requirement for citizens being motivated directly by those terms.

As an empirical matter, some parts of the neoliberal analysis of 'bargaining democracy' are also clearly right. Political officials often do exchange bounty for support. Groups often do exploit asymmetries in the distribution of the costs and benefits of policies. State policies themselves often do encourage the formation of advantage-seeking, choice-restricting and welfare-limiting groups. And state capacities are, in some measure, pushed beyond their limits in affirmative regulation.

Considered as a general framework for studying democracy and associations, however, the neoliberal conception exhibits four principal shortcomings.

First, we have a disagreement on fundamental norms. While we endorse neoliberal concerns with efficiency and liberty as such, we take exception to their single-minded preoccupation with these concerns. As noted earlier, in a system of 'natural liberty', in which the legitimate functions of the state are confined to protecting choice and ensuring efficiency, inequalities rooted in differences of inherited wealth, natural talent or brute good fortune will proliferate. But we see no justice in permitting differences of these kinds to determine life chances. More immediately, such inequalities are in tension with a fundamental ideal of democracy, itself essential to justifying aspects of democratic order that neoliberals value. In a democracy, citizens are treated as equals – with equal standing under the law and full political rights – irrespective of differences in their inherited resources, natural endowments and good fortune. It is difficult to see any rationale for insisting on that equal treatment which is not also a rationale for seeking to reduce the effects of these differences on life-time expectations.[20]

Of course, acknowledging the legitimacy of state action to ensure distributive equity carries with it a willingness to accept restrictions on choice in the name of equality. But we do not find this particularly troubling. While liberty as such is a good thing and ought not to be arbitrarily abridged, there are important distinctions within the class of liberties and correspondingly within the class of reasons for abridgement. Some liberties are more important or fundamental than others, and reasons that suffice for justifying restrictions on the less important are not always sufficient for justifying restrictions on the more important. The fundamental liberties in a democratic order, with a place of pre-eminence in political argument, are liberties of conscience and thought, expression and association, participation and personal privacy. But stringent protection of these liberties is consistent with regulations of and restrictions on market choice in order to ensure political equality and distributive equity.

Now, if one accepts that political equality and a fair distribution of resources are reasonable norms, then one may well have to live as well with some of the inefficiencies that neoliberalism notices. For example, so long as effort is tied to expectations of material compensation, assuring a fair distribution of resources will result in a less than full utilization of resources. But that may simply be the inevitable price to be paid for the important value of a distribution of advantage not hostage to the vicissitudes of inheritance, talent and luck. Furthermore, so long as a fair distribution depends on pressures on the state to correct for unfairness in markets, it will be necessary to devote resources to ensuring that pressure. Neoliberals view such political engagement as a wasteful diversion of resources from productive contribution. It seems more plausible to view it as a way to assure the justice of the society.

Second, the same reasons that lead us to think that distributive equity is a reasonable concern within democratic orders lead us to think that the neoliberal account of group formation is misleading. That account emphasizes the degree to which the formation of groups pressuring the state for benefits is endogenous to the growth of the welfare state itself. The bounty provided by an expansive state creates the incentives to the formation and political actions of advantage-seeking groups.

But this emphasis seems misplaced. It is true that group formation is responsive to the level and kind of benefits provided by the state. But it is also true that at least one important source of group formation is exogenous to the affirmative state, namely ethical concerns about the injustice of purely market-based resource distributions.[21] The history of the welfare state – whether told as the partial triumph of the working class or as a growing series of subsidies to capital, or (more plausibly) as both – is a history of social pressures for the expansion of state functions. Before programs of the modern welfare state encouraged groups to seek resources through the state, social groups fought for the establishment of programs in social insurance, income support and labor market regulation. They aimed to make citizens' life chances less dependent on the contingencies of market success.

There is every reason to believe this history would repeat itself if the neoliberal remedy for faction were implemented. If a more minimal state were achieved, those suffering from material disadvantages of the kind described earlier (that is, inequalities that are at odds with the underlying ideal that citizens are equals) would likely set about pressuring the state to address them. Constitutional bars on redistribution, of the sort neoliberals propose, would clearly increase the political costs and the political stakes of their doing so. But the perception of injustice will lead at least some groups to be willing to bear those costs and to change, as they have done before, the constitutional structure itself.[22] In a word, even a complete enactment of the neoliberal solution appears unstable.

Third, it is unlikely that a complete realization of the neoliberal constitutionalist program can be achieved. One reason for this is simple political power. The welfare state benefits many, business and non-business alike, who can be expected to resist its dismantling. However, even if political power were not an issue, difficulties in definition would intrude. In practice, there is no sharp distinction between programs that provide discrete benefits and those that provide dispersed benefits, between legitimate actions to promote the common advantage and illegitimate interventions in support of particular constituencies. Programs whose benefits are targeted to particular groups – whether the poor or educationally disadvantaged, or farmers, or producers of natural gas – can always be defended by reference to reasons of the general welfare – economic strength, a stable food supply or energy independence and national security. Combining the two points, it is easy to imagine a protracted struggle over the definition of state functions waged via existing programs. In any case, a second-best approximation to the desired neoliberal state seems the 'best' that can be hoped for.

But this second-best approximation would very likely exacerbate certain aspects of the problem of faction. Consider, for example, a scaled-back welfare state, featuring privatization of essential services, more restrictive laws defining the power of secondary associations, the withdrawal of state subsidies to groups performing broad public functions and the exclusion of groups of this kind from policy-making and implementation. Under these conditions, barriers to group formation would be relatively easily negotiated by wealthier constituencies with clearly defined private agendas and the information and other resources needed for collective action. But they would be virtually impassable for would-be organizations of the poor, members of diffuse majorities and other traditionally under-represented classes. The political inequalities that neoliberals associate with groups would thus become worse, not better, on reasonable assumptions about the success of their reform. Even if the total benefits provided by the state were reduced, the share of benefits going to limited populations, and paid for by others, would be greater.[23]

Fourth and finally, we have attributed to the neoliberal constitutionalists the view that when the legitimate functions of the state extend beyond protecting choice and assuring allocative efficiency, factional groups and their mischief inevitably follow. Even crediting the alleged relation between affirmative state functions and group formation, however, the claim that groups formed in the environment of affirmative state action will inevitably be factionalizing does not follow from the existence of that state. Whether a group or group system produces faction is a function of its *qualitative features*. Neoliberal accounts are generally inattentive to such qualitative variation in groups; their analysis of group effects is highly general, and while the impulse to generality is understandable, it can be quite misleading here.

As an illustration, consider the neoliberal claim that group politics produces efficiency losses. To be sure, some groups will engage in redistributive rent-seeking. But more encompassing groups, claiming as members a large share of the population affected by such strategies, will, precisely because they are encompassing, have little incentive to pursue strategies that limit efficiency.[24] They are more likely to pursue productivity growth, forsaking zero-sum conflict for general gain. Similarly, the relations between organized interests and administrative agencies can take different forms. Some groups, certainly, will seek to capture administrative agencies for private purposes. But others are commonly brought into service to act as 'fire alarms', sending signals to legislatures about whether agencies are in fact acting on their legislative mandate. By sending them, they promote the accountability of bureaux to those mandates and reduce the costs of monitoring agency performance.[25]

In response, then, to a general question about the consequences of group formation in a political order characterized by an affirmative state, the right general answer is: 'It all depends.' What it importantly depends on is the range of factors producing qualitative variation in group structure and behavior. But these are exactly the sorts of factors typically neglected in neoliberal accounts.

Strategies of Insulation: Civic Republicanism

A second general approach to democracy and groups endorses a broader scope of legitimate state action than is accepted by neoliberal constitutionalists. At the same time, it recognizes with the neoliberals that the powers of an affirmative state represent a considerable prize and that groups will likely be tempted by the benefits it makes available. To remedy the problems of faction resulting from such temptation, this second strategy proposes institutional reforms that aim to insulate arenas of collective choice from the pressures of particular interests. The recent revival of civic republicanism provides us with a prominent contemporary illustration of this program of insulation.[26]

Background View

Civic republicanism belongs to the species of antipluralist conceptions of politics. Antipluralist conceptions all aim to ensure that the substance of state policy is not fixed by bargaining among interest groups, each seeking its own advantage. Within this broad species – which includes the neoliberal constitutionalism just considered – civic republicanism belongs to the subset of antipluralist conceptions that accept the affirmative state and with it a conception of the state as legitimately advancing a common good that extends beyond the ideal of an efficient allocation of resources.

Within this affirmative subset, civic republicanism is distinguished by two principal commitments. First, it emphasizes the importance of a deliberative politics of policy formation. By a 'deliberative politics' we mean a process of public reasoning that proceeds by reference to considerations of the common good and that shapes the preferences of participants by requiring them to offer reasons for their views that provide such reference. Second, it advances a distinctive institutional program to remedy problems of faction. Specifically, it seeks to secure and *insulate* public processes of orderly political deliberation and efficient achievement of publicly declared ends. In general terms, the strategy is to strengthen institutions, alternative to secondary associations, that have the capacity to consider and act on the common good and to encourage those holding power within such institutions to engage in just such consideration and action. The hope is to increase the degree to which deliberation about and action on the common good proceed autonomously from the pressures of particular interests.[27]

Republicanism and Groups

Civic republicans are not committed to promoting deliberative politics and shielding it from group pressure and bargaining by abolishing groups or excluding them from politics. Quite apart from the impossibility of doing this within a framework of liberal commitment, they recognize that associations can and often do assist public deliberation and the formulation of workable policies to the common advantage.[28] They recognize, for example, that information provided to the state by groups – information on the impact of proposed policy, or the implementation of existing policy, or the intensity of member preferences about either – often aids in public deliberation. They recognize the obvious importance of group representation, particularly in so far as it advances political equality. More controversially, they recognize that the ability of groups to 'deliver' their members in support of a policy once it is enacted can facilitate reasoned deliberation about that policy when it is being formulated. Finally, the fact that associations can serve as 'schools of democracy' promoting habits of other-regarding deliberation has long been honored in the republican tradition.

All this said, civic republicans generally accord groups a distinctly secondary role in deliberative politics. They are generally suspicious of the information they provide, alert to the profoundly unequal character of existing group organization, wary of the conditions that groups impose on policy-makers in exchange for promises of delivering support, and despairing of the selfish habits actually learned within the schools of contemporary group practice. In general, then, they wish to separate public deliberation so far as possible from group influence.

Departing from a combination of opposition to pluralism and commitment to deliberation and insulation, the civic republican embraces both a stronger state and a more sharply delineated one. Accepting the desirability of affirmative state action, civic republicans seek to facilitate 'responsible' performance by state and electoral institutions. Such responsible exercise of public power is understood to require an autonomous reflection on the proper tasks of state action, sufficient capacity to discharge those tasks and accountability to previously declared forms and expectations.

This program has implications for the operation of all major institutions of traditional politics, from political parties and the legislature to the executive and the courts. Parties and party competition should be strengthened with a view to promoting clear and encompassing programs of action, organizing and informing the electorate around them, and holding elected legislators accountable to their performance. To protect against the factional distortion of parties that would arise from their dependence on resources supplied by organized interests, public resources ought to be provided to the parties and their candidates in a system of generally subsidized elections.[29] Similarly, legislators should debate and then legislate clear standards of performance, not simply dollop out vague grants of statutory authority to agencies. In the case of the United States, for example, Congress should spend less time on toothless oversight hearings and routinized constituency service and more on the enactment, codification, and repeal of clear legislation and on genuine review of the performance of administrative agencies in light of a rebuttable presumption of agency disablement.

The executive should also be strengthened, since, as Alexander Hamilton observed, 'energy in the executive . . . is essential to . . . the security of liberty against the enterprises and assaults of ambition, of faction, and of anarchy.'[30] Again in the case of the United States, that strengthening should involve disciplining Congress at the presidential level (e.g. with increased use of the veto power to curb vague delegations), serving Congress at the agency level when it enacts sufficiently precise rules, and coordinating the operations of different agencies to ensure their responsiveness to electoral outcomes.

And finally, the judiciary, the ultimate guarantor of deliberative politics, should insist that the different branches do their job. It should curb accretions of power to the president, invalidate vague delegations of congressional power and apply the principles of statutory construction and standards of review necessary to ensure executive and legislative control over the procedures and substantive decisions of the 'fourth branch' of the agency bureaucracy.

Lowi named this system more than twenty years ago. It is 'juridical democracy', or 'the rule of law operating in institutions'.[31]

Analysis and Criticisms

Much in this conception is plausible and attractive. To begin with, we endorse the civic republicans' acceptance of the affirmative state and mass democracy. From this it follows that we applaud the general form of their question about faction. Unlike neoliberals, civic republicans ask what can be done about faction given this political background. They do not ask how we can eliminate the background itself. We also agree that there can and should be more to politics than the aggregation of preferences given in advance and agree with the republicans' rejection of the reduction of democratic politics to its 'group basis'. Democratic governance requires debate about policy, conducted against the background of explicitly articulated conceptions of the common good. Finally, we agree with the basic constitutional idea that public institutions should have clearly defined responsibilities and the strength to perform them. We are particularly interested in a vigorous electoral system and the recommended strengthening of political parties as alternatives to secondary associations in linking citizens to the state. In brief, we agree that any comprehensive and plausible solution to the problem of faction must include efforts to insulate a politics of the common good from more particularistic aspirations of associations.

But we depart from the civic republicans on three points.

First, the basic strategy of insulation seems unrealistic. The ideal of juridical democracy presumes a greater degree of state autonomy than can be expected under conditions of capitalist democracy – particularly in an affirmative state with the capacity to pursue remedies for social and economic problems. No matter how ingenious the procedural devices of insulation, no matter how vigilant and professional public officials may be, and no matter how resistant courts are to putting their imprimatur on interest group bargains brokered through the state, the state operates within society, and institutional proposals need to be attentive to that fact.

Politics is still largely a game of resources, not a forum of principles. In capitalist democracy, some people have great advantages in the control of strategically important resources, good and clear reasons for wishing to influence the state, and the power to do so. Unless one is prepared to make the implausible assumption that the state can resist the demands and supplications of organized business interests in an environment densely populated by those interests, problems of faction will remain. In particular, as in the case of the second-best neoliberal solution, the fact that the civic republican program of insulation is not attentive to the associational foundations of deliberative democracy can be expected to translate into problems for political equality. If it is implausible to think that any strategy of insulation will be 'group-proof', it is particularly implausible to think that the insulating barriers will not first be negotiated by the best-endowed political players to the further detriment of the less well off.

Second, even as it recognizes some sorts of group contributions directly to deliberation, the civic republican program of insulation neglects the distinctive capacities of groups to facilitate cooperation for the common advantage and remains wedded to an essentially 'zero-sum' understanding of the relation between associations and the state. But that relation can just as easily be 'positive-sum', with an increase in the power of groups contributing to an increase in state capacities to achieve democratic order.

Peak wage bargaining of the kind once practiced in Northern European social democracies, for example, did not diminish the capacity of the state to promote the general welfare. To the contrary, by providing a private mechanism for stable incomes policies, it facilitated state efforts at macroeconomic planning and social support for redistribution. Similarly, the involvement of worker and business associations in organizing systems of worker training need not diminish state capacities to provide all citizens with education. To the contrary, it appears necessary to providing the training best gained through 'hands on' practice, while being equally necessary to ensuring that private training efforts not be narrow and firm-specific and that they be broadly distributed. The enlistment of environmental groups into the development and enforcement of local or regional standards of acceptable use of toxics need not diminish state capacities to state and enforce higher standards of protection. To the contrary, by enlisting the monitoring and enforcement capacities of private associations, it can expand the capacity to achieve better protection of the environment and the public health.

Of course, efforts to enlist associative energies do always threaten the appropriation of public powers by particular interests. But this threat need not be realized. Whether or not it is depends, as we have emphasized, on the organization of the groups, the terms of their interaction with one another, the range of powers that they can exercise and the conditions on which they are granted those powers. In short, it depends on what we have been calling the 'qualitative' characteristics of groups and group systems. Like the neoliberals, civic republicans are insufficiently attentive to such qualitative variation, and its signal relevance to understanding, even defining, the problem of faction.

Our third criticism builds on these two via the observation that the core of the civic republican strategy for addressing issues of faction is to 'design around' groups. Civic republicans take the associative environment as fixed and then seek to design procedures for making and implementing collective choices immune to group pressures. Our first criticism, essentially, was that this strategy of insulation is not feasible. It fails to recognize the centrality of groups, the fact that they are unavoidable as political facts. Our second criticism was that insulation might be undesirable. Noting the qualitative variation of groups, we indicated that groups are not all the same and that some have distinctive virtues in contributing to democratic order. Efforts to protect that order by screening them all out, even assuming the plausibility of that effort, may be self-defeating.

Now one could imagine a position, call it 'reformed civic republicanism', that combined acceptance of both these criticisms in a tragic sense of politics. This reformed view would agree that insulation is difficult and that qualitative variation is important but hold that the determination of group qualities is a matter of social fate. Reformed republicanism agrees, then, that the qualitative character of the group system in a society importantly determines its politics. Nevertheless, reformed republicanism places the group system, the possibilities of insulating politics from it, and therefore the possibilities of achieving a civic republic beyond politics. The reformed civic republican might note, sadly, that unalterable factors – of political culture, ethnic diversity, economic or social structure, population size or some other intractable element – have condemned the United States to a fractious pluralism, even as they permit Swedes or Germans a greater measure of cohesion and so the prospect of deliberative politics.

Our third criticism is that this reformed view is itself mistaken, for it is inattentive to the artifactual character of groups: the fact that there is no natural structure of group representation that directly reflects the underlying conditions of social life. By acting on the environment of group formation (as the neoliberals recommend), or acting on groups themselves, or both, it is possible to change the character of groups and their interaction. It is, moreover, possible to do so along those dimensions of qualitative variation that lie at the source of problems of faction. Northern European incomes policies and training systems were not just inherited but built in significant measure through public policies. Whether unions are more or less encompassing of the working population is not just a matter of national position in international markets or the size of their labor markets but of laws setting the costs and benefits of union membership. And whether environmental groups are merely disruptive of administrative hearings on toxic waste or are co-administrators of its reduction and disposal depends substantially on whether public power is used to facilitate such joint administration.

Like neoliberal constitutionalism, civic republicanism slights the possibility that certain forms of secondary association may be part of the solution for democratic governance and not only a source of its problems. Once this possibility is acknowledged and combined with notice of both the artifactual aspect of groups and their unavoidable centrality, then the need for a politics of associations, and not simply a politics of the reform of political institutions, must be directly addressed.

Strategies of Accommodation: Egalitarian Pluralism[32]

Egalitarian pluralists share, with a vengeance, the doubts just expressed about the possibilities of insulating collective political decisions from the pressures of group bargaining. Assuming the background of mass democracy and associative liberties, they believe that insulation is impossible and perhaps even undesirable.

Background View

Egalitarian pluralism, more positively characterized, is a species of normative pluralism.[33] All members of this genus trace the legitimacy of state actions to their pedigree in procedures of interest representation and group bargaining. Those procedures are set within a political framework that facilitates representation and bargaining, ratifies their results in legislation and enforces the legislative outcomes through executive and judicial action. What distinguishes the different species of normative pluralism are the conceptions of the process that confers legitimacy. What makes egalitarian pluralists *egalitarian* is the central role of the idea of equal representation in their characterization of a legitimacy-conferring process. Thus an outcome is legitimate only if it emerges from a process of representation and bargaining in which all interests have substantively equal chances of being heard and influencing the outcome.

Reflecting this procedural conception of political legitimacy, the egalitarian pluralist emphasizes the importance of assuring liberties of expression, association, and political participation in order to ensure the proper framework of interest representation and group bargaining itself. Other liberties – of conscience, privacy and nonpolitical expression – have a less certain place in egalitarian pluralism. Moreover, the view rejects the generic right to liberty associated with neoliberal constitutionalism, holding that that right would impose an unreasonable constraint on the process of group bargaining.

Finally, egalitarian pluralists are skeptical about substantive conceptions of the common good.[34] Given the diversity of interests characteristic of a pluralistic society, they argue, conceptions of the common good are either vacuous or as controversial as the competing interests that those conceptions are supposed to reconcile. In so far as the notion of the common good has any content, it can be identified procedurally as the outcome of a fair procedure of interest representation and group bargaining. Given this procedural view of the common good, the specifically deliberative aspect of political justification associated with civic republicanism drops out of the egalitarian pluralist conception. Its ideal instead is a political process that reflects the true distribution and weight of social interests. Once opened up in this way, cured of distortion, bargaining in the 'pluralist's bazaar'[35] should proceed essentially unchecked.

The Egalitarian Pluralist Approach to Groups

The value that egalitarian pluralists attach to groups follows simply this characterization of their view of democracy. Groups are primarily good for representing interests effectively. They give individuals of like mind power to bargain with others. This capacity to represent interests

is of particular importance because of its contribution to greater
political equality, the centerpiece of the egalitarian pluralist political
ideal. Groups contribute to greater equality in interest representation
in two ways. They provide a means for individuals with fewer
resources, who might otherwise not be heard, to pool their resources
with others and emerge as potent political factors. And they provide
representation for interests not best organized through territorial
politics based on majority rule. These include functional interests, associated with a person's position or activity within a society; categoric
interests whose intensity is not registered in voting procedures; and,
at least in systems without proportional representation, the interests of
minorities. Briefly, groups can help to provide a more fine-grained
system of interest representation, sensitive to interests that might go
unacknowledged in a system whose only devices of representation were
political parties and representatives with territorial constituencies.

The egalitarian pluralist view of faction also follows straightforwardly from its conception of legitimacy-conferring procedures of
collective choice. Politics is factionally dominated when certain groups
are over-represented in those procedures. So faction arises from the
different capacities of different groups to organize and be heard within
the process of political bargaining. Poor groups tend to be under-
represented because they lack the resources required for organizing;
diffuse groups (e.g. consumers) tend to be under-represented because
the costs of organization are very high; and groups that are the object
of discrimination (blacks, gays) tend to be under-represented because
the hostility and stereotyping directed toward them leads their
interests to be discounted.[36]

To cure faction, then, the egalitarian pluralist institutional program
recommends a more or less radical effort to cure problems of under-
representation in the political process by redressing inequalities in the
conditions of group formation and access. Beginning from the ideal
conception of a procedure for making binding collective decisions that
ensures fair terms of representation and group bargaining, egalitarian
pluralists are customarily attracted to three avenues of reform, the
joint aim of which is to eliminate the pathologies of political inequality
and to ensure a fair, legitimacy-conferring political procedure.

The first strategy is to reform legislative and administrative
processes. Because the problem is inequality in conditions of group
formation and political access, the task of reform is to provide an
encompassing account of the sources of under-representation and
exclusion (race, sex, income, sexual orientation, religion, and so on)
and to make the elimination of all such obstacles a central feature of

policy. Apart from eliminating formal obstacles to participation, that elimination can proceed through strategies of affirmative action for under-represented groups. These might include subsidies for representation of disenfranchised interests (e.g. intervener programs in administrative agencies), enlarged rights of standing to seek judicial review of actions taken by administrative agencies and an extension of rights to participate in administrative processes themselves, or the establishment of specialized agencies that would be directed to represent the interests of under-represented groups and that might provide a focus for efforts to organize those groups (e.g. consumer protection agencies or environmental protection agencies).

Given egalitarian pluralism's correct recognition of the importance of resources in group formation and its correct skepticism about the possibility of insulating politics in a modern democracy from the effects of those inequalities, a second sort of recommendation is to promote significantly greater equality in the distribution of the resources – for example, income, power and information – that are relevant to organization. Robert Dahl, for example, has recommended a scheme of worker cooperatives in part because that scheme would plausibly contribute to background socioeconomic equality in ways that would enhance political equality.[37] More familiarly, the view recommends aggressive use of the taxing power to provide, through the state, compensations for privately generated inequalities of the sort that affect organization. These include compensations for inequalities in the distribution of education, health, housing, other basic goods and income itself.

Finally, in a religiously, ethnically and racially heterogeneous society, there may well be limits on the protections for the representation of minority interests that can be achieved through these two strategies. So egalitarian pluralists commonly favor supplementing the political and socioeconomic strategies with more narrowly judicial ones. Thus there might be more exacting judicial scrutiny of legislation that imposes special burdens on groups that are the familiar object of hostility or stereotyping or that in other ways operate at a disadvantage in the process of political bargaining. The justification for heightened scrutiny is the suspicion that legislative burdens on such groups themselves arise from hostility or other forms of denigration, which are themselves sources of imperfection in processes of political representation.[38] Equally, administrative agencies might be required to consider interests affected by their decisions, irrespective of the participation by affected interests in the process itself.

Analysis and Criticisms

Egalitarian pluralism has two principal strengths. First, it rightly emphasizes that groups defined by common interests and values and not simply by a common territorial basis will inevitably play a central role in the politics of mass democracies. It accepts the centrality of groups that we have insisted on against the other views. Given such centrality, it emphasizes that a program animated by concerns about political equality must address the sources of unfairness or inequality in the group system itself – that is, in the conditions of association formation and access. Second, egalitarian pluralism highlights the artifactual aspects of the group system.[39] It rejects the notion that politics ought to be limited to the transmission of de facto organized social interests into policy. It takes the organization of group interests to itself depend on the structures of political decision-making. And it takes the design of the group system to be an object of political choice, at least with respect to the range of organized interests and the density of group organization.

On the other hand, we disagree with the egalitarian pluralists in part for the reasons that we agreed with civic republicans. More specifically, four considerations lie at the heart of our differences with the view.

First, politics is more than process. A more universalistic concern is needed in politics than is provided by the plurality of interests and aims that define the pluralist bazaar – even an expanded and equalized bazaar. For if politics is defined entirely by the interests of particular groups that bargain with one another over the terms of public policy, then it is unlikely that the framework of pluralist bargaining would itself be stably egalitarian. In the absence of a *direct* concern to ensure the preservation of fair bargaining conditions, those conditions are unlikely to be preserved across changes in economic and social circumstance, particularly since fairness may require alterations in the institutions of bargaining. But the institutional program of the egalitarian pluralist does not address this concern about the formation of such civic sensibilities and the linkages of citizens and state that might plausibly foster them.

Second, we are not persuaded that the fact of a diversity of interests undermines the force of substantive conceptions of the common good. More precisely, we think that reasonable conceptions of the common good fall within a narrower range than the egalitarian pluralist supposes. To recur to a point raised earlier in our discussion of neo-liberal constitutionalism, we take it to be unreasonable for inherited advantage, natural talent and luck to determine differences in lifetime expectations of equal citizens. And we do not see how this can be denied consistent with upholding an egalitarian view of political representation. Legitimate differences of circumstance must be traceable to factors other than these, for example to the choices that individuals make in light of values and preferences formed under free conditions. This constraint on acceptable inequalities does not uniquely determine an account of the common good, but it does impose a significant constraint on acceptable views.

This supposition that there is a substantive common good and that it is a proper aim of politics to advance it adds force to the first point about the need for a direct concern with the fairness of bargaining. Even if conditions of fair political bargaining were self-sustaining, it would not follow that there exists a procedure of fair bargaining among diverse interests that will as a general matter lead to that common good. So achieving it almost certainly requires that it provide a direct aim of political choices.

Third, the ideal of a fair bargaining procedure appears to be so indeterminate as to have limited force as a guide to choices among forms of interest representation.[40] Put otherwise, the ideal of 'fair bargaining', standing alone, is too thin to generate determinate judgments about the appropriate objects of solicitude, subsidy and other sorts of affirmative action. The problems may be clarified by natural questions that might be raised about such affirmative action. Are only interests to be represented? But then what about groups that have aesthetic or other more ideal concerns? Is there a threshold level of intensity of interest that must be reached before interests are represented? If not, then the potential for representational overload is overwhelming; if so, then the scheme of representation is likely to be subject to strategic manipulation. How are interests to be represented? Through representatives of organized groups? Through appointed representatives? In the absence of a more substantive conception of the common good, and relying simply on the ideal of a fair scheme of interest representation, it is difficult to see how these questions could be answered.

Finally, while egalitarian pluralists clearly recognize the centrality of groups, and in some measure recognize their artifactual character, they are as inattentive to the importance of qualitative variation as the neoliberals and civic republicans. This appears, moreover, not to be a matter of oversight, but an ingredient in the egalitarian pluralist conception.[41] The pluralist ideal is to remedy the problems of underrepresentation by ensuring a fair system for the representation and aggregation of interests. Lacking a more substantive view of the common good and the proper terms of political debate, egalitarian

pluralists are concerned principally with whether interests are represented at all. They are not concerned with coordinating interest
representation in the service of some substantive goal, least of all the
goal of reasoned deliberation. Issues about the organization of
groups, about just how they are represented in the state, and about
the effects of the forms of representation on political outcomes and
on civic consciousness fall outside the central range of their view.

Conclusions

Our evaluation of the dominant approaches to democracy and groups
is, then, mixed. We agree with neoliberal constitutionalists on the
importance of self-regulation and choice and the importance of
economic performance and competent and accountable government.
We agree with civic republicans that politics is more than process,
that a substantive notion of the common good is possible and that
that good needs to be aimed at to be achieved. We agree with the
egalitarian pluralists on the importance of equality in representation
and decision-making. And we agree with each of the views that
groups can indeed pose a threat to the satisfaction of their central
aspiration.

At the same time, we dissent from each of these views in different
particulars. And, anticipating central themes in our account of associative democracy, we argue that they have a common limitation in
their failure to give sufficient weight to the simultaneous facts of group
importance, qualitative variation and artifactuality. The sheer importance of groups underscores the need for a more deliberate politics of
secondary associations. Given the associative liberties that partly define
a liberal society, groups will inevitably form, and will inevitably
play an important role. Associative democracy, our deliberate politics
of associations, focuses on improving that role. The artifactuality
of groups, and the roots of faction in the qualitative features of groups,
suggests the possibility and appeal of such a deliberate politics –
directed not merely to one or another aspect of democratic order, but
their reconciliation in a well-ordered egalitarian democracy. We turn
now to filling in the outlines of this suggestion.

2. The Idea of Associative Democracy

Is it possible, and desirable, to promote a deliberate politics of
association directed to egalitarian-democratic ends? In outlining our

affirmative answer to this question here, we begin with those ends themselves – the norms of egalitarian democracy. We then indicate some of the ways that secondary associations commonly act to undermine those norms – in effect, the problem of faction as seen from an egalitarian-democratic perspective – and the ways that groups can and frequently do advance those norms. Finally, we restate the core idea of associative democracy – to cure this factional threat while netting group contribution – and defend that idea against two natural objections: that it is impossible because associations are essentially intractable to political reform; and that it is undesirable because that which is necessary to secure a greater group contribution to democracy raises a ruinous threat of faction.

Norms of Democratic Governance

Associative democracy draws on an egalitarian ideal of social association. The core of that ideal is that the members of a society ought to be treated as equals in fixing the basic terms of social cooperation – including the ways that authoritative collective decisions are made, the ways that resources are produced and distributed, and the ways that social life more broadly is organized.[42] The substantive commitments of the ideal include concerns about fair conditions for citizen participation in politics and robust public debate, an equitable distribution of resources and the protection of individual choice. Lying at the core of social democratic practice in Northern Europe, this conception figures centrally in the most compelling arguments for the affirmative welfare state, including arguments made within such quintessentially liberal orders as the United States. So while we aim here to provide a particular interpretation of both the egalitarian foundations and the more substantive implications, the main ideas that we draw on are familiar and have some roots in common political sensibilities.

For example, we take there to be broad acceptance of the view that opportunities for participation ought to be available to all and that the aspirations of those who do wish to participate ought not to be thwarted by discrimination or limited resources. And while it is widely agreed that some spheres of individual choice ought to remain beyond the reach of public power, government efforts to regulate economic activity with an eye to promoting the general welfare and to securing some measure of distributive fairness and equal opportunity in a scheme of 'ordered liberty' are widely accepted as legitimate functions, even among those who are skeptical about the effectiveness of concerted public action in achieving these aims.[43]

More specifically, we assume that there is broad commitment to the abstract ideal of a democratic society – a society of equals that is governed both by its members and for them. In particular, citizens are understood to be equals in respect of certain basic capacities, including the capacity to evaluate the reasonableness of the rules of association and to govern their conduct in the light of those evaluations and the capacity to formulate and to pursue their aspirations against the background of those rules. Reflecting this abstract democratic ideal and giving it substance are six more specific conditions: popular sovereignty, political equality, distributive equity, civic consciousness, good economic performance and state competence.

These six conditions plainly have different relations to the abstract ideal of democracy. Popular sovereignty and political equality (the popular control or 'by the people' aspect of democracy) are fundamental procedural implications of that ideal. Distributive equity, by contrast, interprets the notion of the general welfare (the responsiveness, or 'for the people' aspect of democracy) in light of the fundamental idea of citizens as equals. Civic consciousness, by which we minimally mean an understanding of and willingness to act to uphold conditions that embody the abstract ideal, contributes to the stability of arrangements satisfying that ideal. And adequate economic performance and state competence are among the conditions required to provide for the general welfare and to sustain confidence in democratic order. For present purposes, however, the precise nature of these connections matters less than the fact that these conditions represent widely shared standards of performance for a modern, democratic society and that they enjoy natural connections to the abstract conception of democratic order. If the problem of faction, then, consists in the threat that secondary associations can present to democratic order, that problem can reasonably be specified by reference to threats to these more particular conditions of democracy.

In the remarks that follow we discuss each of these conditions in more detail, saying only enough about the content of each to give structure to our account of solutions to the problem of faction. We also indicate characteristic measures that democratic states take to satisfy them. This latter feature of our review will be important for later discussion because the attraction of associative democracy partly turns on whether, in meeting the full range of democratic norms, associative forms of governance can be combined with the non-associative measures noted here.

Popular Sovereignty

A central feature of a democratic order is that final authority in fixing the terms of association rests with citizens: that authorization through procedures in which citizens are represented as equals is necessary and, within the limits set by the fundamental liberties, sufficient for the legitimacy of state action. Formally, this requirement of popular sovereignty commands procedures for decision-making which assign citizens or their elected and accountable representatives the legal powers to determine the public agenda, to advance specific proposals for public action, to choose among alternative courses of action and to oversee and enforce the implementation of choices. Meeting these conditions in turn requires rights of expression, association, suffrage and office-holding as well as formal procedures for the oversight of executive bureaux to which enforcement is entrusted. More substantively, popular sovereignty requires that citizens and their elected representatives have at their disposal adequate sources of information and enforcement powers that enable them reliably to control the exercise of governmental power. Good information permits precision in public decisions, including the choice of means for implementing collective choices. The availability of reliable enforcement powers is necessary to ensuring that what is enacted in the name of the sovereign people is in fact done. In addition, the availability of such powers widens the scope of sovereignty. It enables legislatures to enact policies that are judged reasonable but that might not be approved if citizens or their representatives anticipated that the agencies, commissions and departments charged with enforcement would fail to implement the popular will.

Political Equality

A second fundamental element of democratic governance is political equality. We understand this requirement to mandate what Rawls has called the 'fair value of political liberty', or the extension of fair equality of opportunity to the political process.[44] Specifically, the chances to hold office and to influence political choices ought to be roughly equal across citizens. Wealth and other features that distinguish among equal citizens (e.g. race, gender, religious ideals) should not fix the general terms of that process or the weight assigned individual views within it.

As with popular sovereignty, the requirement of political equality has a more formal and a more substantive aspect. Formally understood, it mandates the elimination of legal or other official barriers to political participation, requiring in particular that modes of political representation neither unfairly aggregate individual opinion (e.g. example, through differently sized election districts) nor officially discriminate against certain classes of citizens on grounds of their race, gender or other ascriptive features unrelated to their status as moral equals. But ensuring that citizens are treated as equals in arrangements of collective choice is not simply a matter of barring such official discrimination. So, ensuring political equality also requires measures to correct for the effects that inequalities in wealth, private discrimination or organizational capacity might otherwise exert on the political process. In part, this is a matter of insulating the political process from the effects of de facto economic and organizational inequalities – by, for example, limiting private campaign contributions and establishing public financing of party competition or encouraging the representation of traditionally under-represented groups by lowering barriers to entry into administrative proceedings that bear on their interests and circumstances. In part, it is a matter of limiting those inequalities themselves, through, for example, inheritance taxes, income redistribution and subsidies for the organization and representation of under-represented interests.

Distributive Fairness

In addition to making such adjustments in the distribution of material resources as are necessary to ensure the fair value of political liberty, contemporary states are widely expected to ensure fairness in the distribution of resources. We think that the most suitable understanding of distributive fairness for a democratic society is an egalitarian conception – a conception that condemns inequalities of advantage deriving from differences of inherited resources, of natural endowments or of simple good luck.[45] Even when the imperfections of actual markets are eliminated, differences arising from such factors can be expected to proliferate under the system of 'natural liberty' described by market exchange – for example, income differentials traceable to educational differences that are themselves due to differences of parental wealth or income differentials traceable to the possession of differences in inborn capacity (e.g. for intensive effort). Such differences in market reward may signal genuine differences in the value that others place on individual contributions. They are irrelevant, however, to the moral equality of persons. A concern to respect that equality in the distribution of advantage, therefore, requires efforts to ensure that such factors do not generate differences in lifetime expectations of advantage.

At the level of policy, virtually all plausible egalitarian distributional conceptions will require measures to ensure equal opportunity by limiting the intergenerational transmission of wealth and broadening the distribution of skills – measures including taxes aimed at maintaining a wide dispersion of property (e.g. inheritance and gift taxes) and active labor market policies aimed at ensuring full employment, supporting human capital formation (through education and training) and improving the operation of labor markets (e.g. eliminating discrimination and barriers to entry into trades). These policies would need also to be supplemented by tax and transfer policies aimed at limiting residual distributional effects of the distribution of natural abilities, although the more precise requirements of those policies would depend on the particular interpretation of the egalitarian requirements that one adopts.

Civic Consciousness

Within an egalitarian-democratic order, political decision-making must be deliberative. Public decision-making is deliberative when it is framed by different conceptions of the common good, and public initiatives are defended ultimately by reference to an 'openly acknowledged conception of the public interest'.[46] This requirement does not mean that public debate must exclusively invoke conceptions of the common good or that its terms do not include more mundane expressions of individual benefit. But it does require a general recognition of the norms of democratic process and equity, and a willingness to uphold them and to accept them as fixing the basic framework of political argument and social cooperation – at least on condition that others do so as well. By 'civic consciousness' we mean such recognition and acceptance of these basic democratic norms.[47]

Such consciousness and the forms of deliberative public engagement associated with it arguably have intrinsic value. But that intrinsic appeal is not essential here. For our purposes, it is sufficient that preserving reasonably widespread civic consciousness is required for maintaining conditions of popular sovereignty, political equality and distributive equity. In particular, it is unreasonable to expect these conditions to be sustained as the stable equilibrium outcome of political bargaining among particular interests under changing social circumstances. However satisfactory the initial situation of such bargaining, changes in population, occupational structures, social roles and expectations, and external involvements and pressures will likely lead to a decline in the satisfaction of such norms, without some remedial reform of institutional arrangements. And it is implausible that the appropriate changes in institutional arrangements will be made unless the norms themselves function as guides to public deliberation. The stable satisfaction of the fundamental conditions of democratic order, in short, appears to require that the conditions themselves provide the basic norms of political justification and the conscious object of political choice – that arenas of collective choice serve as a 'forum of principle' and not simply as an occasion for high stakes bargaining. This is the requirement of civic consciousness.

As a matter of policy, efforts to foster civic consciousness are familiar enough. Virtually all school systems require attention to national civic practices and institutions in programs of compulsory instruction. Mandatory programs of public service are routine, public subsidy of private programs serving public functions even more so. However, the encouragement of an ongoing and popular civic consciousness can be treated as an explicit goal of institutional design, affecting both public and private institutions. To strengthen public allegiance to arrangements of political equality and popular sovereignty, for example, the satisfaction of democratic norms must itself be manifest to the public. So, for example, inspiring confidence in the scheme of public deliberation and the widespread embrace of its terms may require a visible independence of that scheme from private interests. Rules limiting the 'conflicts of interest' faced by public officials are only the most obvious way to do this. Rules on limiting and disclosing private contributions to campaigns for public office, or more ambitious schemes to finance party competition largely out of public funds, are another way in which public confidence is sought. Or, to express the importance of the norms of distributive equity and equal opportunity, states may condition grants of support to private institutions on their own demonstration of allegiance to them. Research grants to universities or contracts to government suppliers, for example, may be conditional on demonstrated fairness in their hiring procedures.

Economic Performance

Good economic performance is not constitutive of the notion of a well-ordered democracy. But policies directed to its achievement are important in enhancing the general welfare and in giving substance to the ideal of popular sovereignty. This is particularly true of policies aimed at increasing productivity – the measure of economic perfor-mance that we adopt here – for two reasons.

First, productivity improvement is typically necessary to promote the general welfare. Other measures of economic performance (e.g. non-inflationary growth) might be proposed here, but we take productivity growth to be of especially fundamental importance both because of the direct welfare benefits conferred by the reduction of toil that it makes possible and because its satisfaction permits a choice among a variety of different welfare-enhancing strategies. These prominently include low growth, high quality of life strategies for welfare improvement of the sort that present environmental disasters recommend.

Second, and following on the point about choice among different welfare strategies, by reducing the amount of effort per unit of output, productivity growth reduces the constraints of material necessity. It thus makes more possible a social choice between economic and other sorts of activity. In doing so, it gives substance to the democratic ideal of free deliberation about the ends and conditions of social association.

Competent Government

Some measure of competence and efficiency in government performance also appears necessary to public confidence in, and ultimately to the stability of, democratic arrangements. Even a minimal state needs to engage in a range of activities, particularly the provision of a variety of public goods, whose costs are borne by the public. In modern democratic welfare states, public budgets account for a substantial portion of total economic activity. In expending such publicly appropriated resources, competent and efficient performance is needed to maintain public confidence in the democratic process – a point underscored by a massive literature in political economy and mountains of opinion polls, which have emphasized that 'government failure' is not a suitable remedy for market failure.

In addition to these implications for public confidence, competent and efficient government performance directly contributes to the general welfare and, as noted earlier, to satisfying the condition of popular sovereignty. It does so by removing one constraint on deliberation and the application of public authority that might otherwise be compelling: namely, that the 'inevitable' waste, corruption or incapacity of government bars its use to address public ends.

'Egalitarian Faction'

In the everyday politics of contemporary mass democracies, these norms of democratic order are routinely frustrated by groups. The 'natural' pattern of group formation reflects the unequal distribution of conditions favorable to group formation – including the control of strategic resources, the size of the populations with common concerns, the density of interaction among persons with shared interests and the intensity of concern about an issue. The groups that form typically seek to advance the specific interests of their members and not any more comprehensive interest (including the interest in maintaining democracy itself). With powers exerted in both public and private arenas, unrepresentative and particularistic groups promote a politics far removed from the democratic ideal of popular control, by equal citizens, of a government promoting the general welfare.

By way of illustration, consider the ways that group organization, operating in the areas of agenda formation, political choice and policy implementation, might raise factional threats to three of the conditions of democratic order just noted: political equality, popular sovereignty and state competence and efficiency.[48]

The factional threat to political equality is straightforward. Organization confers power. But as just noted, the distribution of group powers tends to reflect inequalities in the conditions favorable to group formation. As a result, some classes of citizens will be over-represented in the group system, whereas others – principally the poor, those whose size and/or dispersion produces high organizational costs, and those sharing aims whose expression is less easy to negotiate or compromise – will be under-represented. The political importance of such inequalities in group representation rises as the political process relies more on groups. That organized groups commonly use the benefits they extract from the state to bolster their organization, of course, only makes matters worse.

The threat to popular sovereignty arises from the possibility of a de facto transfer of public power, as groups intercede in the policy formation process, over-representing the interests of their members within it.[49] That over-representation undermines the faithful representation of the interests of citizens within the process – both the preferences of the constituencies of the separate representatives and the general welfare that transcends private aims.

In particular, groups distort the process of agenda formation by exploiting the 'rational ignorance' of both the people and their representatives. In the selection of items from that agenda, they develop de facto veto powers. These are secured through a variety of threats to legislators, from contingent withdrawal of campaign support to more ominous and general failures of group 'confidence'. Distorted by group powers, the political process may devolve to the exploitation by organized groups of asymmetries in the benefits and burdens of public action. This is perhaps most clearly displayed in the case of distributive policies that feature concentrated benefits (to particular groups) and diffuse costs (spread over all taxpayers). Finally, in policy implementation, groups may continue to obstruct fidelity to the popular will. In cases of regulatory 'capture', groups dominate administrative rule-making and implementation. But even in those cases of reasonably independent agencies with reasonably clear legislative instructions, groups may exercise effective veto powers over effective enforcement of policies running contrary to their private interests. As a result of all these intercessions and distortions from secondary group activity, government action comes less and less to reflect the free deliberation of a sovereign people.[50]

Narrowly defined groups threaten government competence and efficiency, finally, through the same sort of self-seeking. In their promotion of concessions to particular interests in the policy-making and implementation process, they can complicate and enfeeble general programs of action. In their exploitation of private information and the dispersion of program costs, they engender wasteful expenditures of public resources ('pork') on private ends. And through agency 'capture' or more discrete interventions in the administrative process, they can cripple enforcement of policies they oppose.[51] The result has been described as a 'feudal' version of the administrative state, simultaneously feeble and oppressive: an agglomeration of discrete centers of privilege that literally corrupts concerted national action in the public interest even as it takes public monies to do so.

The Potential Contribution of Groups

But if the dangers that groups pose to egalitarian norms are familiar enough, so too is the fact that groups can make substantial contributions to egalitarian-democratic order. In the ordinary of mass democracies, groups are generally acknowledged as capable of performing at least four useful, democracy-enhancing functions.

Information. Associations can provide information to policy-makers on member preferences, the impact of proposed legislation or the implementation of existing law. As the state has become more involved in regulating society and extended the reach of its regulation to more diverse sites, technically complex areas and processes subject to rapid change, this information function has arguably become more important. Good information is needed to assess the effectiveness of a myriad of state policies, commonly operating at some distance from the monitoring of state inspectorates, and to adjust policies to changed circumstances or behaviors. This is especially so given social and policy interdependence – the interaction of social welfare policy and economic growth, for example, or environmental regulation and technical change – that underscore the value of accurate timely intelligence on policy effects. Because of their proximity to those effects, groups are often well positioned to provide such information. When they do, they contribute to satisfying the norm of popular sovereignty because good information improves citizen deliberation, facilitates the enforcement of decisions and clarifies the appropriate objects of state policy.

Equalizing representation. Politics is materially conditioned, and inequalities in material advantage of the sort definitive of capitalism translate directly to inequalities in political power. Groups can help remedy these inequalities by permitting individuals with low per capita resources to pool those resources through organization. In making the benefits of organization available to those whose influence on policy is negligible without it, groups help satisfy the norm of political equality. Similarly, groups can promote a more equitable distribution of advantage by correcting for imbalances in bargaining power that follow from the unequal control of wealth. Groups can also represent interests not best organized through territorial politics based on majority rule. These include functional interests associated with a person's position or activity within a society; 'categoric' interests of the sort pursued by the new social movements, interests whose intensity is not registered in voting procedures; and, at least in systems without proportional representation, the interests of political minorities. Here, groups improve an imperfect system of interest representation by making it more fine-grained, attentive to preference intensities and representative of diverse views. This too furthers political equality.

Citizen education. Associations can function as 'schools of democracy'. Participation in them can help citizens develop competence, self-confidence and a broader set of interests than they would acquire in a more fragmented political society. De Tocqueville provides the classic statement of this educative power of associations: 'Feelings are recruited, the heart is enlarged, and the human mind is developed only by the reciprocal influence of men on one another', and under democratic conditions this influence can 'only be accomplished by associations'.[52] In performing this educative function, associations help foster the 'civic consciousness' on which any egalitarian order and its deliberative politics depend. That is, they promote a recognition of the norms of democratic process and equity and a willingness to uphold them and to accept them as fixing the basic framework of political argument and social cooperation, at least on the condition that others do so as well.

Alternative governance. Associations can provide a distinctive form of social governance, alternative to markets or public hierarchies, that permits society to realize the important benefits of cooperation among member citizens. In providing a form of governance, associations figure more as problem-solvers than simply as representatives of their members to authoritative political decision-makers, pressuring those decision-makers on behalf of member interests. They help to formulate and execute public policies and take on quasi-public functions, which supplement or supplant the state's more directly regulatory actions.

Such associations facilitate cooperative dealings in two ways. First, their very existence reduces the transaction costs of securing agreement among potentially competing interests. The background of established forms of communication and collaboration they provide enable parties to settle more rapidly and reliably on jointly beneficial actions. Second, groups help establish the trust that facilitates cooperation. They effectively provide assurances to members that their own willingness to cooperate will not be exploited by others. Often directly beneficial to society, associative governance can also support public efforts to achieve egalitarian aims.

The Core Idea of Associative Democracy

The core idea of associative democracy is to curb faction through a deliberate politics of association while netting such group contribution to egalitarian-democratic governance. It seeks neither to abolish affirmative governance nor to insulate the state from society nor simply to open a bazaar of bargaining among more equally endowed groups. Instead, it proposes to act directly on the associative environment of public action in ways that make associations less factionalizing and more supportive of the range of egalitarian-democratic norms.

The tools of this reform project would be the conventional tools of public policy (taxes, subsidies, legal sanctions), as applied through the familiar decision-making procedures of formal government (legislatures and administrative bodies, as overseen by the courts).[53] In general terms, the aims of the project are given by the norms of democratic governance. More specifically, this means action in three sorts of area. Where manifest inequalities in political representation exist, associative democracy recommends promoting the organized representation of presently excluded interests. Where group particularism undermines popular sovereignty or democratic deliberation, it recommends encouraging the organized to be more other-regarding in their actions. And, where associations have greater competence than public authorities for achieving efficient and equitable outcomes, or where their participation could improve the effectiveness of government programs, it recommends encouraging a more direct and formal governance role for groups.

This last point about governance may be the most immediate. In many areas of economic and social concern – from the environment and occupational safety and health to vocational training and consumer protection – egalitarian aims are badly served by the state-market dichotomy, which still dominates mainstream debate about how those aims should be pursued. Often, the right answer to the question 'Should the state take care of the problem, or should it be left to the market?' is a double negative.

This seems so in three ideal-typical classes of regulatory problems. In the first, non-market public standards on behavior are needed, which government has the competence to set, but the objects of regulation are so diverse or unstable that it is not possible for the government to specify just how those standards should be met at particular regulated sites. Much environmental regulation presents problems of this sort. In the second, public standard-setting is needed, which government has the competence to do, but the objects of regulation are sufficiently numerous or dispersed to preclude serious government monitoring of compliance. Consider the problems of occupational safety and health enforcement. In the third, uniform public standards are needed, but it lies beyond the competence of either markets or governments to specify and secure them, as doing either requires the simultaneous coordination of private actors and their enlistment in specifying the behavior sought. Here, consider the difficulties of getting private firms to agree on standards for vocational training and to increase their own training efforts.

Where these sorts of problem are encountered, associative governance can provide a welcome alternative or complement to public regulatory efforts because of the distinctive capacity of associations to gather local information, monitor behavior and promote cooperation among private actors. In such cases, the associative strategy recommends attending to the possibility of enlisting them explicitly in the performance of public tasks.

Basically, then, associative democracy departs from the observations that groups inevitably play a fundamental role in the politics of mass democracies, that the threat of faction is real and that groups could make a substantial contribution to democratic order. It observes further that the 'right' sorts of association do not arise naturally. It then proposes to supplement nature with artifice: through politics, to secure an associative environment more conducive to democratic aims.

Natural Objections: Impossibility and Undesirability

This core idea of associative democracy may be clarified by considering two natural objections to it. Both accept, at least for the sake of argument, the attractiveness of egalitarian-democratic norms and the possibility of group contribution to their satisfaction, but they reject the use of an associative strategy to engender a democracy-enhancing associative environment. According to the first objection, it is not possible to create a favorable associative environment through politics; according to the second, efforts to create such an environment are more dangerous than the disease they aim to cure.

Impossibility. The argument for impossibility begins with the assumption that groups are a product of nature, or culture, or some other unalterable substrate of a country's political life. Just as some countries are blessed with good topsoil or a temperate climate, others are blessed with the 'right' kinds of group at the right level of organization. In countries that are so blessed, group contributions of the sort we note are observed. But because patterns of group organization and behavior lie beyond politics, the observation provides no support at all for an associative strategy for addressing the problems of egalitarianism. Indeed, precisely by highlighting the importance of a favorable social basis for egalitarian democracy, they explain why equality does not travel well.

For reasons already suggested in our treatment of conventional cures for faction, however, we think that this objection exaggerates the fixity of the associative environment. Groups are, again, importantly artifactual. Their incidence, character and patterns of interaction are not merely the result of natural tendencies to association among citizens with like preferences; they reflect structural features of the political economy in which they form, from the distribution of wealth and income to the locus of policy-making in different areas. And they reflect variations across the members of that society along such dimensions as income, information and density of interaction. Existing political institutions and culture may crystallize around certain structural features and patterns of variation along these dimensions. But those features and variations are in no sense natural: they are themselves in part a product of opportunities and incentives that are induced by the structure of political institutions and the substance of political choices and so can be changed through public policy.

Public policy can, for example, make the background distribution of wealth and income more or less uneven. It can shift the locus of public decision-making from regional to national levels or concentrate it in a single department in ways that encourage different sorts of group formation and discourage others. The availability of information can be widened or constricted. The density of interaction among similarly situated citizens can be increased or decreased. The cost of administering joint efforts or navigating the negotiation antecedent to them can be subsidized or not. Those subsidies can simply be provided to the most powerful, or tied to antecedent satisfaction of certain requirements of behavior. Consistent with the continued supremacy of formal political institutions, groups can also be assigned public functions – for example, including the power to issue complaints for violations of administration regulation, to take emergency action in correcting violations, to establish standards for licensing and training in different occupations and industry standards on production, to establish eligibility criteria for receipt of other sorts of benefit including welfare benefits, and to apply such licensing procedures, standards and eligibility criteria as part of a general regulatory regime. All such changes in the environment of group formation, the incentives available to individual groups and the governing status of groups can manifestly change the group system.

In claiming that associations are artifactual, we do not mean to suggest that they are simply political creations or that they ought to be treated as such. But it is both an empirical and normative mistake to treat the extent and forms of group organization as a scheme of private ordering to which politics must simply adapt. In part reflecting political choice, the incidence and structure of groups and the patterns of group representation can be changed through political choice.

Undesirability. Even accepting this, however, efforts to enlist associations in democratic governance may be undesirable. While groups can contribute to democratic order, they always carry the risk of faction. If our associative strategy entails the further cultivation of groups and recommends that further public powers be ceded to them, what is to keep that risk under control? Won't associative democracy invite a truly ruinous faction? The second objection to associative democracy concludes that it will, and thus finds the scheme undesirable.

But this conclusion, we believe, is premature. As already suggested in our treatment of faction, that threat is posed not by groups per se but by particular kinds of groups interacting in particular ways with the more traditional processes of public decision-making. In thinking about groups, recognition of this is the beginning of wisdom and of the hope that group energies might be enlisted without ruinous faction. We come back, then, to the fact of qualitative variation. Groups and group systems differ not only quantitatively but qualitatively with respect to such features as the pattern of their internal decision-making, their inclusiveness with respect to potential membership, their relations to other associations, and the nature and extent of their powers. The art of associative democracy consists in matching group characteristics with assigned functions and – now admitting the fact of artifactuality – cultivating those characteristics appropriate to functions consistent with the norms of egalitarian democracy. Just how this might be done in particular policy areas we explore in sections 3 and 4. To frame that discussion, however, we shall sketch here seven important features of qualitative variation in groups that are worth keeping in mind:

1. *Accountability of group leadership to members and leadership powers over those members.* For example, a union membership may or may not have a right to prior consultation in the negotiation of a collective bargaining agreement or a right to withhold approval of the agreement once negotiated. Similarly, strikes may or may not require approval from leaderships, which may or may not have powers to sanction wildcatters or scabs. Variation along such dimensions affects the scope and content of collective agreements and the incidence of strikes.

2. *Centralization of authority in group decision-making.* Distinguishable from variation in the accountability and powers of leadership, centralization is a matter of concentration of leadership or decision-making authority. Continuing with the union example, a union with a highly centralized leadership, negotiating a national agreement with employers, can be expected to pursue a strategy different from a union in which bargaining is handled by numerous locals negotiating with separate firms or plant managements. In the centralized case, assuming some accountability to membership, the union is more likely to be attentive to the range of member interests. At the same time, the negotiating team can make compromises and tradeoffs across diverse interests within that membership. Ceteris paribus, an agreement is more likely to be reached (both because of the possibility of concerted force and the possibility of tradeoffs before applying that force), and it

is more likely to be one that represents the aggregate interests of the membership.

3. *Encompassingness or completeness of group membership relative to affected populations*. The encompassingness of an association is the proportion of the affected population that it counts among its members. A less encompassing business association claiming 10 percent of the firms in a particular industry, region, or national economy will behave differently from an association claiming 90 percent of the firms. In the first case, possibilities of 'free-riding' on other social actors (including other firms) is greater than in the second. A proposal for a taxbreak for oil companies, funded out of general corporate tax revenues, is more attractive to an organization consisting only of oil companies than it is to an organization representing all firms. In the first case, all the benefits of the proposal will be internalized to the organization's members, but they will bear only a small portion of its costs. In the second case, both the benefits and burdens of the proposal are internalized. Also, an organization representing 90 percent of some class of actors is more likely to be recognized as representative by other actors and institutions (including the state). In combination, the disincentives to free-riding and the greater security that comes of social recognition tend to encourage more responsible organizational behavior vis-à-vis other social actors.

4. *Scope of responsibility assumed by, or assigned to, associations*. By this we mean the range of policy areas or concerns in which a group or group system pursues an interest, that is, the particularity of its concerns. As with encompassing groups that must be attentive to the diverse interests of their membership, so groups with relatively wide scope must be attentive to the interaction of different elements that fall within the range of their powers. Again, possibilities for tradeoff, compromise or synergy between different aspects of group activity are more likely than in more narrowly defined groups.

5. *Relation to the state*. This can range from bare toleration to active state promotion through the endowment of the association with public powers. Critically important here, of course, are the terms of 'political exchange' where such exists (i.e. the quid pro quo of group recognition, licensing, subsidy, etc.) and the state's demands upon associations in return for such support.

6. *Characteristic modes of interaction with other groups*. Here we have in mind the degree of competition and cooperation among formally independent groups – for example, the degree to which they respect each other's programmatic boundaries and membership bases, share information, pool resources and elaborate joint programs. The

political consequences of a high level of associability in a population will depend on these characteristics of the associations. For example, a population of associations, each of which encompasses only a small portion of an affected population, might, through intense cooperation with other groups, achieve results parallel to a single encompassing group.

7. *Equality in the distribution of powers across groups*. Finally, the strength and distribution of groups inevitably reflects such 'background' conditions as the distribution of material resources, the proximity and density of interaction of memberships with convergent interests and other familiar conditions of collective action. Underlying inequalities tend to translate into inequalities in group power. Systems of group representation vary in the degree of such background inequality, in the extent of translation and, as a consequence, in policy outcomes. A system that features strong employer organizations and churches but extremely weak unions, consumer groups and women's federations, for example, will have different effects from a system in which all such groups are flourishing.

If artifactuality is admitted, the trick of associative democracy is simply keeping such features in mind, and using conventional policy tools to steer the group system toward one that, for particular problems, has the right sorts of qualitative features. Of course, there is nothing 'simple' about this. Doing it right involves judgment. But in this it is no different from any other politics. And in principle – and that is all we have sought to establish here – it can be done.

It remains to be shown just how it could be done and what it might be done about. That is the task of the remainder of this essay.

3. Associative Regulation

We began by noting a concern with the growing mismatch between the present regulatory institutions and the tasks of democratic regulation. In brief, 'promoting the general welfare' now requires a serious alternative to the policies and practices of the Keynesian welfare state, but that alternative is now lacking. In this section, we propose to use this observation as a basis for deepening our consideration of associative democracy. Specifically, we ask two questions. First, how might an associative strategy be used to correct this mismatch? In particular, how might associations be used to enhance government competence and improve economic performance? Second, how might these associative solutions to problems of government competence and economic performance be reconciled with other democratic norms? Before addressing these questions directly, however, we provide some background on the mismatch itself.

Problems in the Welfare State

Since the early 1970s, economic performance in advanced capitalist economies has seriously deteriorated, with productivity and growth rates lagging and employment/inflation tradeoffs becoming more severe. This decline in economic performance is associated, perhaps causally, with sharply increased competitive pressures, resulting from increased internationalization of capital and product markets, and the emergence of a range of new competitors from poorer countries. It has also coincided with a continued shift in the composition of employment away from manufacturing and toward service and public employment; a series of changes in gender relations occasioned principally by sharp increases in female labor market participation; and the advent of the 'fourth industrial revolution' of microelectronics and (often related) changes in transportation and communications technologies.

These changes have seriously weakened the powers of public regulative institutions. Variations in national style, economic structure and political institutions permit only the most abstract characterization of those institutions. But, as a general matter, the earlier arrangements – commonly referred to as the 'Keynesian welfare state' – provided a framework of macroregulation of the economic environment and class compromise and conflict, within national economies. In the model most closely approximated in the most 'developed' welfare states (e.g. the Scandinavian social democracies), such regulation proceeded through national government fine-tuning of fiscal and monetary aggregates, centralized bargaining over wage/profit/employment shares between encompassing peak associations of workers and capitalists, and political bargaining over a 'social wage' which took more or less explicit notice of traditional family structures (and low male unemployment) as a benchmark.

In retrospect, it appears that some substantial measure of integration into the rest of the world economy was a condition for the elaboration of this model. Dependence on foreign markets limited the appeal of narrow sectoral political strategies of economic gain (e.g. trade protection) and thus drove even the most powerful economic actors toward alliance with weaker ones in national political compromises and strategies of gain. At the same time, however, the

elaboration of such national strategies was premissed on the ability of
the national government to 'deliver the goods', which was in turn
dependent on its ability to extract payment from a captive tax base.
This in turn was dependent on the stability of that base, and the ability
to work out terms of cooperation among taxable actors within it (e.g.
on restricting the flow of capital and labor out of the country and
spreading the 'overhead' costs of the state sufficiently so as not to
impair the international competitive position of particular sectors or
firms).

Now, virtually all the ingredients in this model have been thrown
into question in the new environment.

Internationalization of capital and product markets coupled with
increased possibilities for firms to migrate from national economies
has limited the capacities of states to maintain control of their tax
bases and monetary policies. The very idea of a national economy, as
distinct from the international one, is increasingly remote from
policy-makers whose monetary interventions are swamped by global
capital movements and whose tax base is continually threatened by
the exit of capital and (increasingly) labor.

Within what is left of national economies, moreover, the appropria-
teness of general macroeconomic regulation is increasingly uncertain,
given changes in the organization of economic activity. In particular,
firms' responses to increased competition have taken at least two
divergent forms. This divergence itself is disturbing to generic forms
of regulation, as it introduces significant new elements of heterogeneity
into the regulated system. More immediately, however, neither
characteristic path of response is favorable to national strategies of
regulation.

Along one path of restructuring ('flexible specialization' or 'diversified quality production'), firms are producing high value-added items
tailored to niche markets. In the search for flexibility and higher
quality, those pursuing this first path typically also aim for tighter
integration of design, engineering, marketing and production functions within and often across cognate firms. Such 'flexible integration'
has often served to erode the stability of internal labor markets (in
particular, those whose operation was premissed on relatively narrow-
banded job classifications and career ladders). It has also increased the
relative returns to education and skill in the external labor market,
exacerbating inequalities within the workforce. Most immediately
for macroregulatory institutions, however, it has simply increased
the diversity of production needs within the economy and altered
intrafirm and interfirm organization, resulting, for example, in a

declining dominance of the M-form, the rise of regional economies, and a variety of joint activities by firms. The upshot is that the most helpful forms of state regulation are less macro than 'meso' (i.e. sectoral or regional) or micro (i.e. tailored to individual firms or small clusters thereof). Furthermore, the pace of change implies that substantive 'command and control' regulation increasingly risks immediate obsolescence.

On the second path, firms retain an orientation to price competition in relatively low value-added goods and then make those adjustments needed to compete with ultra low-cost Third World producers – that is, 'sweating' their own labor forces, outsourcing as much production as possible to low-wage havens abroad, automating at home. Here the barrier to regulatory institutions intent on high social welfare is, if anything, more straightforward. The tax base declines, as departure from the national economy is deployed not merely as a threat but as a strategy.

In practice, of course, the two sorts of strategies are pursued in combination. But whatever the precise mix, generic regulation appears less suitable either because of the inability of the state to impose national terms or because of the perverse effects of those national terms on increasingly heterogeneous production, or both.

The same changes that threaten the capacities of states to pursue national projects also threaten the capacity of the most typical encompassing organizations of the Keynesian era – national unions and employer associations – to integrate and manage broad class interests. For them, too, there is a growing divergence between the political arenas in which their power is concentrated and the arenas in which their membership has its strongest attachments or concerns. On the one hand, the operation of business proceeds increasingly on an international plane, beyond the reach of national organizations. On the other, the requirements and politics of the intensive organizational innovation now under way are best appreciated at more local or particular sites, such as the community, firm, region or state. Remote national organizations of employers and workers thus suffer in their capacity to address the concerns of members.

With capacities for international management even more remote than capacities for national regulation, the effect is a natural devolution of responsibility and an erosion of solidarity on both sides of class divisions to subnational levels. Both the members of employer organizations and those of unions wish their organizations to be more attentive to their particular needs and bargaining capacities. Concerted programs of employer cooperation, in particular across more narrowly defined sectors or product markets, erode. So too do concerted programs of worker cooperation across particular circumstances of employment – as reflected, for example, in new forms of productivity syndicalism focused on particular firms, as well as declining union membership and activity, threats to solidarity bargaining and decreasing support for public efforts at redistribution.

These economic developments, especially when combined with the disruption of traditional family structures to which they contribute, also have consequences for the state's capacity to provide effective national social welfare regulation. In the Keynesian welfare state, it was in some measure justified to organize welfare provision through broad categoric programs and politically understandable that such programs were developed along separate lines. But indifference to variation and lack of integration are less tolerable under present circumstances. Conceptions of a 'traditional' family, job or life course make increasingly less sense, even as approximations. The expanded rate of labor force participation by women has pressed into focus a whole series of needs once met by their household labor. And movements into and out of social services and between services at any given moment or over a life course are as a consequence greater. The rate of technological change is such that education now needs to be available throughout working lifetimes, not only at their start, and means that those without marketable skills are at increased risk for a string of other social problems (unemployment, health problems, family unrest, etc.). Increased diversity within the economy means that generic programs of assistance repeatedly under- or overshoot their target. Regionalization of economic production leads to clumping not only of economic activities but of the needs occasioned when they do not go well.

In this context, national welfare programs and administration are, like other aspects of state macroregulation, mismatched to circumstances. The old arrangements performed reasonably well in a world of relative stability, mass markets, more clearly defined national economies and more narrowly defined class politics. But each of those conditions has changed, and the old institutions are not doing so well now. A need for new structures of citizen involvement in decision-making, for more flexible means of adjusting to rapid change and for institutions capable of extending public capacities for regulation into the interstices of the economy and social life are all implied. How to supply such in a way that respects liberal commitments to individual autonomy, is attentive to the new requirements of the economy and enjoys public support but that at the same time advances egalitarian aspirations is the difficult political and administrative question.

Associations, we believe, are a large part of the answer. Their capacities for information-gathering and dissemination, the construction and enforcement of standards and, more generally, the enlistment of private actors as supplementary supports for public regulatory efforts are at this point especially valuable. The question for an associative democrat is, can those capacities be harnessed for public purposes in a way consistent with other democratic commitments?

Associative Solutions

Faced with the sketch just offered, and recognizing the limits of national economic policy-making, someone committed to democratic ideals and associative forms of governance might suggest a wide variety of arrangements to address problems of economic management and the capacity/efficiency of state regulation. We do not know, and do not propose here to attempt to specify, the full range of appropriate new institutions and organizations. What we will do, however, and what is sufficient for the basic task of displaying the content of the associative conception, is to indicate a significant range of such institutions, performing various functions at different levels of society.

The functions that we have in mind are (1) the formulation of policy, (2) the coordination of economic activity in the shadow of the law, and (3) the enforcement and administration of policy. These would, as a practical matter, be distributed over organizations operating at national, regional/sectoral and local levels, creating nine cases for analysis. But for convenience, we suppress these complexities in our presentation here, concentrating on one function for groups at each level. Thus we offer suggestions for national groups performing policy formulation functions, regional groups coordinating economic activity and local groups helping with enforcement – providing in each case a characterization of certain desired features of the groups, their potential contribution, and a few examples of the sorts of areas in which that contribution might be most evident.

To begin, then, with national policy formulation, we imagine a range of national-level associations engaged in more or less ongoing bargaining among themselves and with the state. These groups might be understood as lineal descendants of the traditional 'social partners' of unions and employer associations. As in the case of the social partners, it would be important that they be relatively encompassing, accountable to membership and possessed of significant powers of sanction over their memberships. And like the social partners, they would enjoy quasi-public status and even direct state subsidy in exchange for observing a series of behavioral constraints. Unlike the traditional social partners, however, the functions of these groups would be more clearly restricted to a demarcated set of specifically national concerns, and their number would be greater. In particular, they would extend to include organizations not organized along class lines (e.g. environmental groups, women's groups, representatives of the aged). The range of such officially represented groups would (as discussed shortly) be determined by citizen choice, as expressed through the party system.

The policy formulation role of such groups would consist in their assistance in the formulation of authoritative standards, their advancing of new programs or reforms of state initiative and their contribution of information and advice for state actors. As pertains narrowly to the questions of economic performance and state efficiency, the chief institutional advantage of individual associations would consist in their ability to provide more detailed and accurate information about social needs than that available from more comprehensive and less socially rooted forms of representation and in their ability to coordinate social actors in welfare-enhancing projects – in part through their communication capacities and in part through sanction. As a system of ongoing bargaining among social interests, moreover, gains would be realized from the attending visibility – to representatives and the state – of the interdependence of interests. This can reasonably be expected to facilitate the coordination of initiatives, tradeoffs across interest domains and continual adjustment of appropriate policy mixes.[54] Finally, by establishing terms of co-operation among affected actors, such a system can contribute to the willingness of those actors to experiment with initiatives that disrupt old patterns.

As examples of areas in which these contributions might be especially welcome, we offer incomes policies, active labor market policies and environmental policies.

In incomes policy, the advantage of encompassing centralized labor and employer associations, with power of sanction over members, are already known. This structure of groups, and their bargaining, permits more or less authoritative exchange between the two great classes through the state. Because groups can sanction free-riders, they facilitate cooperation between those classes. And because that cooperation proceeds with the aid of the state, the feasible set of cooperative outcomes is enlarged. The general structure of such cooperative outcomes is that unions exchange nominal wage restraint for employer investment assurances and provision by the state of a high social wage.

As a consequence of such cooperation, all parties can gain. Employers and the state achieve greater stability in prices and production; workers enjoy real income gains realized either through primary or social incomes.

In active labor market policies aimed at creating new demands for labor, or increasing its supply, quality or mobility, the presence of encompassing associations again makes possible the forging of cooperative arrangements. It also contributes to the simple coordination of interests, with greater flexibility and precision achieved in the formulation of policies. Thus cooperation among worker and employer representatives, again in the context of the availability of state assistance, can help in (1) targeting new skill needs in the population and identifying the necessary public and private components of skill delivery; (2) establishing feasible incentive structures across firms and regions – for workers, unions, employers and the unemployed – for developing or upgrading skills within such a structure; (3) providing early warning on the distributive consequences of policy choices; (4) devising programs of subsidy across different regions, or even firms, to respond to leads and lags in labor market adjustments; and (5) hammering out minimal national standards for the transferability of credentials across different local labor markets. In all these areas, the existence of encompassing national organizations, operating with state sanction, provide useful information and assurances against suckering.

In environmental policies, many of the same sorts of possibility are available. Again, the problems feature high levels of interdependence across different regions of the national economy, thus underscoring the need for more encompassing organizations. There are severe information problems – both in determining the dimensions of problems and in determining appropriate variation in their solution – thus underscoring the need for structures capable of eliciting and organizing the widest possible range of relevant information. And there are severe cooperation and coordination problems attendant on any constructive policy, thus underscoring the need for organizations capable of providing assurance against defectors. What was just said of active labor market policy could be repeated here for environmental policy. Again, concentrating narrowly on economic performance and state efficiency criteria, encompassing environmental organizations, and especially environmental organizations in active negotiation with representatives of 'productive' interests (labor and capital), could contribute to the development of national standards, specification of appropriate programs and incentives, development of experimental initiatives, and the like.

There is, moreover, every reason to believe that the usual sorts of comparative advantages of groups, and in particular the advantages of national bargaining among encompassing groups, will be more pronounced in the years ahead in the area of environmental policy. Heretofore, national environmental controls have been principally directed to limiting the most noxious consequences of the most noxious production processes and consumption decisions. But the limits of past policies have underscored the need for more ambitious efforts within national economies – efforts that would take aim not only at mitigating the consequences of relatively uncontrolled production and consumption decisions but at altering those decisions themselves through 'source reduction' of toxics and other environmentally damaging elements. Here, even more clearly than in the past, the address of environmental concerns would implicate these concerns directly in production and consumption decisions.

But as environmental policy moves closer to these sources, the difficulties of state 'command and control' regulation will increase, and socially rooted organizations, ideally a series of socially rooted organizations in negotiation with one another, will become more helpful. Implementing programs of toxic source reduction requires eliciting information from employers and workers about the costs of different technologies, cooperation from them and other social groups in implementing the use of less polluting production techniques, diffusion of knowledge about the program to consumers, the organization of new markets to provide additional incentives to program development (e.g. secondary markets in recycling or 'full use' of production side-products), and the like. It is simply implausible to think that state administrators will be able, even in the best of circumstances, to perform this range of tasks. Associations, including associations at the national level, are needed.

We move now to our second class of organizations: regional/sectoral groups. Here we wish to highlight the function of coordinating economic activity in the shadow of national policy. Because much that might be said here has already been anticipated, we shall be more brief.

As a general matter, sectoral and regional organizations are key to industry adjustment and the coordination of interests pursuant to industrial policies. And they play an important role in facilitating supply-side adjustment in economies featuring flexible specialization, which again commonly have a 'lumpy' geographic aspect. As with other associations, their effectiveness requires that they be relatively encompassing of affected interests and have powers over their memberships while remaining accountable to them. This enables them

JOSHUA COHEN AND JOEL ROGERS

to ease the adjustment of firms to national policy initiatives. More generally, it enables firms to respond to the pressures of competition, and the spread of flexible specialization, without turning their surrounding society into a nightmare of inequality and particularism – a latter-day version of the 'Bourbon kingdom of Naples, where an island of craftsmen, producing luxury goods for the court, was surrounded by a subproletarian sea of misery.'[55]

Associations do this by helping construct an institutional infrastructure attentive both to the need to be maximally responsive to technological and product market changes and capable of limiting individual firm free-riding. They provide mechanisms for pooling resources for training in particular regions or trades and for developing and sharing research and development funds, particularly among smaller firms. The coordination and cooperation they provide help correct a variety of problems that firms face for familiar market failure reasons: deficiencies in the supply of training (in particular, training that creates more generalized and easily transferable skills), suboptimal pooling of research and development funds and product information among competitors, inadequate links in product design between primary producers and suppliers, and the deadweight losses and excessive caution associated with more arm's length forms of coordination, which are especially damaging in the current economic environment.

Our third example is local or intrafirm organizations that contribute to the enforcement and administration of policy. The by now familiar requirements of relative encompassingness with respect to affected interests, accountability and leadership power again apply, as do the typical sorts of advantages of association – facilitation of cooperation through sanctioning and facilitation of coordination by better knowledge, itself gained from social rootedness and consequent 'local knowledge'. We move directly to some examples of the sorts of association we have in mind and the different roles they can play in administration and enforcement in different policy areas.

The first would be in-plant organizations for workers. Such committees or works councils, like the committees and councils that presently exist in many countries, would provide additional 'voice' for workers in dealings with management; they would, further, of necessity be coordinated in some way with other forms of worker representation. Here, however, we focus exclusively on their contribution to the enforcement and administration of state policy.

What is important here is that, for workplace regulations presumptively enforced across a large number of dispersed and heterogeneous sites, such organizations have advantages over state inspectorates in enforcing those regulations in efficient ways. They are 'on the ground', close to the activity being regulated, and thus better informed about conditions in particular sites and the different local ways in which noxious conditions might be remedied. As organizations of workers, they typically have capacities to elicit cooperation from fellow workers in devising such remedies. If appropriately empowered – as in, for example, Swedish work environment committees or West German works councils – they can bring diverse sites into line with minimum generic standards without requiring uniform process in doing so.

Then there are any number of local groups with declared interests in particular policy areas (e.g. environmental groups, women's groups, housing co-ops, churches, etc.). Depending on their configuration, these too can be recruited to a variety of administrative and enforcement tasks. They can monitor state enforcement, communicate new problems to legislative bodies and help negotiate the means of meeting uniform standards that are attentive to local variation in circumstance. Local associations can also be of use in the delivery of social services. The fact that such groups are already established means that delivering benefits through them is commonly less costly than it would be through newly created bureaucracies. The fact that they have alternative sources of support (alternative to the fee charged the government for such service delivery), moreover, makes it easier for the government to vary levels of support for particular programs and thus increases flexibility. Again, the fact that such associations are 'on the ground' means that they know more about the needs of the intended recipients of those services than do distant government officials, and the fact that they are integrated into communities and local economies leaves them better equipped to see the connections, for individuals, of different policy initiatives.

In combination, these features of local organizations (or, for that matter, regional ones) make them especially attractive additions to the governance of social welfare. As noted earlier, recent economic changes, especially in conjunction with increased labor market participation by women, have immeasurably complicated the discharge of traditional welfare tasks. Rapid economic change, increased heterogeneity in production, and ever greater relative returns to human capital, combined with the destruction of 'traditional' family patterns to which they all contribute, create a universe of problems quite different from that which confronted welfare policy even fifteen years ago. In this context, effective policy needs to be especially attentive to variation across cases, to the interdependence of different categories of need among individuals, and to the integration of welfare delivery into plausible career programs for recipients. This in turn favors a devolution of welfare administration from more to less centralized bodies. As in the case of specializing firms, such devolution brings with it obvious dangers of an oppressive federalism of neglect. But as with firms, socially rooted associations can serve as an effective counterweight to such pressures for particularism while reaping the advantages, for welfare design, of being integrated into their communities and thus knowledgeable and flexible in fitting programs to individuals.

Our contention is that these (and related) associational initiatives would have desirable effects on economic performance and state efficiency. In support of this contention, we offer two sorts of consideration. First, drawing on the earlier discussion of qualitative variation, there are several attributes of the associative scheme that appear important in generating gains along these dimensions: (1) the most important groups have significant power over their members, and are accountable to them, and at the same time have relatively clear understandings with the state about the range of their powers and responsibilities; (2) the groups involved are relatively encompassing with respect to potential membership (defined as those with interests that are plausibly convergent with actual group members); (3) at least some organizations have relatively wide scopes of authority and concomitantly encompassing memberships; and (4) some associations, particularly those with wide scope of authority, are relatively stable and generally accepted, so that members can expect the same associations to continue to serve as collaborators and negotiating partners.

The expectation, then, is that the combination of these features would generate a favorable environment for cooperation among relevant actors, thus helping to avoid a chief source of 'mischief' in secondary associations, namely, their narrow and shortsighted defense of particularistic interests. In particular, greater encompassingness in organization, in conjunction with accountability, reduces temptations to free-ride on others because members of encompassing associations would themselves likely feel the effects of such free-riding and transmit their dissatisfaction to leaders (here the assumption of accountability is crucial). The relative stability of bargaining partners establishes a common, institutional memory of past behavior and at the same time lengthens the shadow of the future. The scope of authority enables trades across different areas of policy, thus enhancing flexibility in particular areas of policy. And the quasi-public status of some of the groups enables negotiations to proceed against the background of an expectation of enforcement and, at the same time, under conditions that promote responsible (because publicly visible) behavior. Altogether, the result is to generate the usual gains from cooperation – easier access to relevant and reliable information, a reduction in deadweight losses due to contention, reduction in the costs of enforcement and an expansion in the range of options to include joint strategies.

In addition to these more abstract considerations, there is some evidence that aids our case. The evidence is spotty and its relevance might reasonably be contested – a point that we shall come back to. Still, an examination of the performance of systems with associational forms analogous to those sketched earlier does suggest some support.

On economic performance, a range of studies of macroeconomic performance show more corporatist systems, featuring national-level bargainers of the sort suggested here, exhibiting more stable growth, better inflation/employment tradeoffs, higher rates of investment and productivity growth, and, as a consequence, higher and steadier rates of income growth than do systems with more classically pluralistic forms of interest organization. And recent studies of industrial adjustment and the reemerging 'regional economies' of Western Europe show in more qualitative ways the contribution made by sectoral and regional groups to the competitive performance of diversified quality production.

On state efficiency, measurement problems are particularly notorious, but again the evidence is accumulating. The more organized systems from which we draw our examples deliver a much higher 'social wage' than more pluralist systems and appear to do so at lower cost. Gains are realized through better planning and prevention and economies of scale in administration (e.g. monopolies in the provision of health services, where more pluralist systems feature large amounts of waste due to marketing among competitors). Studies of compliance also indicate better performance in cases featuring the sorts of 'on the ground' local enforcers we are suggesting. Occupational safety and health legislation sets higher standards, with better compliance and at less cost to government where significant responsibilities for information and enforcement are devolved to in-plant committees.

To conclude the case for the associative approach to the problems of post-Keynesian regulation, we need finally to address the objection mentioned above to the relevance of this evidence to our case. The difficulty is that much of the evidence is drawn from systems – for example, democratic corporatist systems – with characteristics, potentially relevant to the capacity of groups to make such contribution, which are absent from our associative scheme. Two characteristics in particular – stable monopolies of groups within their respective categories of interest and sharp limitation of the number of categories of interest represented in the policy process – are characteristic of liberal corporatism but not of the associative scheme. Why, then, do we suppose that advantages that have been associated with corporatism would also pertain to the arrangements described earlier? We shall address the concern about monopoly now and come back later to the issue of the number of categories of interest that are represented.

The objection is this: while the evidence we cite is drawn in part from democratic corporatist systems, it is crucial to the contribution of associations in corporatist systems that they have a stable monopoly of powers of representation within their respective categories. But the associative scheme increases the level of challenge to them, thus depriving them of the source of their virtue and depriving us of the alleged evidence.

By way of response, we note that the objection appears to make one of two assumptions, neither of which seems compelling. First, it may assume that the associations in liberal corporatist systems make favorable contributions to policy because their representational monopoly implies that they do not need to be responsive to the interests of members and so could assist the state in achieving its aims. But if this is the assumption, then it faces its own straightforward problem of empirical support, namely, that there does not appear to be any evidence that, as a general matter, the monopoly associations in liberal corporatist systems do display a lesser degree of accountability or responsiveness.[56] Alternatively, the objection may be assuming that a representational monopoly enables associations to play a constructive role because it places them beyond political challenge. But this is plainly not right because groups with formal representational monopolies are commonly the object of opposition and protest.[57]

What may underlie these assumptions is the more fundamental idea that the benefits of associations in liberal corporatist systems with representational monopolies derive, as a general matter, from their capacity to exclude certain interests from being represented. An alternative view, which seems to us more plausible, is that the benefits derive from the capacity of such associations to coordinate the actions of a diverse range of individuals who might otherwise have gone un(der)represented. But as this advantage is retained by the associative scheme, we do not accept the contention that evidence drawn from liberal corporatist systems is irrelevant to our case.

Problems and Prospects of Associative Democracy

Suppose that this account of group contribution to economic performance and state efficiency is plausible. It remains to be asked how
the group structure contributing to such performance comports with
other (more constitutive) features of democratic governance – popular
sovereignty, political equality, distributive justice and civic consciousness. This is the question we take up in this section.

Apart from its intrinsic interest, this normative issue has important
practical implications. Both for the stability of performance-enhancing
group structures in those regimes where they now exist or for their
encouragement in those systems (like the United States) currently
featuring more 'liberal' regulation of economic affairs something more
than an economic or state efficiency argument is almost surely
required. This is especially so in the reform case. The institutionaliza-
tion of a system of dense associative activity would inevitably face
opposition and would be fraught with uncertainties about effects,
potential reversals, and the like. In such circumstances, proposed
changes in group design cannot only promise (what and who does
not?) increased economic productivity and efficiency but something
linked more deeply and immediately to constitutive democratic ideals.
For in this circumstance, if not in the ordinary workings of capitalist
democracy, Schattschneider is right – 'consent is no longer enough.'[58]
Active popular support is needed, and that is unlikely to be forthcoming
unless an associative democracy connects with deeper aspirations to
democratic order.

To get at this question about linkage, we proceed straightforwardly. Taking each of the remaining conditions of democratic
order in turn, we ask how arrangements of the sort just claimed to
improve performance contribute to or infirm their satisfaction.
Remedies for the problems identified here will then be introduced in
the next section.

Popular Sovereignty

Does the existence of the groups characteristic of our associative
scheme contribute to, or create problems for, the ultimate authority
of the people in the formation of policy? Two observations frame
our answer to this question. First, the quasi-public, functionally
demarcated bodies exercising power within that scheme do so against
the backdrop of encompassing political organizations that organize
representation along traditional territorial lines. A basic possibility

of 'exit' from the group-based system of representation to the more traditionally organized system thus exists. Moreover, the group system is itself regulated by the traditional system, depending on it, for example, for subsidies. Second, we take it as clear that the delegation of powers to arrangements of group bargaining does not by itself pose a problem for popular sovereignty any more than the existence of specialized agencies of governance poses such a problem. Rather, the concern arises when there is an 'irrecoverable delegation' that places those powers beyond the review of encompassing institutions.[59]

With these background assumptions in mind, we want first to indicate three sorts of positive-sum relationship between associations and the democratic state – three ways, that is, that the fuller and more explicit incorporation of groups into governance roles might actually enhance the exercise of popular sovereignty through the traditional institutions and practices of territorial representation.

First, groups provide the state with information, thus permitting better definition of problems and greater precision in the selection of means for addressing them. By thus sharpening policy instruments and enabling them to be applied with greater precision, groups promote the capacity of the people to achieve their aims. Second, groups provide additional enforcement power, thus increasing the likelihood that decisions made by the people will be implemented.[60] Third, in mitigating enforcement problems, groups remove one important constraint on political debate. Instead of proposals being shortcircuited with the claim that they are unenforceable, a wider range of proposals can be discussed seriously. In combination, better and more flexible means, better enforcement and, as a consequence, less constrained debate about ends and their achievement count as powerful pluses for popular sovereignty.

These three contributions are, however, accompanied by three sources of serious concern – of negative-sum relations between the powers of associations and egalitarian-democratic order.

First, there are problems of disjunction of interest between the leaderships of groups and their members – the problem of the 'iron law of oligarchy'. A dense world of association may make the government more informed about, and more responsive to, the interests of group 'oligarchs' but not group members. Second, there is the problem of independent powers – what might be called the 'Frankenstein' issue. Endowed with quasi-public status, and commonly subsidized by the state, groups that at one point in time contribute to decent policy may continue to exercise power after outgrowing their usefulness, use that power to freeze their position and so work to distort future debate and choice. Third, increasing the extent of policy-making outside of formal legislative arenas increases threats of improper delegation. In particular, powers delegated to associations are bound to be vague. As in the context of legislative delegations to administrative agencies, then, there are problems about the abuse of the discretion permitted by such vagueness.

Political Equality

With respect to political equality, three contributions of the associative order are important. First, the forms of association described earlier improve the representation of workers and other less well-endowed citizens. As a consequence, the capacity to influence political outcomes becomes less dependent on position in the distribution of material resources, a direct gain for political equality. Second, and closely related, improved representation of the less well-off can be expected to provide support for programs of distributive equity (discussed shortly), and that in turn will serve to provide more stable foundations for equality of political influence. Third, greater material equality and security, combined with enhanced capacities to enforce legislation, mean reduced concern about the capacity of powerful private interests effectively to veto public policies. This, as we just noted, is a major gain for popular sovereignty. But because such vetoes are typically exercised by the best-off members of the order (e.g. through the private control of investment), it is also a gain for political equality.

The bad news is twofold.

First, there is a potential for sclerosis. Powerful functioning groups in place at any given point, already performing governance functions, are likely to be looked on favorably by the state as partners in governance tasks. Assuming this to be the case, the result may be that the initial organization of group interests would become quasi-permanent, thus replacing private wealth with public favor as a source of political inequality.

Second, and more critically, even if the associative scheme improves interest representation, it appears to impose important limits of its own on achieving a genuinely fair representation of social interests. Again, background inequalities in the conditions favorable to group organization (resources, etc.) intrude. Even abstracting from these inequalities, some interests – for example, those of consumers – are intrinsically more difficult to organize than others. Still other interests do not lend themselves to representation within a bureaucratic system of representation. For example, those who oppose bureaucracy itself will find little solace in the organizational environment suggested by our associative proposal. Further, concerns of 'principle', which often are intractable to negotiation and compromise, may be under-represented. Here we think of the 'new social movements' and 'single-issue groups' that pursue matters of what are regarded as moral principle. Finally, the effective operation of a system of peak bargaining among encompassing groups plausibly requires the exclusion of some interests, for it is precisely the limits on the number of 'social partners' that permits such groups to function effectively. To the extent that any of these departures from the equal representation of interests is significant, the fact that our associative democratic scheme enhances the powers or those groups that are organized threatens to worsen the prospects for political equality.

Distributive Equity

The contribution of group organization to distributive equity appears straightforward. There is a strong empirical case (stronger even than the case on economic performance) that systems featuring such higher levels of group organization and coordination of group interests are more equitable than classically pluralistic systems; this appears to be the case on a wide range of plausible egalitarian conceptions (including those that focus on the minimum and the dispersion and whether the conception is resourcist or welfarist). The basic reason is that they feature higher levels of organization and more powerful forms of organization of workers and other citizens whose 'natural' level of welfare is lower and who otherwise can be expected to be grossly under-represented in the policy process.

Such organization contributes to distributive fairness in at least two ways. First, by gaining representation and power at the national level, union federations representing workers can use that power to press for more favorable incomes policies, labor market policies and social welfare policies for their members. This reduces the dependence of individual welfare on market performance and thus reduces the dependence of distribution on the ethical contingencies that shape such performance. Second, by offering enforcement and administrative mechanisms 'on the ground', the organization of such groups reduces the cost of making a 'welfare effort', thus contributing to an increase in that effort.

It might be noted too that the wage and social welfare policies within such systems tend to be more 'solidaristic' and generic, presumably because of the organizational support for them. Greater reliance on generic social welfare programs – rather than a patchwork of means-tested programs and favorable government treatment of the gains of a minority of fortunate workers – tends to equalize receipt of government largesse. What may be lost in the targeting of the least advantaged appears to be more than made up for in the encompassing-ness of these social programs, which can be expected to translate into long-term political support leading to greater and more stable efforts.

Two concerns about equality stand out. First, where the less well-organized interests are also the interests of the less well-off, the gains for the bulk of the working population may be unmatched, or worse, among minorities within it. Second, and more serious, functional representation systems are ill-designed to cope with regional inequalities. To the extent that functional representation is relied on as a guide to policy, then, questions about the treatment of regional inequality legitimately arise.

Civic Consciousness

We have already indicated some contributions that associations, including those that we propose, can make to civic consciousness. By facilitating cooperation between, and coordination of, interests, they can encourage less narrow group programs, greater awareness of the interdependence of different aspects of policy, and less steep rates of time discount than is common in more pluralistic systems. This seems particularly the case for the largest and most encompassing of organizations. Because they are not narrowly organized, the solidarity of their memberships approaches a social solidarity. Because they are involved in the widest range of activities, they promote awareness of interdependence. And because they engage in peak bargains with other social partners that are explicitly conditioned on promises of performance some distance into the future, they encourage longer time-horizons.

Arguably, however, such contributions can also be made by groups operating at our two other functional levels (that is, coordination, and administration and enforcement). In the area of supply-side coordination of education and training programs, for example, dense networks of association among union, business and community groups, interacting with state officials, create something approximating a 'public sphere', in which public-regarding criteria of action achieve institutional form. Even in the narrowest of arenas – for example, a workplace safety and health committee that acts to enforce nationally legislated norms – citizen involvement in a responsible role in the

maintenance of publicly declared norms of order arguably promotes
sensitivity to the rewards, and necessity, of such an order.[61]

In these latter two cases especially, the degree to which group
organization promotes civic consciousness depends heavily on the
precise role those groups are assigned and the surrounding framework of articulate public authority. In particular, it depends on their
having a relatively clearly defined scope of discretion and obligation
and on their operating with clear standards and mechanisms of
accountability to fully public authorities. This point granted, however,
the encompassingness of groups and their increased participation in
appropriately structured acts of public governance appear to carry
benefits for civic consciousness.

The dangers here are familiar. By officially delegating more public
authority to functionally defined groups, an associative democracy
may exaggerate a tendency to devolve public authority to less politically encompassing organizations by placing a public imprimatur on it.
Further, if these groups are successful, the centrality of their operation
can undermine respect for more encompassing organizations. Finally,
some narrowness in group representation remains in such a system,
and associated with that, there is encouragement of forms of group
'consciousness' that compete with and may take precedence over civic
sensibilities.

Reconciling Association and Democracy

In sum, the sorts of groups associated with gains in economic performance and state efficiency appear both to contribute to and potentially
to threaten the satisfaction of other conditions of democratic governance. In short, it is not yet clear, on balance, how democratic
our associative proposal would be. To address that issue we propose
now to devote exclusive attention to the threats, examining them
more closely, assessing their seriousness, suggesting remedies where
the problems appear serious and remediable, and considering how
damaging any residual difficulties are.

Throughout, we are guided by three background assumptions,
aspects of which have already been emphasized but which merit
explicit notice here. First and all-important, our scheme assumes that
final authority continues to rest with more traditional, encompassing,
territorially-based systems of representation. Among the objects of
debate within this system, then, is the degree to which groups will be
accorded a quasi-public status in governance. Both individual citizens
of the order, and, as it were, the people itself, can choose to 'exit'

from reliance on groups in this quasi-public role or to transfer public support from some groups to others. Second, while we assume that the capacities of the state are constrained, we assume as well that some measure of refashioning of conditions of association is possible. Third, we aim at some measure of 'realism', by which we mean that the deformations in our associative scheme should be compared to alternative systems of governance (among mass capitalist democracies), and not to an ideal that lies beyond the reach of human beings as they are and institutions as they can be.

Popular Sovereignty

Turning first to sovereignty, then, recall that there were three potential difficulties: the problem of disjunctions between member and leadership interests within groups, and thus a 'misresponsiveness' of the state; the Frankenstein problem of independent powers; and standing concerns with vague delegation in systems featuring much delegation.

To begin on a note of realism, we assume that there are always some problems of disjunction. The issue is whether our associative proposal worsens the problem. It might appear to, as it seems intuitively plausible that the problem of disjunction would be especially pronounced in the largest, most encompassing and most bureaucratic of organizations. A recurrent example used in critical discussions is the distant, professionalized leadership of centralized trade union federations, whose 'social responsibility' in dealings with employers and the state is seen to come at the expense of the concerns of actual members. In fact, however, there is little evidence that forms of organization necessary to meet the demands of peak bargaining bear negatively on responsiveness. It is not that centralized encompassing union federations are more responsive to their memberships than decentralized union movements, only that there appears no clear relation between opportunities for voice and exit on the one hand, and centralization and encompassingness on the other.

On a variety of measures of international union democracy, for example, the Norwegian union movement, among the most centralized and encompassing in the world, is more democratic than unions in the United Kingdom, comprising one of the least centralized union movements, which are in turn more democratic than the unions of West Germany, which are intermediate in their level of centralization. Two conclusions of immediate relevance are suggested by this work. First, there is a variety of mechanisms that can be used, in different combinations, to enhance internal responsiveness – including election to union councils, intermediate organizations and national office; the encouragement or permission of informal caucuses; procedures for debate and vote on strikes, contracts and other sorts of concerted action; and so on. Second, the use of these mechanisms is fully compatible with the requirements of peak bargaining.

The natural response to the problem of disjunction, then, is to require greater use of such mechanisms of responsiveness among groups that are granted quasi-public status. Operationally, the requirement should be that groups accorded this status provide evidence that they, in fact, represent their members by showing that they actually use some mechanism of responsiveness. Infinite gradations in degree and differences in judgment are certainly imaginable here, just as they are in ongoing disputes over the representativeness of electoral systems. But as the case of electoral systems also suggests, it is possible to articulate a general principle of legitimacy, in this case internal responsiveness, and to debate specific proposals in light of that principle.

The Frankenstein problem of independent powers also carries a natural response, namely, some variant of 'sunset legislation'. The quasi-public status of groups should be reviewed on a regular basis, with a rebuttable presumption that status will be withdrawn or amended as group behavior or perceived social needs warrant. The general requirements are reasonably clear, although their precise elaboration is not. On the one hand, the threat of withdrawal must be sufficiently credible and the gains associated with public status sufficiently great to induce satisfaction of accountability and other conduct requirements. On the other hand, the requirements must not be so exacting as to preclude relatively stable satisfaction of them and thus the continuity in bargaining relations that, as we noted earlier, is an important prerequisite of the system.

The ultimate guard against independent powers, however, is the vitality of the system dispensing powers in the first place. Systems relying heavily on group-based representation should always be systems of dual, and juridically unequal, powers. Final authority should reside in encompassing territorial organizations, and both they and the electoral system that generates them should be sufficiently strong to permit social exit from group representation. This essential point emphasized by the 'insulating' Republicans seems right and especially suggests a need to strengthen the party system.

To the pervasive problem of vague delegations of power and attendant risks of abused discretion we offer two responses. Beginning on a note of realism, with what are the vague delegations of powers in our associative scheme being contrasted? If we consider contemporary legislation in liberal systems, the comparison does not seem damning, as there is already much vague delegation to and exercise of discretion by administrative agencies. If we consider a scheme of more limited government as a means to cabin discretion, then we need to keep in mind that such a scheme is unlikely to serve the egalitarian-democratic aims at issue here. If we consider a scheme with stronger legislative controls – less vagueness in delegation and more sharply formulated legislative standards – then we should consider familiar cautions that it may lead to an unwelcome politicization of legislative instruction, reflected in unreasonable goals, improbable deadlines on their achievement or simple legislative deadlock.[62] Nor is there any reason to think that such reasonable requirements as clarity in the statement of statutory goals would be inconsistent with the associative scheme. And to what are the problems arising from vagueness to be compared? If to the fact of regulatory capture, again the comparison is not damaging to the associative scheme.

More constructively, however, the problem of delegation may be treated separately for our three levels of group operation. At the level of policy formulation, and in particular in the case of peak bargaining, there does not appear to be a very great problem. The descendants of the social partners, each with considerable powers, are 'naturally' curbed in any intended abuse of discretion. At the level of decentralized enforcement and administration, the problem appears to have more punch. Here, the most plausible solution to the abuse of discretion is for public institutions to formulate clear performance standards for groups to enforce and administer (while avoiding detailed specification of the means to be used in meeting those standards). For example, in the area of workplace health, there might be performance standards in the form of permissible exposure limits for hazardous chemicals, with decisions about the means for implementing those limits falling to health and safety committees. At the level of coordination, we would again address problems of discretion by conditioning grants of quasi-public status on performance criteria – for example, minimum standards for skills, knowledge, courses and examinations in vocational training programs whose operation is coordinated by labor and business in particular sectors. Even where groups do not enjoy subsidies for their performance of quasi-public duties, they should be regulated in the conduct of those duties. Where they are officially granted quasi-public status, and/or material state assistance, then performance criteria can be more exacting.

In sum, then, our response to the concerns about popular sovereignty is that dangers of faction in this area could be mitigated by requirements on internal democracy, legislative and judicial oversight, 'sunset' laws that threaten a group with competition for its position, and performance standards.

Political Equality

Earlier, we noted two threats to political equality: the over-representation of groups already in place by virtue of their quasi-permanent status and the more foundational problem of inequalities in the interests organized into groups. On the first, the remarks on 'sunset' review entered in the discussion of sovereignty again apply. Groups should be evaluated at regular intervals for renewals of their grants of public status, holding in reserve a credible threat of exit from the group system into other alternative (territorial) mechanisms of representation and governance.

On the foundational problem of inequality, we note again the importance of realism. However distorted the representation process within systems saturated with group organization, it appears on balance, and for the reasons discussed earlier, to be eminently more inclusive and fair than under less group-oriented systems. Furthermore, certain of the interests invoked as 'under-represented' within more group-based systems – such as interests that are hostile to bureaucratic forms of organization – appear unlikely to do well under any imaginable system of representation in a mass democracy.

Turning to a more direct engagement with the problem, different modes of address appear appropriate for different sources of inequality. For those interests whose collective representation would threaten their very expression (e.g. consumer interests), there is a case for establishing a government agency for their protection (perhaps with monitoring support from those consumer groups that are formed). The more difficult issue is that of exclusion, especially in peak bargaining. For that bargaining to proceed in the 'virtuous' way sketched above, most observers see the need for a severe limitation on the 'quantity and variety of recognized interlocutors' in order to preserve the 'properties of small-group interaction, specialized competence, reciprocal trust, and propensity for compromise' featured in successful societal corporatist systems.[63] Such limitation implies exclusion of some interests, thus raising the specter of exacerbated political inequalities.

The problem of exclusion has two components – the extent of the requisite exclusion and its legitimacy – and we consider them in turn.

First, then, the necessary severity of the limits on inclusion is plainly an unsettled empirical issue. It is clear that increasing the number of parties to negotiations complicates them, generating 'diseconomies' of scale. What is less clear, however, is what peak bargaining with three groups instead of two, or four instead of three, might look like and how it would affect outcomes on the performance versus exclusion dimensions. Discovering the scope and limits of the space of representation appears, quite simply, to be a matter of institutional tinkering.

The second issue concerns the legitimacy of exclusion. It appears to us that in mass societies with heterogeneous social interests the possibilities of achieving a group system of functional representation that provides equal representation of all interests is more and more remote. But this is less a problem for democratic governance than it might be if decisions about the range of interests to be represented, in particular the range of groups to be accorded quasi-public status, are themselves made under conditions in which the views of each citizen are accorded equal weight. This might be done, as we have suggested at several points, by making the choice of groups, the groups selected, the appropriate criteria of selection, the rules on their external and internal accountability, the tasks they are selected to discharge, and so forth themselves the object of authoritative popular political choice through conventional political institutions. In that case, the groups so authorized inherit the legitimacy of the authorization.[64]

Distributive Fairness

Our discussion of distributive fairness indicated two problem areas: (1) possible coincidences between excluded or under-represented interests and less well-off citizens; and (2) regional inequality. It is not at all clear that the first is a major problem, especially when compared to existing alternatives. This aside, all that we have to say about its address has been said in our discussion of mitigating inequalities in representation.

The second issue appears to us important but not intractable. That is, it does seem to be the case that functional systems of representation, by their very nature, will be less responsive to territorially defined inequalities. In addition, it appears that heavier reliance on 'private government' in promoting supply-side adjustments in regional economies will itself tend to favor those regions that already have some organizational infrastructure in place.

By way of response, we begin by invoking once again the continuing authority of traditional modes of representation, and in particular the fact that such traditional modes are territorial. This should provide some counterbalance to regional inequality, by ensuring a sphere of decision-making more attentive to the proliferation of such inequalities, and to the need to encourage greater balance in associability across regions. Thus the state should encourage group organization in regions where the requisite organizational structures are not developed. In providing 'encouragement', the state could use an array of familiar incentives and sanctions – preferred tax treatment of cooperative ventures and grants to communities and regions contingent on demonstrations of efforts to so organize – to achieve the desired result.

Civic Consciousness

Troubles for civic consciousness came from three sources: the problem of encouraging extant tendencies to erode public authority by according public status to groups; the undermining of respect for encompassing organizations; and residual problems with group narrowness. To these objections, we offer three responses.

First, many of these alleged effects derive from the unequal representativeness and lack of public accountability in the group system. With greater efforts (of the kind recommended here) to ensure both, these aspects of the problem can be mitigated. Thus, with the supremacy of the 'traditional' forms of representation clearly established – through the more explicit discussion within that system of appropriate delegations of power to groups, regular review of group action, the articulation of standards of public accountability, and the like – both devolution from and declining respect for public authority seems a less pressing concern. Similarly, with the satisfaction of new standards of public accountability and internal responsiveness set as the precondition of grants of quasi-public status to groups, and a range of recommended remedial measures in place for assuring suitably wide representation of interests, the problem of residual narrowness appears to have less force.

Second, we resort again to our realist criterion. Consider the case of the United States. Here, civic consciousness is already woefully 'deformed' by (among other things) ineffective government, gross inequalities and weak parties that appear to be uninterested in mobilizing citizens into popular discussion or in demonstrating fidelity to articulated programs. It is further eroded by the general lack of opportunities for citizens to engage in acts of self-government other than the occasional act of voting, to participate in ways that bear more direct consequences for their daily lives. It is against this backdrop that the suggested greater use of groups in governance should be assessed, and in this context, the proposed contribution to civic consciousness may seem more plausible. Assuming that more associative forms of democracy do deliver performance benefits, the obstacle to the development of civic consciousness represented by general public cynicism about the effectiveness of public institutions would be weakened. With the sorts of internally accountable association imagined here, along with greater reliance on decentralized groups in administration and enforcement, citizens would have enhanced opportunities to engage in just those concrete acts of politics that strengthen and encourage citizenship.

Third, and perhaps most generally, we offer a point about the state of public debate. Reforms of associability in the direction of a more associative democracy would make explicit a condition that is already a standing feature of even the most liberal of societies, namely, that secondary associations do in fact perform a variety of functions that affect the conditions of political order. As Jaffe observed in his classic article on 'Law Making by Private Groups' written at the height of New Deal constitutional controversy:

> Participation in law-making by private groups under explicit statutory 'delegation' does not stand . . . in absolute contradiction to the traditional process and conditions of law-making; it is not incompatible with the conception of law. It exposes and brings out into the open, it institutionalizes a factor in law-making that we have, eagerly in fact, attempted to obscure.[65]

Such exposure would, we think, itself represent an advance over present conditions. For individual citizens, it might serve as an immense act of public education, bringing the understanding of groups and their role in society into the sphere of public knowledge and debate. For groups themselves, it would represent a call to look beyond the immediate concerns of their members, to recognize the consequences of their actions for the larger society, and to consider those consequences in devising their own strategies for action. As proposed here, of course, the formal assignment of public authority will carry public sanctions for malfeasance, sanctions that do not exist at present. Even abstracting from such sanctions, however, explicit recognition of such a role is plausibly a condition for, and powerful spur to, its responsible performance, for, as Jaffe also observed, 'tolerated, covert monopolies – power exercised indirectly – may be much more difficult to attack or to ameliorate than the edicts of majorities arrived at openly and according to forms of law'.[66] And one of the conditions that defeats civic consciousness is precisely the sense that the most significant exercise of power is 'covert' and 'indirect'.

To summarize this entire discussion of associative democracy, then, we have argued that there is a variety of pressing problems of economic performance and state regulation to the solution of which secondary associations can make important contributions. These contributions, moreover, need not come at the expense of other conditions of democratic order – provided that sufficient attention is paid to encouraging those features of groups consistent with such order. Although countless details are absent from the discussion and many legitimate questions remain, the account is, we believe, sufficient to support the plausibility of wider use of associations in contemporary governance.

4. Reforming a Liberal Polity

Thus far we have argued that associative solutions are, in the abstract, attractive ways of advancing democratic ideals and that the factional potential of such solutions can be tamed by the same strategy of constructive artifice that enlists group contributions. Still, the idea of associative democracy may seem of little relevance to the United States. More than any other economically advanced mass democracy, the United States has a strongly anti-collectivist political culture, a weak state and a civil society dominated by (relatively disorganized) business interests. The potential for artifice granted, this context poses obvious problems for the associative strategy. At best, it might be thought, the absence of any initial favoring conditions make the strategy irrelevant. There is simply not enough to get started down the path of democratic associative reform. At worst, it might be feared, pursuit of the strategy under these conditions would be a political nightmare. Giving new licence to a congeries of group privilege and particularism would exacerbate inequalities and further corrupt and enfeeble the state.

Such concerns have considerable force and deserve a fuller answer than we can provide here. Briefly, however, while we acknowledge the anti-collectivism of much of US political culture, we also see considerable experimentation now going on with associative solutions to policy problems in such areas as regional health and welfare service delivery, local economic development, education and training, and environmental regulation, among many others.

There is, for example, a tradition of delivering many welfare and social services through secondary associations – community organizations, churches, volunteer agencies, and the like. While such organizations often have substantial autonomy in designing the appropriate service mix for the communities they are asked to serve, they are also increasingly inextricably dependent on government fees for such services for their own survival.[67] Much 'public' input in local economic development is decided, for good or ill, in 'community development corporations' heavily subsidized government grants representing different admixtures of independent neighborhood associations and business firms.[68] In education, parent-teacher associations are commonly vested with substantial powers in determining the budget and curriculum of elementary and secondary public schools, and those schools increasingly look to local business interests for support in setting standards on student performance.[69] In training, the largest single training program in the United States, the Job Training Partnership Act (JTPA), is almost wholly administered through 'private industry councils' dominated, by statute, by local business interests.[70] In environmental regulation, from the deliberate promotion of bargaining among industry and environmental groups as a prelude to standard-setting at the federal level to the promotion of bargaining between business and community organizations over the appropriate implementation of environmental standards in local neighborhoods and regions, policy is rife with secondary associations exercising de facto public powers.[71]

Some of these efforts display the great strengths of associative governance; others display its many dangers. Our point here is simply that such governance in fact goes on widely, even in this liberal culture, and its incidence provides a natural basis for more deliberate, and democratic, associative strategies.

Moreover, while we acknowledge the weakness of the US state, we think that at least some sorts of associative reforms can make it stronger. Particularly given a weak state, it is important that group empowerment proceed in a way that is reliably positive-sum with state power. But this merely requires judgment in the choice of associative strategies. It does not generally bar their pursuit. And while we acknowledge, finally, the overwhelming business dominance of the US polity, we think this again simply constrains choice in the groups that are advantaged through the associative strategy. If business is too powerful, then associative resources should be provided to labor or other non-business dominated groups; the current imbalance is not an argument for abandoning the general idea.

Generally, we agree that the United States has high levels of inequality, a less than competent government, and weak cooperative institutions – that, in brief, it does not work well as a democracy. This, in fact, is the very problem that provides our point of departure. We move, then, to some examples of how an associative strategy might proceed from this point of departure in this distinctive polity. We offer illustrations of the general look and feel of associative projects of reform in three areas: worker representation and industrial relations; vocational training; and occupational safety and health administration. In each case, we sketch some problems that need to be addressed; indicate the ways that a richer associational setting might help in addressing them; and discuss some measures that might now be taken to promote that setting.

Worker Representation

Our goal here – controversial and surely bitterly contested – would be to improve the organization of American workers. Such improvement would plausibly contribute to the satisfaction of democratic norms in a variety of ways. By extending and deepening the benefits of organized representation to those who are now unorganized or underorganized, it would advance the goal of political equality. It would also have a fair chance of improving distributive equity and of improving economic performance in the United States. At the same time, properly structured worker organization is of particular importance because work is important. The associative framework that determines how it is organized, distributed and rewarded sets the background and tone for associative action throughout much of the society. So other reforms are more likely to succeed if reforms here succeed.[72]

The system of worker organization in the United States currently suffers from two related problems. First, very few substantive benefits are provided to workers simply as citizens. We have a low 'social' wage. Most benefits are instead provided through individual firms. But benefits are costly and firms compete. So there are obvious incentives to skimp on the provision of benefits. The result is comparatively low and uneven substantive protection for workers.

Second, the system discourages cooperation between employers and employees. Part of the reason for this is the generally low level of worker organization. Genuine cooperation is based on mutual respect, which typically depends on recognition of mutual power. With the disorganization of workers limiting their power, however, employees are commonly incapable of extracting from employers the sorts of institutionalized respect for their interests (e.g. a serious commitment to job security or consultation in advance of work reorganization) needed to elicit genuine cooperation. The other part of the reason has to do with the structure of union organization. In general, mimicking the decentralized benefit system, unions themselves are highly decentralized. Where they have power, then, they have incentives to free-ride on the interests of others and to seek maximum reward for their particular labor. Decentralization does permit wildcat cooperation. More commonly, however, it – in conjunction with the low social wage – promotes an economistic job control unionism unfavorable to cooperation. Altogether, then, an environment featuring a low social wage, low union density and highly decentralized union organization is dense with incentives for collectively irrational conflict.[73]

This diagnosis suggests four related steps of associative reform of this system: (1) lower the barriers to unionization, (2) encourage alternative forms of self-directed worker organization, (3) raise the social wage, and (4) promote more centralization in wage bargaining while permitting high levels of decentralization in bargaining over specific work conditions. We consider these in turn.

Even within the current framework of current US labor law, which centers on collective bargaining between elected and exclusive worker representatives (unions) and employers, strategies for reducing barriers to worker representation are clear enough. Elections of representatives could be simplified and expedited, bargaining obligations could attach early and survive the arrival of successor employers, the right to use economic force could be enhanced, and, throughout, violations of labor regulation could be remedied with compensatory damages rather than toothless 'make whole' remedies. In a more ambitious scheme of reforms, representation might be awarded on the basis of a simple demonstration of support from a majority of affected workers rather than the elaborate demonstration elections now required; the individual rights of workplace members of unions without majority status might be enhanced; restraints on the coordination of unions in using economic force could be relaxed; greater attention could be given to the practical requirements of union 'security' in maintaining a workplace presence; and current restraints on the use of member dues for organizing the unorganized, and for political action, could be relaxed.[74]

Even with such reforms in place, however, most of the economy will remain non-union, leaving most workers without representation. We would suggest, then, that forms of workplace representation alternative to, though not in direct competition with, unions also be encouraged. This could be achieved directly through a mandate of workplace committees with responsibilities in, for example, occupational health and safety or training or areas of concern apart from wages. Alternatively, or as supplement, government purchasing contracts might be used to enhance worker voice. Eligibility for such contracts could be conditioned on successful employer demonstration of the existence of a works council or some other acceptable form of autonomous employee representation with real powers in the administration of the internal labor market.

The increased levels of worker organization that could be expected to follow on these two changes would mitigate one of the barriers to cooperation noted earlier, namely, the weakness of labor organization. With labor stronger, it is possible to imagine a new social contract in the internal labor market, one that would promote cooperation. The terms of the contract are simple enough: labor offers flexibility on internal labor market work rules and greater job commitment in exchange for management's commitment to consultation and heightened job security.

To ensure fairness, however, and to promote the stability of associations that contributes to their beneficial effects, a system of multiple worker organizational forms would need an increase in the social wage, our third initiative. For workers, an increased social wage would provide some assurances of fair treatment and security external to the firm. Aside from its direct distributional benefits, this increase would relieve pressures for the internal rigidity and defensiveness associated with job control unionism. It would make more flexible, productivity enhancing strategies of work organization more appealing. For employers, the mitigation of job control consciousness (and the likely reduction of labor costs) among organized workers would remove one powerful incentive to resist worker association in their firm.

Finally, greater coordination of wage contracts would be needed to overcome a second barrier to cooperation and to reap the full benefits for economic performance. As noted earlier, the American system of contract negotiation is highly decentralized. It is unreasonable to expect the United States to approximate the corporatist peak bargaining of the late 1970s (especially since corporatist systems themselves no longer approximate that). Still, some measures could be undertaken to encourage more encompassing associations than now exist, thus generating an environment better suited to some greater centralization and coordination of wage negotiations (at least on a regional basis).

One step would be to amend the law governing multi-employer bargaining, shifting the presumption away from the voluntariness and instability of such arrangements and toward their requirement. In addition, pressures within the union movement for consolidation could be strengthened by selective incentives, for example, in the form of funds for (re)training, conditioned on inter-union cooperation. Government support for business cooperation – for example, consortia pursuing joint research and development strategies – could be conditioned on efforts to consolidate wage policies. Or, following common practice in most systems, 'extension laws' on bargaining contracts could be enacted, generalizing their results to non-union settings.

The effect of this combination of increasing the social wage and promoting more generalization of wage patterns across firms would be to discriminate more sharply between the focus of bargaining within the firm and the focus of bargaining outside it. Within the firm, unions would come to look more like employee participation schemes, and employee participation schemes would look more like unions. Worker representation would be secured, but with a particular focus on regulating the internal labor market and increasing productivity within it through innovation on issues of job design, work organization, access to training on new firm technology, and the like. Outside the firm, more encompassing organizations, suitable to handling matters affecting workers in general, rather than workers in a particular firm, would be more empowered to pursue that object. They would focus more on securing generalizable wage agreements and the content of the social wage.

Such a system, which relies on associative empowerment and artifaction throughout, would likely be a vast improvement on current US industrial relations. It would improve representation, increase productivity, generalize the benefits of cooperation and better integrate the industrial relations system with state economic and welfare policies.

Vocational Training

Our second example of constructive group artifice comes from the area of vocational training. In the United States, as in most other rich countries, intensified international competition and rapid technological change have underscored the need for improvements in workforce skills. To preserve living standards in the face of low-wage competition from abroad, labor must be made substantially more productive and firms must become increasingly adept at such 'non-price' aspects of product competition as quality, variety, customization and service. Success here will require, inter alia, that 'frontline' production and non-supervisory workers be equipped with substantially higher and broader skills than they presently possess.

The vocational training problem in the United States consists in the fact that such skills are being provided in insufficient quality and quantity by US schools and firms, and in so far as they are provided, they are directed to college-bound youths and managers. In the public school system, very little occupational training is provided for either the 'forgotten half' of each high school cohort that does not go on to college or the 'forgotten three-quarters' of each cohort that do not complete it. Also, US employers provide their frontline workforce with far less training than do leading foreign competitors. Moreover, the training they do provide is generally narrower than is desirable – for the economy as a whole, for innovative firms drawing from the external labor market, and for individual workers, who typically change employers several times in their working lifetime.[75] With skills more essential than ever to compensation, the failures of US training have powerfully contributed to the decline in production and non-supervisory worker wages experienced over the past generation and to rising inequality in US market incomes.[76]

The problems in the US training system lie on both the 'demand' and 'supply' side. We shall concentrate here on the supply-side aspect, focusing in particular on two central issues.[77]

First, the quality of public [i.e. state] school vocational training is limited by the absence of effective linkages with the economy itself. Most such vocational training in the United States is essentially 'stand-alone' classroom-based instruction, and while such instruction is certainly important for any training system, it has intrinsic limits.[78] As a general matter, the system will lag behind industry practice in its provision of skills. It will be baffled by the need to make large expenditures on capital equipment, of the sort needed to replicate factories inside schools. And it will have difficulty conveying to students the active knowledge they need to flourish in, and can only acquire from, real-world production situations.

To remedy these problems, denser linkages must be forged between schools and students on one side, and employers and their workers on the other. Through such linkages can flow that which the classroom system now lacks: up-to-date knowledge on industry trends, loans and grants of current equipment on which to train, and all-important access to actual workplaces and their principals for work-based instruction complementary to what goes on in the classroom.

Second, while the quantity of training supplied by government could be expected to increase as a result of the reform of worker representation discussed earlier, the effort by employers must also be substantially increased and improved. Here, the problem is partly that employers are uncertain about the sorts of broad-banded skills that would be appropriate to provide and partly that they have no confidence that they will capture the returns to training in such skills. Employer training suffers, that is, both from a lack of agreed standards for coordinated training and from the positive externalities that accompany an open external labor market in which workers are able to move freely among firms, and so one firm's trainee can become another firm's asset. The externalities problem is particularly acute for high and broad skills. By definition of use in a wide variety of work settings, their possession increases the potential mobility of workers, enabling one firm to appropriate the benefits of another firm's training efforts. This is part of the reason why when firms do train, they train narrowly in job-specific or firm-specific skills.

To remedy the problem of coordination, a mechanism for setting common standards and expectations is necessary. To remedy the externality problem, there are two basic solutions. One is to reduce worker mobility across firms. This permits firms to train workers with the confidence that they recoup any investments made. In effect, this is what is done in Japan. The other solution is to socialize the costs of private firm training, so that individual employers will not care about worker mobility. This can be done with the assistance of the tax system in, for example, the form of 'train or tax' rules requiring firms either to train or to pay into some general fund. Or it can be done through the private collective organization of employers to a point that they can discipline free-riders or, at high levels of joint participation (where close to all relevant competitors or poachers train), become indifferent to them. In effect, this is what is done in successful European training systems, which, like the United States, operate with relatively open external labor markets and high rates of interfirm worker mobility.

As the second European strategy makes clear, the presence of competent, encompassing employer and labor associations immensely aids both in addressing the problem of linkage between the worlds of school and work and in increasing the level and quality of employer-sponsored training.

Facilitating linkage, associations provide the state with timely information on emerging industry trends and practices, new technologies, skill needs and access to the insides of firms. They permit industries to speak with a unified voice to public training providers, to negotiate authoritatively with the state over training curricula, access to firms, requirements on skills certification, rules on the use of equipment, and the like. They permit the state to get closure and enforcement on decisions once made – 'If you don't like it, talk to your association' being a far more effective retort to second-guessing firms than 'Well, that's just what we decided to do' – while providing monitoring and enforcement capacities to supplement any public training effort. Thus by being broad in their representation and accountable to members, they are natural vehicles for developing general standards of wide applicability, of the sort that protect the training investment made by employees themselves.

As facilitators of employer training efforts, industry associations help in part by setting general standards on skills, something no single firm can do. The identification of commonly desired competencies assures workers that acquiring those competencies will improve their position on the external labor market. This leads to increased takeup rates on training, assuring employers of a large pool of workers with high and common skills. And this assurance encourages more proactive industry strategies of upgrading and interfirm cooperation in implementing those strategies.

But associations also act to facilitate employer training efforts by mitigating the externality problem that discourages those efforts. They require training as a condition of membership, or receipt of its benefits. They monitor the training that goes on, relieving fears of 'suckering'. They ease the flow of information about new technology and work practices among members, providing a natural vehicle for voluntary industry benchmarking that creates upward pressures on existing standards. They share training facilities and curricula among them-selves, reducing per capita training costs. More elusive but not less important, they help define and sustain – through means ranging from social gatherings and award dinners to insider gossip and plum subcontracting deals – common norms of 'accepted practice'. As such norms congeal into obligatory industrial cultures, those who undersupply training come to be seen less as clever businessmen than as social pariahs to be punished with loss of status and business. This can powerfully discourage even temptations to defection, making the consideration of cooperation more familiar, extending and secur-ing its reach, and lowering monitoring costs. In all these ways, a strong employers' association, especially one 'kept honest' by a strong union, can provide a powerful boost to the quality and extent of firm training efforts.

How might associative supports be enlisted for a revamped

vocational training system in the United States? In general terms, the problems and the instruments at hand to solve them are clear enough. Both labor and employer associations are relatively weak in this country and need to be strengthened, at least in their capacity to discipline their own members and to deal effectively with one another and with the state on training matters. Very little public money now goes directly to these purposes, even though the lessons of comparative experience clearly indicate their virtue. Public supports – in the form of direct cash assistance, technical assistance, a greater role in curriculum development and/or increased legal powers to enforce obligations against their own members – can be provided in exchange for help in carrying out the important public task of training the workforce.

For example, significant improvement in the quality of vocational training will require some recognized occupational standards. But outside a few specialized trades, these do not exist. Joining with public training providers, existing unions and employer associations could be invited, on an industry-by-industry basis, to develop such standards. Their work could be facilitated by the state in the form of modest financial supports and technical assistance. And it should not be accepted by the state without independent vetting. But some product should finally be accepted and enforced as a standard. Such enforcement will naturally be advanced by the primary authors themselves. Employers would look to demonstrated competence, according to these standards, in the award of jobs in internal labor markets. Unions would center on them in wage negotiations or in rules governing job assignments in those markets. But such private actions can also be supplemented through public means. The standard can be made applicable to all federally funded vocational training programs, for example, and adopted as a standard in arbitration and judicial decisions in labor and employment law.[79]

The competency of labor and trade associations to provide training services to members may be explicitly promoted by public policy as well. Public subsidies and technical assistance to such organizations for this purpose, utterly routine in other countries and already tried with some success with a handful of trade and labor organizations in the United States, would be a natural supportive policy. Antitrust law could be relaxed for joint training activities of member firms;[80] additional amendments may be needed in labor law to permit union-management cooperation in training activities involving nonunion firms.[81]

Both of the examples just presented involve efforts to improve training by strengthening existing associations. But the formation of new associations around training might be encouraged as well. Industry or regional training consortia composed of firms and unions, for example, could be encouraged through demonstration grant assistance, technical aid and discounts on public training services provided to their members.[82] These supports would properly be conditioned on those associations providing training services, participating in standard-setting, mounting outreach programs to public schools, providing such with technical assistance, expanding existing apprenticeship programs (the best, albeit much neglected, example of vocational training in the United States), and otherwise cooperating with public providers and each other to move a more aggressive and inclusive training agenda. The goal again would be to bring both more order and a critical mass to private training efforts and to improve effective linkages to schools.

Given the present weakness of associations in the United States, addressing the externality problem probably requires direct government efforts at socializing costs – through unqualified payroll levies or 'play or pay' levy structures. The revenues, however, can be used in ways that strengthen future private capacities for self-governance. Funds might, for example, be given to associations for redistribution. The effect would be to create enormous temptations to associations to organize themselves to take a more active role in training and for firms and unions to join associations – in effect, an inducement to encompassingness of the sort desired. Or, in a 'play or pay' scheme, tax relief could be granted to firms that demonstrate that the training they provide conforms with the standards set by industry associations. This would have the same effect of strengthening a collective associative hand in standards and strengthening associations themselves.

There are many paths to virtue, but this should be enough to make the point. In principle, at least, the associative supports for a more successful vocational training system could be achieved in the United States with fairly standard policy instruments. Those supports would benefit both workers and 'better' (i.e. interested in upgrading) firms. And far from engendering further corruption of the state, they would strengthen public capacities to address problems of manifest public concern.

Occupational Safety and Health

Finally, we consider an example of how associations can operate to enhance state capacity and advance egalitarian norms in a more overtly regulatory activity.

We said earlier that in many areas of regulation the right answer to the question 'Should the state take care of the problem, or should it be left to the market?' is a double negative – because neither institution is well suited to delivering the result desired on egalitarian grounds. Vocational training is one such area: uniform public standards on behavior are needed, but neither markets nor the state have the competence to specify and secure them. There are, however, also situations where non-market public standards on behavior are needed and government has the competence to set them, but the objects of regulation are either so diverse or unstable that it is not possible for the government to settle just how those standards should be met at particular regulated sites or so numerous or dispersed that it is not possible for government to monitor compliance effectively. In the latter sorts of cases, the deficiencies of 'command and control' specification of process and the reliance on government inspectorates for enforcement become pointed. The protection of occupational safety and health represents one such case.

Consider the Occupational Safety and Health Act (OSHA). By all accounts – left and right, management and labor, state and academic – OSHA has had only limited success in improving workplace health and safety. The sources of this problem owe in part to the OSHA standard-setting process. That reflects the under-representation of worker interests and the failure to enlist the 'social partners' (as well as community and environmental groups) in joint decision-making. More immediately, however, it illustrates the difficulty of enforcing heavily procedural standards over diverse and numerous sites.

The chief problem with enforcement is that, in a system that relies chiefly on an inspectorate, there are too many plants and too few inspectors. Several million commercial establishments, employing countless specific mixes of different production techniques, cannot be successfully monitored by a few thousand federal officials. So long as federal inspectors remain the chief enforcement mechanism, either the law will be – as at present – narrow in its objects and woefully under-enforced or the process of production will need to be more closely regulated through a qualitatively greater federal presence. The former is unsatisfactory, and the latter, whatever its merits (which are not obvious), is not in the cards.

An alternative, however, is to supplement the federal enforcement mechanism through the enlistment of existing (or encouragement of new) but alternative mechanisms available 'on the ground', namely, workplace committees on occupational safety and health. Such committees, used widely and with good effect in Western Europe,[83] would be selected by employees themselves, trained by the government (again working with unions and business) and empowered to make decisions and conduct activities contributing to workplace safety and health. Certain generic aspects of health and safety training, indeed, could be part of standard vocational education programs. Such powers might include taking air samples or conducting other tests of plant environment to detect hazardous levels of exposure, performing certain routine forms of health monitoring (e.g. pulmonary function tests), consulting with management about how best to satisfy or supplement generic performance standards (e.g. permissible exposure limits for chemicals), shutting down plants in cases of imminent danger, reporting back to central federal administration on problems, educating colleagues on health and safety, and collaborating with health professionals, academic researchers and environmental activists to detect emerging problems. The hope is that a stable, quasi-public group, accountable to its members, and set within a framework of national standards, would combine the power to enforce and the capacity to generate specific, local information in ways that would help to reduce workplace hazards.

A problem with any system of self-administration of costly standards is that the self-administering actors face tradeoffs between the benefits of effective administration and the costs that it imposes on them. In the case of workers in dependent bargaining relations with employers, clearly, such tradeoffs can become pointed. Workers' interest in eating may exceed their interest in staying healthy. In addition, because the groups involved in decentralized administration may not be sufficiently encompassing, interests not best organized from the standpoint of the particular administrative unit might be selected out. More simply put, workers may be concerned with their own health but not with the pollutants that the factory discharges into the ambient environment.

Such problems would have to be addressed in any plausible scheme. As just suggested, it is important to establish reporting requirements back to an authoritative government agency, to be clear that local negotiation around the satisfaction of minimal performance or specification standards cannot extend to negotiated reductions in those standards, and to encourage (perhaps by requiring) the exchange of information between committees and actors outside the firms. In principal, however, none of these problems appears intractable. And in practice, as the Western European cases make clear, a workplace committee system of administration delivers more effective, and efficient, administration of occupational safety and health than in the United States.

Moreover, what is true in the OSHA case might be plausibly extended to other areas of regulation in which monitoring must be extended to numerous and diverse local sites. Environmental regulation is one such case, but there are many others: for example, all manner of social programs (in health, housing, welfare services) and economic development programs. Fairly generally, that is, it would be helpful to supplement public efforts at securing certain standards of behavior with private multipliers on enforcement, local negotiation on process and monitoring of those standards.

Conclusion

The examples just given provide only a few illustrations of the directions an associative democratic strategy might take in the United States. But they suffice to underscore the sorts of concerns that define that strategy and the considerations relevant to its execution. What we have argued in this essay and what is displayed in the examples just given is straightforward enough. To proceed, egalitarian politics must once again be shown to work. To work, it requires associative supports. Those supports can be developed. And developing them, and realizing their contribution to democratic governance, does not require a naive view of associations as free from the threat of faction or a dangerous view on the surrender of encompassing public authority. Faction can be mitigated through the same artifice that enlists associative contributions. And the strength and competence of public authorities can gain by their enlistment.

More broadly, by assuring greater equality in organized representation among private citizens and by more effectively recruiting the energies of their organizations into public governance, the aim of the associative strategy is to forge an egalitarian-democratic order without an oppressive state. That is nice work if you can get it – and we have suggested that you can.

Acknowledgment

Drafts of this manuscript have been presented at meetings of the American Political Science Association, Princeton University Political Theory Colloquium, Social Organization Colloquium at the University of Wisconsin-Madison, Society for Ethical and Legal Philosophy, UCLA Center for History and Social Theory, University of Chicago

Colloquium on Constitutionalism, University of Maryland Seminar on Political Theory, PEGS (Political Economy of the Good Society), and CREA (Ecole Polytechnique), at the conference on 'Post-Liberal Democratic Theory' held at the University of Texas, Austin, and at the 'Associations and Democracy' conference held at the Havens Center, University of Wisconsin-Madison. We are very grateful to participants in those discussions, and especially to Bruce Ackerman, Suzanne Berger, Owen Fiss, Charles Sabel, Wolfgang Streeck and Erik Olin Wright. Shorter versions of this paper appeared in *Market Socialism*, ed. Pranab Bardhan and John Roemer (Oxford University Press, 1993), and *Social Philosophy and Policy*, 10, 2 (summer 1993), pp. 282–312.

Notes

1. The phrase comes from James Madison, Federalist paper no. 10, in *The Federalist*, New York: G. P. Putnam 1907, pp. 51–60. We are concerned here only with what Madison called 'minority' faction, or the exploitation of the many by the few – the problem that Madison thought (incorrectly, in our view) would be fully addressed through enactment of the 'republican principle'. We have very little to say here about the problem of 'majority' faction – conflicts of the 'ruling passion or interest' of the majority with 'both the public good and the rights of other citizens'. Moreover, what we do have to say about it is generally limited to the case of majority decisions that fail to advance the 'public good', thus leaving unattended the problem of majority suppression of the 'rights of other citizens'. This is an important limitation on our treatment of faction, which would need to be remedied in a more comprehensive discussion of the subject. But we believe that our proposals for addressing those aspects of the problem of faction that we consider here do not carry untoward implications for addressing issues of oppressive majorities. In addressing the problem of faction, then, the narrowing of our focus does not, we think, make the resolution of that general problem more difficult.

2. We do not distinguish here between secondary associations, which represent the interests of their members to, and in other ways interact with, the state, and those that do not. However, as the following makes clear, we are chiefly concerned with the former.

3. See E. E. Schattschneider, *The Semi-Sovereign People: A Realist's View of Democracy in America*, Hinsdale, IL: Dryden [1960] 1975; V. O. Key, *Politics, Parties, and Pressure Groups*, 4th edn, New York: Crowell 1958; Grant McConnell, *Private Power and American Democracy*, New York: Vintage 1956; and Charles Lindblom, *Politics and Markets: The World's Political-Economic Systems*, New York: Basic Books 1977.

4. See Theodore Lowi, *The End of Liberalism: The Second Republic of the United States*, 2d edn, New York: Norton 1979.

5. See, in particular, Philippe C. Schmitter, 'Still the Century of Corporatism?', *Review of Politics* 36 (1974), pp. 85–131; Suzanne Berger, ed., *Organizing Interests in Western Europe: Pluralism, Corporatism, and the Transformation of Politics*, Cambridge: Cambridge University Press 1981; and John H. Goldthorpe, ed., *Order and Conflict in Contemporary Capitalism*, Oxford: Clarendon 1984.

6. Charles F. Sabel, 'Flexible Specialization and the Re-emergence of Regional Economies', in *Reversing Industrial Decline: Industrial Structure and Policy in Britain and Her Competitors*, ed. Paul Q. Hirst and Jonathan Zeitlin, Oxford: Berg 1989,

17–70; and Wolfgang Streeck, 'On the Institutional Conditions of Diversified Quality Production', in *Beyond Keynesianism: The Socio-Economics of Production and Employment*, ed. Egon Matzner and Wolfgang Streeck, London: Edward Elgar 1991, pp. 21–61.

7. Philippe C. Schmitter, 'Interest Intermediation and Regime Governability in Contemporary Western Europe and North America', in Berger, ed., *Organizing Interests*, ch. 10.

8. We share the term 'associative democracy' with John Mathews, *Age of Democracy: The Political Economy of Post-Fordism*, New York: Oxford University Press 1989, but arrived at the term independently.

9. See John Rawls, *A Theory of Justice*, Cambridge, MA Harvard University Press 1971, whose own work is an exception to the generalization made in the text. Another prominent exception is Roberto Unger's *False Necessity*, vol. 2 of *Politics*, Cambridge: Cambridge University Press 1987.

10. Our discussion of neoliberal constitutionalism is based, in particular, on James M. Buchanan, *The Limits of Liberty: Between Anarchy and Leviathan*, Chicago: University of Chicago Press 1975; Milton Friedman, *Capitalism and Freedom*, Chicago: University of Chicago Press 1962; and Friedrich A. Hayek, *The Constitution of Liberty*, Chicago: University of Chicago Press 1960; *The Mirage of Social Justice*, vol. 2 of *Law, Legislation, and Liberty*, Chicago: University of Chicago Press 1976; and *The Political Order of Free People*, vol. 3 of *Law, Legislation, and Liberty*, Chicago: University of Chicago Press 1979. We draw as well on the constitutional argument associated with the 'Lochner era' in US constitutional law, in particular the idea that the constitution's due process clauses impose substantial barriers to the exercise of the police powers of the state in areas of economic activity. For examples of such argument see *Lochner v. New York*, 198 U.S. 45 (1905); *Coppage v. Kansas*, 236 U.S. 1 (1915). For general discussion of the Lochner era, see Cass R. Sunstein, 'Lochner's Legacy', *Columbia Law Review* 87, no. 5 (1987), pp. 873–919. Our presentation and criticism of the view is indebted to John Rawls's critical discussion of the 'system of natural liberty' in Rawls, *A Theory of Justice*, pp. 66–72.

11. Neoliberal constitutionalism is not the only plausible historical continuation of the liberalisms of John Locke and Adam Smith. Moreover, in associating the term 'liberal' with neoliberal constitutionalist views, we do not mean to suggest either that such liberals as Alexis de Tocqueville, John Stuart Mill, Emile Durkheim, John Rawls or Ronald Dworkin really agree with the neoliberal constitutionalists, or that because they disagree they should not be called 'liberals'.

12. For qualifications, see Samuel Bowles and Herbert Gintis, 'Contested Exchange: New Microfoundations for the Political Economy of Capitalism', *Politics and Society* 18, no. 2 (June 1990) pp. 165–222.

13. A central theme of neoliberal constitutionalism is that the fact of market failure is not sufficient to justify state action, because political action may produce still greater inefficiency. For discussion of this issue, see Gary S. Becker, 'Competition and Democracy', in *The Economic Approach to Human Behavior*, Chicago: University of Chicago Press 1976, ch. 3; Charles Wolf, Jr, 'A Theory of Nonmarket Failure: Framework for Implementation Analysis', *Journal of Law and Economics* 22 (1979), pp. 107–39; and Kenneth A. Shepsle and Barry R. Weingast, 'Political Solutions to Market Problems', *American Political Science Review* 78 (1981), pp. 417–34.

14. Hayek emphasizes the virtues of voluntary associations in *The Mirage of Social Justice*, pp. 150–52.

15. Adam Smith, *Wealth of Nations*, New York: Modern Library 1937, p. 128.

16. The 'rational basis test' for the constitutionality of economic regulation in post-New Deal constitutional law provides one way to articulate this reduced burden. For cases that define and illustrate the reduced burden, see *United States v. Carolene Products Co.*, 304 U.S. 144 (1938), *Williamson v. Lee Optical Co.*, 348 U.S. 483 (1955), and *Ferguson v. Skrupa*, 372 U.S. 726 (1963).

17. See Smith, *Wealth of Nations*, book 4, ch. 2, esp. pp. 429, 438.

18. Hayek, *The Political Order of Free People*, pp. 13, 15 (emphasis added).

19. Ibid., p. 14. A more direct route to the limited government conclusion proceeds without a detour through (partially) democratic legislatures, semi-autonomous bureaux, or even the actions of groups. The direct argument is that all regimes require popular support and that appropriation and redistribution of the surplus to the public is a principal means of securing that support. Given this political criterion for resource allocation, however, the state's allocation of resources will be less efficient than the market's. There will be deadweight losses, violating the fundamental norm of efficiency. While such losses will increase under democratic conditions with organized groups (since democracy institutionalizes the requirement of support and since organized individuals are better able than unorganized ones to extract benefits), neither democracy nor groups are necessary to creating problems of waste. States with extractive powers and even minimal dependence on popular support (e.g. dictatorships) will do that alone. Once that is recognized, the basic solution for public order again follows: limit rents at their source, by constitutionally constraining the functions of the state to those needed to preserve formal individual liberty and a robust market.

20. See Joshua Cohen, 'Democratic Equality', *Ethics* 99, no. 4 (July 1989), pp. 727–51.

21. For a suggestive discussion of this issue, see Jon Elster, 'The Possibility of Rational Politics', *Archives Européennes de Sociologie* 18 (1987), pp. 67–103.

22. Here we are thinking of the example of the New Deal constitutional revolution which was directed against the constitutional understandings set in place by the line of Supreme Court decisions beginning with *Lochner* v. *New York*. On the New Deal as a fundamental constitutional change carried through by a mobilized citizenry, see Bruce Ackerman, *We The People*, Cambridge, MA: Harvard University Press 1991.

23. Schematically, imagine a world with tariffs but without unemployment insurance or social security. State outlays will be smaller, but their distribution will be even more skewed toward select populations.

24. Mancur Olson, *The Rise and Decline of Nations: Economic Growth, Stagflation, and Social Rigidities*, New Haven, CT: Yale University Press 1982, pp. 47–53.

25. See Matthew D. McCubbins and Thomas Schwartz, 'Congressional Oversight Overlooked: Police Patrols vs. Fire Alarms', *American Journal of Political Science* 28 (1984), pp. 165–79.

26. See, for example, Cass R. Sunstein, 'Constitutionalism After the New Deal', *Harvard Law Review* 101 (1987), pp. 421–510.

27. On the issue of institutional program, different republican conceptions diverge considerably, depending on where precisely they put the locus of deliberative politics. Confining attention just to contemporary debate in US constitutional law, there are at least four proposals in the field. Sunstein, whom we follow in the text for purposes of concrete illustration, emphasizes the deliberative role of elected legislators. See Cass R. Sunstein, 'Beyond the Republican Revival', *Yale Law Journal* 97 (1988), pp. 1539–90. Michelman locates deliberative politics in the Supreme Court. See Frank I. Michelman, 'The Supreme Court, 1985 Term – Foreword: Traces of Self-Government', *Harvard Law Review* 100 (1986), pp. 4–77. Ackerman finds deliberative forms of mass politics in moments of constitutional transformation, and argues that the role of the judiciary is to preserve the results of those periods of popular political engagement. See his *We the People*. Brest argues that republican self-rule ought to be extended outside the arena of narrowly political institutions, even in periods of normal politics. See Paul Brest, 'Further Beyond the Republican Revival: Toward Radical Republicanism', *Yale Law Journal* 97 (1988), pp. 1623–31.

28. Issues about associative contributions to democracy have not played a prominent role in the recent 'republican revival'. So, when we say in the text that republicans 'recognize' certain possibilities of contribution, we mean only that such recognition would be a natural extension of their views.

29. Sunstein, 'Republican Revival', pp. 1576–78. Strategies of strengthening

political parties played a particularly prominent role in an earlier generation of anti-pluralist political conceptions. See, for example, Key, *Politics, Parties, and Pressure Groups*; Schattschneider, *Semi-Sovereign People*; and Committee on Political Parties of the American Political Science Association, 'Toward a More Responsible Two-Party System', *American Political Science Review* 44 (1950): Special Supplement. Parties are featured less prominently in the current wave of republican antipluralism perhaps because parties in the United States look increasingly implausible as vehicles of reform or perhaps because the republican revival has come to be so closely associated with law schools and with the more formal-institutional concerns of constitutional lawyers.

30. *Federalist Papers*, p. 423.

31. See Lowi, *The End of Liberalism*.

32. This section draws in particular on Robert A. Dahl, *A Preface to Democratic Theory*, Chicago: University of Chicago Press 1956; *Dilemmas of Pluralist Democracy*, New Haven, CT: Yale University 1982; and *Democracy and its Critics*, New Haven, CT: Yale University Press 1989; and John Hart Ely, *Democracy and Distrust: A Theory of Judicial Review*, Cambridge, MA: Harvard University Press 1980.

33. Pluralism, of course, is not only a normative view, but an empirical one. Empirical pluralism is sometimes said to assert or assume that existing societies do in fact approximate a complete, proportional representation of interests. The strength and distribution of interest groups is taken to match closely the actual strength and distribution of citizen preferences. We doubt that this is a correct characterization of empirical pluralism. In any case, egalitarian pluralists make no such assumption, and the extent of their concerns about faction is defined by the degree to which they suppose it to be false.

34. See, in particular, Dahl, *Democracy and its Critics*, ch. 21.

35. Ely, *Democracy and Distrust*, p. 152.

36. See, for example, Ely, *Democracy and Distrust*; and Bruce Ackerman, 'Beyond Carolene Products', *Harvard Law Review* 98 (1985), pp. 713–46.

37. See Robert A. Dahl, *A Preface to Economic Democracy*, New Haven, CT: Yale University 1985, pp. 105–7.

38. See Ely, *Democracy and Distrust*.

39. Pluralism is sometimes criticized for treating the group system as natural or pre-political. Perhaps this is true of empirical pluralism or of some formulations of that view. But it is not a fair assessment of normative pluralism.

40. On the problem of indeterminateness as it applies to the context of US administrative law, see Richard Stewart, 'The Reformation of American Administrative Law', *Harvard Law Review* 88 (1975), pp. 1776–81. On the more general problem of the indeterminateness of procedural conceptions of democracy, see Ronald Dworkin, 'The Forum of Principle', in Dworkin, *A Matter of Principle*, Cambridge, MA: Harvard University Press 1985, pp. 33–71.

41. Dahl, *Dilemmas of Pluralist Democracy*, pp. 68–80, 193, is an important exception.

42. The egalitarian tradition, as we characterize it here, begins with Rousseau and includes both Marx and John Stuart Mill among its principal nineteenth-century exponents. In *A Theory of Justice*, Rawls gave new philosophical life to the central ideas of this tradition.

43. Such classical liberals as Hayek and Friedman would not accept the account of political equality or the egalitarian conception of the general welfare that we present below, although they agree that ensuring formal equality of opportunity (keeping 'careers open to talents') and promoting the general welfare are legitimate public functions, and they are not hostile to the idea that public policy ought to seek to assure a decent minimum. See, for example, Friedman, *Capitalism and Freedom*; and Hayek, *Mirage of Social Justice*. Only the most extreme forms of libertarianism deny this. See Robert Nozick, *Anarchy, State, and Utopia*, New York: Basic Books 1974. We are not troubled by the disagreement with the classical liberals, both because we do not think that their views are coherent or plausible and because we think that some of their

current popularity reflects more a judgment about the efficacy of certain strategies of public policy than an agreement with the classical liberal conception of the legitimate functions of the state.

44. Rawls, *Theory*; and Rawls, 'The Basic Liberties and Their Priority', in *Tanner Lectures on Human Values*, vol. 3, Salt Lake City: University of Utah Press 1982.

45. In asserting this natural fit between an egalitarian conception of distributive fairness and democratic order, however, we do not mean to embrace any particular egalitarian conception – such as Rawls's maximin criterion, or a conception that imposes constraints on the dispersion of resources, or a mixed view combining attention to the minimum and to the dispersion – or, to take another dimension, a resourcist as distinct from a welfarist interpretation. We mean only to underscore the connection between the democratic ideal of an association of equal citizens and the family of distributive conceptions that seek to limit inequalities to those that can be justified without regard to the factors that distinguish among equal citizens.

46. Committee, 'Toward a More Responsible Two-Party System', 2. On the connection between this substantive characterization of deliberation and a more abstract characterization in terms of finding reasons that are acceptable to others who share that commitment, see Joshua Cohen, 'Deliberation and Democratic Legitimacy', in Alan Hamlin and Phillip Petit, eds., *The Good Polity*, Oxford: Blackwell 1989.

47. Erik Wright has urged us repeatedly to call this requirement 'democratic consciousness'. Sheer stubbornness prevents us from taking the suggestion.

48. We shall say more about threats to each of the six norms when later in the essay we consider the ways that an associative democratic scheme might handle the problems of faction.

49. Here we are assuming that the representatives of groups do faithfully represent the interests and aims of the members, thus abstracting from 'iron law of oligarchy' problems.

50. The threats to popular sovereignty noted here do not depend on inequalities in group organization, as there is the possibility of mutual exploitation by different groups equally situated.

51. It might be thought that rational legislators, anticipating such results at the administrative level, would resist making policy that would require delegation to unreliable agencies. If true, this simply returns us to the problems that faction creates for sovereignty, as popular political choices would be thwarted by the anticipated opposition of privileged groups.

52. Alexis de Tocqueville, *Democracy in America*, vol. 2, New York: Vintage 1945, p. 117.

53. Throughout, respect for the associational liberties of group members, recognition of the resistance of many groups to change, and rejection of concessionist views of associations mean that the strategy stops well short of legislating associative practice or its relation to the state. Associative democracy is not a distinct form of order but a strategy to reform aspects of current practice.

54. Harold L. Wilensky and Lowell Turner, *Democratic Corporatism and Policy Linkages: The Interdependence of Industrial, Labor-Market, Incomes, and Social Policies in Eight Countries*, Berkeley: Institute of International Studies 1987, p. 1.

55. Michael J. Piore and Charles F. Sabel, *The Second Industrial Divide: Possibilities for Prosperity*, New York: Basic Books 1984, p. 278.

56. See Peter Lange, *Union Democracy and Liberal Corporatism: Exit, Voice, and Wage Regulation in Postwar Europe*, Cornell Studies in International Affairs, Occasional Paper no. 16. The measures include rules governing election to union councils, intermediate organizations and national office; the incidence and support of informal caucuses; and procedures for debate and vote on strikes, contracts, and other sorts of concerted action.

57. An example is the principal French agricultural union, the FNSEA (*Fédération Nationale des Syndicats d'Exploitants Agricoles*). The sole agricultural union recognized by the state, the FNSEA was a regular target of protest by rank-and-file farmers,

prompting the president of the FNSEA to say at a 1969 Congress that the leadership had been 'the object of permanent criticism' for its 'excessively intimate' connections with the French state. See John T. S. Keeler, 'Corporatism and Official Union Hegemony: The Case of French Agricultural Syndicalism', in Berger, *Organizing Interests*, pp. 185–208, at pp. 187.

58. Schattschneider, *Semi-Sovereign People*, p. 109.

59. Dahl, *Dilemmas*, p. 47.

60. See, for example, the discussion of 'fire alarm' enforcement in McCubbins and Schwartz, 'Congressional Oversight Overlooked', pp. 165–79.

61. Again, see de Tocqueville, *Democracy in America*, p. 117.

62. These effects are noted in Sunstein, 'Constitutionalism', pp. 480–81: 'The movement toward increased congressional control is not without risks of its own [since] . . . undue specificity may produce regulation riddled by factional tradeoffs.'

63. Philippe C. Schmitter, 'Democratic Theory and Neo-Corporatist Practice', *Social Research* 50 (1989), pp. 885–928, at p. 918.

64. Consider, by way of clarification and contrast, a proposal by Schmitter about how to address the problems of the limited space of representation in a corporatist association. He argues that an assurance of fair authorization, specifically attentive to inequality in representation, might be provided by a voucher system. Citizens would receive vouchers, representing a promise of funds to be generated out of general tax revenues, to spend on quasi-public groups. They could then 'vote' these vouchers on groups of their choice. At a very general level, our suggestion is similar, as we also are thinking of the system of favored organizations as itself a matter of collective choice. But whereas Schmitter proposes a collective choice through a new form of political market, the choice that we have in mind would be made under more conventionally political circumstances. Citizens would vote through the electoral system on party programs, one aspect of which would be party positions on the appropriate forms of associative governance, and then would hold elected officials accountable to the conduct of those programs. See Philippe C. Schmitter, 'Corporative Democracy: Oxymoronic? Just Plain Moronic? Or a Promising Way Out of the Present Impasse?' (mimeo, Stanford University 1988). We prefer our proposal to Schmitter's because we think that the decisions in question ought to be made through institutions that make a deliberative collective decision possible. But whatever the advantages of the more political method of choice, both proposals appear to provide promising approaches to the problems that our associative scheme faces in the area of political equality, suggesting that however serious those problems are, they may not be entirely intractable.

65. Louis Jaffe, 'Law-Making by Private Groups', *Harvard Law Review* 51 (1937) pp. 202–53, at pp. 220–21.

66. Ibid., p. 221.

67. For an instructive discussion of the role of non-profit organizations in welfare state service delivery, emphasizing the increased dependence of many of these agencies on their ties to government, see Steven Rathgeb Smith and Michael Lipsky, *The Age of Contracting: Nonprofit Agencies and the Welfare State*, Cambridge, MA: Harvard University Press forthcoming.

68. A useful (though not impartial) recent survey of local economic development strategies is provided in R. Scott Fosler, *Local Economic Development*, Washington, DC: International City Management Association 1991.

69. For an enthusiastic review of some of the emerging linkages between schools and private business associations, see Anthony Carnevale, Leila Gainer, Janice Villet and Shari Holland, *Training Partnerships: Linking Employers and Providers*, Alexandria: American Society for Training and Development 1990.

70. The Job Training Partnership Act (JTPA) has been widely criticized as insufficiently accountable to public needs. Among others, see John D. Donahue, *Shortchanging the Workforce: The Job Training Partnership Act and the Overselling of Privatized Training*, Washington, DC: Economic Policy Institute 1989; and US General Accounting Office (GAO), *Job Training Partnership Act: Inadequate Oversight Leaves Program*

Vulnerable to Waste, Abuse, and Mismanagement, rep. no. GAO/HRD–91–97, Washington, DC: General Accounting Office 1991.

71. Some of the federal experience is reviewed in Charles W. Powers, *The Role of NGOs in Improving the Employment of Science and Technology in Environmental Management,* New York: Carnegie Commission on Science, Technology, and Government, May 1991; the experience of local communities in fostering such environmental bargaining among organized groups is reviewed in Valjean McLenighan, *Sustainable Manufacturing: Saving Jobs, Saving the Environment,* Chicago: Center for Neighborhood Technology 1990.

72. The force of this claim will emerge in our discussion of the role of associations in vocational training.

73. For a general review of the US industrial relations system emphasizing these interactions, see Joel Rogers, 'Divide and Conquer: "Further Reflections on the Distinctive Character of American Labor Law"', *Wisconsin Law Review* (1990), pp. 1–147. For a recent review of the state of the American labor movement, see the contributions to George Strauss, Daniel G. Gallagher and Jack Fiorito, eds., *The State of the Unions,* Madison, WI: Industrial Relations Research Association 1991.

74. There are many such statements of possible labor law reform. A good guide to the issues involved, containing both more and less ambitious recommendations for reform, is provided by Paul Weiler, *Governing the Workplace: The Future of Labor and Employment Law,* Cambridge, MA: Harvard University Press 1990.

75. For general reviews of US training problems, making all these points, see US Congress, Office of Technology Assessment, *Worker Training: Competing in the International Economy,* rep. no. OTA ITE–457, Washington, DC: GPO 1990; and Commission on the Skills of the American Workforce, *America's Choice: High Skills or Low Wages!,* Rochester, NY: National Center on Education and the Economy 1990.

76. For a good review of wage trends in the United States and the more general decline in living standards among non-supervisory workers, see Lawrence Mishel and David M. Frankel, *The State of Working America,* 1990–91 edn, Armonk: M. E. Sharpe 1990.

77. A word of explanation on the focus. Demand by US employers for high and broad frontline workforce skills is extremely weak and uneven. Unless this changes, supply-side innovations geared to improving skill delivery to frontline workers will have all the effect of 'pushing on a string'. Moreover, the needed changes cannot come from competitive pressures alone, as employers can choose to respond to those pressures by reducing wages, increasing firm productivity through changes in work organization that 'dumb down' most jobs while increasing the human capital component of a well-paid few, or simply moving away from high-end markets. Most US firms, in fact, have chosen some combination of these 'low wage, low skill' competitive strategies. To remedy the demand-side problem, it is essential to foreclose this option. The most obvious way to do this is to build stable floors under wages and effective linkage between productivity improvements and wage compensation, thus forcing employers to be more attentive to strategies for increasing the productivity of their labor (e.g. skill upgrading). Direct state action can help here by increasing minimum wage floors. As regards more specifically associative reform, however – and this is why we do not linger on the demand side – we believe the most important actions are those already outlined in the recommendations just made on improving industrial relations. Deeper and more encompassing worker organizations, especially ones shaped by social interests in proved cooperation (discussed earlier), would help create the needed wage floors, wage-productivity linkages and pressures within firms to upgrade. Moreover, they could be expected to do so in a way that not only raised the aggregate demand for skills and their compensation but improved the distribution of both. The basic problem on the demand side is that the interests of the bulk of the population – workers – are simply not now centrally in the picture. They are barely represented in the economy and only very imperfectly represented in the state. The basic solution to under-representation is to improve the conditions of their organization in ways consistent with other democratic norms.

78. The importance of these limits rises where, as in the United States, the public training system lacks any effective industry-based training complement.

79. The Department of Labor's Office of Work-Based Learning is already making qualified moves in this direction, 'qualified' in that, outside more heavily unionized industries, it remains unclear what, if any, organized voice workers in the industry will have.

80. Following current practice for joint research and development activities.

81. Recommendations on how to do this are made in Margaret Hilton, 'Shared Training: Learning from Germany', *Monthly Labor Review* 114, no. 3 (March 1991), pp. 33–7.

82. An experiment along these lines is now under way in Milwaukee, where several firms (non-union and unionized), unions and public training providers have come together around a Wisconsin Manufacturing Training Consortium designed to do just these things. See Joel Rogers and Wolfgang Streeck, 'Recommendations for Action', Madison: Center on Wisconsin Strategy 1991.

83. For a review of worker participation in safety regulation focusing on Europe, see the contributions to Sabastiano Bagnara, Raffaello Misiti and Helmut Wintersberger, eds., *Work and Health in the 1980s: Experiences of Direct Workers' Participation in Occupational Health*, Berlin: Edition Sigma, 1985; for a particularly useful country study, see Bjørn Gustavsen and Gerry Hunnius, *New Patterns of Work Reform: The Case of Norway*, Oslo: Universitetsforlaget 1981; for the contrast with the United States, see Charles Noble, *Liberalism at Work: The Rise and Fall of OSHA*, Philadelphia: Temple University Press 1986; and Eugene Bardach and Robert Kagan, *Going by the Book*, Philadelphia: Temple University Press 1982.

PART II

Commentaries, Criticisms, Extensions

2

Can Secondary Associations Enhance Democratic Governance?

Paul Q. Hirst

There is no doubt that the problem Joshua Cohen and Joel Rogers have addressed in the opening paper to this volume is a very important one: the failure of strongly market-oriented liberal democratic polities like the United States to develop a system of effective governance through collaboration with sufficiently representative, interest-based secondary associations. Their claim is that secondary associations are neither inclusive enough, nor representative of the major interests in the society that they serve, to be an effective link with the formal structures of political decision-making. Yet such a link would enhance both the quality and the fairness of public policy.

They identify a connection between most of the major failings of the US social and political system and the weakness of secondary associations in democratic governance: limited citizen participation in the formal institutions of democracy; weak and unrepresentative political parties; the excessive influence of exclusive, narrowly self-interested associations in government and policy generally – in particular the over-representation of particular corporate business interests and the weakness of inclusive organizations representing the general interests of employers and organized labor; the exclusion of large sectors of society, specifically unorganized labor, the poor and welfare recipients, from effective political influence; an imperfect and fragmented welfare state; and the absence of effective national policies to enhance economic performance through supply-side measures like training.

This is a daunting list and most of these unsatisfactory features are widely recognized by political commentators and social scientists concerned with reform. Like Philippe Schmitter,[1] Cohen and Rogers are distinctive in their focus on the crucial role of the revitalization of secondary associations in democratization. Many commentators have recognized and lamented the fact that the economic competitiveness of the United States has suffered from its individualistic social and political culture. Commentators such as Michel Albert[2] have argued that US firms lack the forms of social solidarity characteristic of Japan or the forms of societal corporatism characteristic of Western Europe. However, the problem with such a diagnosis, as Cohen and Rogers recognize it, is that it is difficult to identify existing foci of social solidarity that would enable the United States to evolve in such a direction. The United States is unlikely to evolve spontaneously in such a collaborative/cooperative direction, nor do its political institutions enable it to adopt an external 'model' and convert itself wholesale into a version of Japan or West Germany. Therefore, reforms are needed that are adapted to US conditions as well as a process of active democratic-governmental involvement in reforming its associational culture. Can secondary associations be transformed into a means of more effective and equal interest group representation and, therefore, into a vehicle for more collaborative governance? If they can, this may provide the key to solving some of the problems that beset the United States. Such changes can work only if they are compatible with US political institutions and the continental scale of the US economy.

In an earlier version of their paper Cohen and Rogers gave particular emphasis to an aspect of organizations that appeared to provide the basis for such an active reform strategy by government, that is, their *artifactuality*. Associations are not merely the given and spontaneous products of social life; rather, the forms that they take and the powers that they have are in large measure the product of public policy. Therefore, the conditions under which organizations operate, the balance of power between them and the degree to which they compete or cooperate can all be shaped by the deliberate reform interventions of the democratic state. This strong version of the artifactuality thesis seems to offer a promising basis for such an active reform strategy, evening up the conditions of democratic representation between associations. If associations were substantially the products of public policy, then they could also be changed by it.

I shall continue to refer to these stronger and starker formulations, since they highlight the problems of a strategy of active state intervention. They define artifactuality as follows: 'What we mean by this is that there is no natural structure of group representation that directly reflects the underlying condition of social life.' I would agree wholeheartedly with this statement: social interests are not given, nor are the forms of organization in which such 'interests' are articulated. They go on to argue that the conditions of group formation, intergroup interaction and the resources groups possess 'are in part a product of opportunities and incentives that are induced by the structure of political institutions and the substance of political choices'. Therefore, groups can be made the objects of public policy: 'a deliberate artifaction of groups, using the tools of public persuasion ... (taxes, subsidies and sanctions), can be used to encourage those qualities of groups contributing to democratic governance, and to discourage those qualities that infirm it.' They quote E. E. Schattschneider[3] to the effect that the institutions of the political process are as much subject to public choice as substantive policy issues: 'The public has a choice of strategies and theories of political organization as well as a choice of issues. As a matter of fact, the choice of issues is apt to be meaningless unless it is backed up by the kind of organization that can execute the mandate.'

Artifactuality, therefore, appears to be a matter of public choice, of political agents executing the mandate of a sovereign people. However, while 'the associative conception recognizes the importance of groups, and the need for congruence of state agendas with group agendas', it 'seeks to alter these agendas, and the structure of group representation, through the use of state powers.' The state is the agency of group transformation, acting on a popular mandate. However, the state is seen to be clearly more than a relay of popular decisions: 'the state, and citizens acting through it, should be alert to the possibilities of such associative solutions to policy problems, and willing to *act on groups* to achieve desired results ... policy-makers should ask if the problem is one where *properly designed* associations could make a contribution ... ' The issue here that needs to be emphasized is that state action by policy-makers to act on groups to ensure that they are 'properly designed' will always be something quite different from a simple, popular choice or democratic mandate; it will involve a far more autonomous series of actions by 'policy-makers', who are far more specific agents than a sovereign people.

This stark version of their thesis implies the proposition that if associations are artifactual, then they can be re-artifacted. The state can choose to change the types of association, their roles and powers. The problem is that this implication of their thesis by no means follows. Artifactual associations and organizations created by public policy can prove remarkably resistant to deliberate change and active political re-engineering. Consider the corporation. At one time both US and UK laws were hostile to the widespread granting of corporate powers and privileges; corporations were considered a danger to the interests of individuals and gave undue powers to some citizens to protect their property against risk. In the latter part of the nineteenth century legal and political opinion changed and corporate status with limited liability became widely available. No one imagines that we could now radically alter the rights of private corporations, removing limited liability or greatly increasing the public responsibilities of corporations, without the most fundamental change in political attitudes and public opinion.

The same may hold true for other aspects of associative life and the capacity of the state to reshape the existing structure of secondary associations. I would claim that the capacity of the sovereign power of the democratic state may be less than they assumed and that there is a tension between two radically different conceptions of democracy in their analysis. The six criteria Cohen and Rogers advance to define democracy – popular sovereignty, political equality, distributive equity, civic consciousness, good economic performance and state competence – encapsulate these two different conceptions. The latter two criteria are not wholly coincident with the first four. Those four relate to a classic radical republican definition of democracy as the majoritarian power of decision of sovereign citizens (subject to the protection of individual rights and minorities). But the concerns for which they raise associative democracy as a solution involve a rather different conception of democracy, which is at best understated in their criteria. That is, the conception of democracy as effective governance based on an adequate flow of information from society to government and the coordination of social affairs through the collaboration of the state with secondary associations representing the major, institutionally constructed social interests.

This latter conception defines democracy not in terms of the rule of majorities but in terms of the *quality* of decision-making which results from the interaction of the state and other social organizations. It is the basis for neocorporatist conceptions of governance and was probably best expressed by Emile Durkheim in his *Lectures on Civic Morals*.[4] For Durkheim the majoritarian principle and formal territorial representation of individual citizens are not the most significant phenomena in defining what is 'democratic' about the modern capitalist state – democracy is a process of effective two-way communication between an independent public power (the state) and organized social groups representing the main occupational interests. In his conception of democracy Durkheim emphasizes the state as a distinct organ of social coordination, *not* of majoritarian decision: 'the state is nothing if it is not an organ distinct from the rest of society'.[5] Only an independent public power can ensure that the state does not become a medium for the conflict of distinct social interests, in which the majoritarian principle serves merely to enable one set of interests to prevail over another. He argues that accurate information, objectivity and rationality in policy-making are the hallmarks of an effective democracy. Group participation is only effective if the interaction of groups with the state enables public policy to be made on such a basis: 'The more deliberation and reflection and a critical spirit play a considerable part in the course of public affairs, the more democratic the nation'.[6] Communication makes possible enhanced social solidarity because it requires groups to put their objectives in a rational form, capable of mediation by the public power. Groups, therefore, are able to act together. Such enhanced solidarity makes possible effective group coordination through the state; the state is able to act in an informed and efficient way, and thus enjoys consent for its policies.

This view of 'democracy' may appear idealistic if we expect pluralistic political competition to take the form of knock-down, drag-out conflicts between exclusive and self-interested groups. It emphasizes, however, that the state must be more than a medium of decision if effective coordination in the attainment of long-term and common social goals like good economic performance and state competence are to be achieved. This view of 'democracy' emphasizes that the separateness of the state from the organized social interests is a condition for its function as an organ of social solidarity. The state in this conception must be neither captured by certain organized social interests, nor become a mere forum for group conflict and antagonistic bargaining. The state, while distinct, must interact with society and not stand over it as an absolute power. This conception, for all its apparent idealism, does capture the political processes at work in more consensual and collaborative policies, and there is considerable evidence that such group coordination does enhance economic performance. This type of state is a key component in those *political* conditions that enable a balance to be struck between the cooperation and conflict of interest groups, firms and other agencies, such that market societies can produce satisfactory outcomes for both welfare and long-term competitiveness.

It seems to me that this conception of the state as a distinct public power capable of a substantial measure of objectivity in policy-making is implied in Cohen and Rogers's own analysis. On the one hand, this emerges from their emphasis on the need to ensure that the state is not so permeable to outside influence that it cannot be captured by certain powerful, exclusive and narrowly self-interested associations. Associations are not given agencies that emerge from underlying and natural divisions in social life; rather, they are political *constructs*. That means that they can be crafted by deliberate public policy. As we have seen, such crafting cannot be simply a matter of giving effect to the popular will; it involves a process of 'design' by state agencies.

If we accept that associations are to be *crafted* by public policy, then the question of the *agency* that accomplishes such crafting becomes crucial. Such an agency requires both a measure of neutrality and objectivity to act in the common good. It also requires a measure of legitimacy so that its actions will evoke consent. How can state agencies acquire the competence, neutrality and legitimacy to perform this function of crafting? They must be autonomous enough to act on society and yet must possess sufficient public support that those actions can be sustained. The artifactuality of organizations seems an attractive thesis to a reformer, yet it raises a host of problems. Crafting can be neither the recognition of already given interests by the state nor can it be the creation de novo by the state of secondary associations as forms of social solidarity. Durkheim argues that the state must function as a directive organ of social intelligence if it is to be both an effective and yet not excessively authoritarian means of societal governance: he does not explain how it acquires both the capacity to act on society and the neutrality to do this constructively.

Such a state cannot be subject to citizen sovereignty and the majority principle, for that would undermine its separateness and neutrality. Its agencies and servants must be autonomous enough to function and yet not too independent that it dominates society as an authoritarian power. Can such a state of objective and effective public servants exist? On what basis can it claim to craft group representation in the interests of the whole? The legitimacy of 'majority' support is hardly helpful, since the role of the state is to act on and craft the very associations that serve to create that support. Moreover, the very necessity of crafting arises because the existing associations are deficient in certain important respects: weak political parties, exclusive interest groups, etc. A 'majority' may be regarded as itself an artifact of the very associational structure and culture which is at default. If the state is seeking the support of a 'people's will' independent of the existing secondary associations which act to form it, does it not court the plebiscitarian danger of an over-strong state and associations which are crafted to suit its objectives and therefore provide it with manufactured support? How does the state acquire the independence from an artifactual but deficient 'society' to act in the 'general interest' against narrowly self-interested associations?

I ask these questions in a sharp form, not because I wish to dispute the thesis that secondary associations are in some substantial degree artifactual, nor because I dispute that the more inclusive and equal representation of the major social interests would be a good outcome. The thesis of artifactuality and the process of reform in the direction of the equalization of the influence of secondary associations both involve a very difficult balancing act. Place too much emphasis on artifactuality and the task of public policy either becomes impossible – the state is acting in a vacuum of legitimacy – or the risks of the state acquiring too much power become too great – it shapes associations to its own purposes.

In fact, the only way out of these dilemmas is to downgrade the thesis of artifactuality a good deal, while accepting that associations are political constructs. The crafting of associations by state agencies can only work if there are existing foci of quasi-constructed and quasi-political group solidarity to work on. The state enters into a partnership with weak organizations to enhance their capacities and it also enables weakly articulated and fragmented interests to acquire a more effective definition and voice. What is entailed here is something radical informers in the United States have often hankered after – a new New Deal, in which a majoritarian democratic decision enables state agencies to have the power to act on the political system in order to enable and empower the weak and excluded. This supposes that the existing system of associations is neither too deficient nor too corrupt to produce such a result.

Serious problems remain, however, even if we entertain the premiss that such an outcome is possible. We accept in this analysis that there are pre-existing (if constructed) foci of solidarity with which a demo-cratically renewed state enters into partnership. If newly enhanced associations (based on pre-existing sources of solidarity) are artifactu-ally generated by state aid, will they not be heavily dependent on state aid in order to function? The problem here is less that of the state crafting associations in its own image, and, therefore, skewing the process of political communication excessively in the direction of the state, than of weakening associations by the very process of strengthening them. If secondary associations become creatures of public policy, then danger lies in their fragility and vulnerability to shifts in public policy.

The only way to avoid this danger is if the state were to engineer an 'irreversible shift in power', simultaneously promoting certain organizations and weakening others in order to undercut their capacity to campaign against this process and win elections. This would court the opposite danger of political mobilization from above, and would be regarded by the threatened organizations as a 'totalitarian' manipulation of the political process. There is no prospect of such a radical redistribution of power aided by the state in the United States, the established and exclusive parties and interest groups are simply too strong and well resourced. A reform initiative could only proceed and avoid being derailed if the strong and exclusive organizations capable of reversing a 'majority' in favor of such change actually accept the need for a reform which produces a fairer and more open system of associations. The odds of such interest groups doing so, of accepting even modest changes in the status quo, is probably small, however articulate and sustained the advocacy of the collective benefits of such changes. Without such a broad political consensus for reform and the acceptance of common national goals, the fragile new capacities of groups are at the mercy of the formal representative system with all its defects. Thus there may be reversals of policy long before the benefits of such crafting are felt and the 'artifactual' associations are capable of standing on their own feet. The fate of the poverty programs of the 1960s and 1970s is an all too obvious reminder. They were reforms from above and dependent on state bureaucracy. But reforms that aim to produce action and governance from below may be equally vulnerable to failures of implementation of and subsequent changes in state policy.

Durkheim assumed that groups were far from artifactual. He supposed that the state could bring itself into relation with independently solidaristic secondary associations, occupational groups. The objective was to persuade all groups to cooperate and for key groups to come to recognize the futility of non-cooperation. A corporatist state could thus overcome both the pathological tendencies of an unregulated market society and the threat of conflict that arose from such tendencies. In Cohen and Rogers's case the threat is not socialism as it was for Durkheim; rather, it is the continued decay of social solidarity through an excessively anarchic and individualistic capitalism which threatens to destroy the conditions for effective and more equal group representation and which undermines its own international competitiveness in the process. I have tried to show that the problem is that this process of crafting an alternative throws an excessive weight either on the capacity for reform of the state or the possibility of a consensus about the virtues of reform on the part of existing parties and associations. However accurate Cohen and Rogers's diagnosis of the problems may be, however attractive their thesis of artifactuality, it does not follow that a satisfactory political mechanism to solve them is at hand in a liberal capitalist state like the United States.

The nation-state is far from completely losing its salience in the face
of globalization and the formation of supranational economic blocs
like the European Union.[7] The mechanisms of national economic
regulation are changing, but governmental policies to sustain national
economic performance can retain considerable relevance, even if their
nature, level and functions have changed radically. The problem
is that, unlike Keynesianism, the new strategies of regulation are not
techniques of macroeconomic management available to every competent state administration in an advanced industrial country. Rather,
these new strategies place a premium on the specific inheritance of
social institutions and, in particular, on the solidarity and common
commitment of effectively organized associations.

Nation-states are no longer (if they ever were) 'sovereign' economic
regulators able to alter macroeconomic aggregates at will. Instead,
national economic management depends increasingly on the capacities
of *political* communities at national and regional level to sustain
certain policies: cooperation to enhance supply-side performance,
commitment to fiscal policies that enable effective public investment in
human capital and infrastructure, restraint in wage bargaining by
organized labor and the commitment by a cohesive core of the business
community to continued investment in the territory in question.
These policies require forms of solidarity between social actors and the
capability of organized interests to put long-term, territorially-based
outcomes first. Organizations may be both artifactual and the outcome
of specific histories, but all states are not equally well endowed in this
respect. One must qualify the capacity of states to reverse unfavorable
institutional inheritances by means of deliberate public policy. This
may be possible – inheritance is not fate – but then again, it may
not. The conditions of building the political prerequisites of effective
cooperation are not available to all states.

As Scharpf[8] indicates, organized labor has the greatest interest in
such collaborative policies. It is collectively less mobile than capital
and must regard its own national or regional situations as a community of fate. Where organized labor is both strong enough and able
to adopt the necessary policy measures, then it can offer the conditions
for an ongoing national or regional pact with capital. Where capital
has the minimum solidarity and national commitment to respond,
such initiatives by organized labor are capable of creating the political
conditions for effective economic partnership. Organized labor has
to make three long-term commitments which are difficult to sustain
and which put a premium on its capacity for concerted action: the
acceptance of tax levels high enough to sustain public spending to

assure economic competitiveness, and in particular investment in human capital; the recognition of the need for ongoing responsibility in wage bargaining to secure price stability and the profitability of firms; and a partnership with management at national and firm levels to promote the ongoing improvement of productivity. In this sense 'social democracy' is a core component of a viable national strategy for economic management in the changed conditions of the post-Keynesian era. States that can draw on and preserve strong social democratic traditions have the best chance of adapting to the changed conditions. As we can see from the cases of Germany and Sweden, such adaptation may prove difficult even where the traditions of coop-eration and common action are strong. Other countries, like Japan, have effective – if politically and institutionally divergent – substitutes for social democracy. Certain regions can also develop policies that compensate for the weakness of their national political systems (e.g. the more successful Italian regions), although here too the difficulties of deliberate adaptation are formidable. The countries at the greatest disadvantage are those whose manufacturing sectors lack broad-based competitiveness and which lack the political conditions to compensate for the disintegration effects of internationalization. The UK and the US are obvious examples, and the prospect of their continued economic decline into the twenty-first century must be greater than that of a politically directed process of collaboration to restore competitiveness.

If this gloomy analysis is correct, then its *political* consequences are disturbing. Lack of cooperation between the major social interests and of coordination by the state leads to poor economic performance. Poor economic performance leads to social fragmentation as success-ful firms, sectors and regions pull away from the national norm and are unwilling, at the price of their own competitiveness, to pay for general programs of economic revitalization or social compensation for the effects of economic decline. Such firms, sectors and regions adhere to exclusive interest organizations and pursue a narrowly protective policy, which aims to direct public policy toward their own advantage. They gain in influence since they have the resources to campaign and the state is fearful to overburden the remaining islands of success. Economic failure leads to social fragmentation, and the consequence is political blockage – consensus policies become impossible as social interests become more and more internally divided and mutually antagonistic. This process is more likely where the political inheritance is one of *laissez-faire* and competitive individualism. The process of fragmentation legitimizes the 'winners'

PAUL Q. HIRST 111

and stigmatizes the 'losers'. The odds are that the *social* sources of competitive failure are likely to be self-reinforcing and to inhibit an effective political response.

This latter outcome appears more likely than that failure will evoke a radical political response and strong action by the state to change the terms on which associations operate. Moreover, the US political system has specific features which are likely to inhibit effective and sustained state action. The difficulties with a practice of crafting associations toward new focus of democratic governance are that it requires both a strong state and a cohesive political class of representatives and officials. The Federal government seems woefully deficient in this respect. Political parties exhibit weak discipline and are not effective mechanisms to generate carefully constructed policy platforms. The separation of the legislative and executive branches means that cabinet posts are headed by short-term political appointees who are usually not experienced career politicians. The US lacks both a stable and competent political class and an autonomous and experienced administrative stratum.

How, then, should one respond? I am constitutionally hostile to making pessimism the basis for a gospel of political despair. I have two suggestions to make, neither of which will adequately address problems at the national level. Both rely on giving greater scope to associations in democratic governance. The first is to advocate a process of rebuilding associations from below, by political campaigning and voluntary action in civil society. Resources for associations may be unequally distributed, but they do not altogether exclude efforts to construct or rebuild means of campaigning on behalf of the poor and excluded. Voluntary and campaigning associations of this kind are still quite effective in the United Kingdom and they continue to attract able and determined members of the professional classes as leaders and staffers. Churches in the United States are possessed of considerable resources and great public influence. Perhaps they might be vehicles for campaigns to support marginalized constituencies. Such action will be long-term and its outcomes partial, but this kind of voluntary action to craft artifactual associations may create foci for support of a more general politics of reform while also acting in the meantime as agencies for addressing social problems. The second is to work at the regional level and to build on and attempt to generalize the efforts of state and city governments to promote programs of economic revitalization and to create agencies to carry out these programs. Obviously, there are severe budgetary constraints to such programs in the United States and the problems of many localities are massive, but in the absence of appropriate Federal programs there seems little alternative.

There are rationales for such strategies that are more than a gospel of despair. There is a strong English associationalist tradition which gave precedence to voluntary action in civil society.[9] This tradition overemphasized the organic nature of associations and denied the thesis of artifactuality advanced by Cohen and Rogers. However, we need not subscribe to this tradition uncritically nor believe associations are simply spontaneous outgrowths of social life. The great strength of this pluralist and associationalist tradition – represented by such thinkers as J. N. Figgis, G. D. H. Cole and H. J. Laski – was that it was all too aware of the danger of dependence on the state. They were opponents of centralization and bureaucracy. They believed that associations are most effective when they are constructed by citizens rather than by the state, and they challenged the 'concessionist' theory of associations as entities that are dependent for their existence on state recognition. As libertarians they feared the dangers of giving more and more tasks to central state agencies and officials. They were aware of both the formidable difficulties of accountability of big government and of the tendencies of a public service state to appropriate and redefine social objectives in its own image and interest.

The voluntarist and libertarian current in associationalism was, however, not inherently hostile to extended cooperation between associations or to the coordination of social activities through the interaction of associations and (decentralized and more accountable) state agencies. The problem is that those most open to such conceptions tended to see such processes in terms of a guild socialist society. That was utopian then and beyond credibility now. But this current of associationalism is a valuable corrective to certain aspects of the corporatist conception of the role of associations in democratic governance. It makes clear against Durkheim – that the idea of the state as a 'distinct organ' of the community and separate from it – has real dangers, unless the state is pluralized and decentralized as far as is practicable. Against the theorists of societal corporatism, it warns of the dangers of inclusive 'peak' organizations with strong disciplinary powers, unless they are constrained by active and democratically self-governing subsidiary organizations below them.

As it happens this voluntarist and libertarian current of associationalism, which emphasizes self-governing organizations freely formed of citizens, is in many ways more compatible with the individualistic tendencies of 'Anglo-Saxon' politics than is the more centralist and statist conceptions of Durkheim or the neocorporatists. This may seem to be making a virtue out of necessity, but, given the inherent difficulties of reform from above, it is worth considering the prospects for revitalization from below. Such prospects are far from rosy. One cannot imagine that voluntary action in civil society can address all the problems of national economic performance, but at least it can mitigate the consequences of such problems for marginal groups and serve as an advocate of their concerns. Given that ambitious programs of crafting associations through the state are unlikely to be realized, such a strategy has the merit that the partial successes it achieves will be real ones.

Notes

1. P. Schmitter, 'Corporative Democracy: Oxymoronic? Just Plain Moronic? Or a Promising Way out of the Present Impasse?' mimeo, Stanford University 1988.
2. Michel Albert, *Capitalisme contre capitalisme*, Paris: Seuil 1991.
3. E. E. Schattschneider, *The Semi-Sovereign People*, Hinsdale, IL: Dryden 1960.
4. E. Durkheim, *Professional Ethics and Civil Morals*, London: Routledge & Kegan Paul 1957.
5. Ibid., p. 82.
6. Ibid., p. 89.
7. P. Hirst and G. Thompson, 'The Problem of Globalization: International Economic Relations, National Economic Management and the Formation of Trading Blocs', *Economy and Society*, vol. 21, no. 4 (1992), pp. 357–96.
8. F. Scharpf, *Crisis and Choice in European Social Democracy*, Ithaca, NY: Cornell University Press 1991.
9. P. Hirst, *Associative Democracy*, Amherst, MA: University of Massachusetts Press 1994; P. Hirst, ed., *The Pluralist Theory of the State: Selected Writings of G.D.H. Cole, J.N. Figgis & H.J. Laski*, London: Routledge 1989.

3

Some Skeptical Considerations on the Malleability of Representative Institutions

Claus Offe

What we are dealing with in the discussion of the work by Cohen and Rogers is the relationship of rational actors and social order. Let me first distinguish four solutions to the problem of how rational actors can achieve social order.

Rational Actors and Institutional Order

Solution (1) follows a Hobbesian logic. Given the essential equality of human actors, their capacity to act rationally and the scarcity of goods they need for their survival, the result will be eternal, violent conflict and a state of nature governed by fear. Having experienced this state of nature, rational actors will look for ways to overcome it. The only solution will be concluding an irreversible contract of domination. This contract involves the collective self-disarmament of all members of society in favor of a third party, the absolute authority of the Leviathan, who himself is not part of nor bound by the contract. The exchange is rational because what the actors sacrifice (the natural 'right' to use violence against others plus obedience to an absolute authority) is clearly inferior in value to what they gain (namely, the secure enjoyment of life and property). This collective exchange of *obedience* and the forbearance of the use of violence for *protection* is clearly and self-evidently rational so that the actors' capacity for rational action alone, without any further commitment to moral norms, will suffice to effect and sustain the contract – at least, that is, if we assume general compliance with *pacta sunt servanda*.

Solution (2) replaces macro-contractarianism with micro-contractarianism, known as market liberalism. Its proponents raise doubts concerning both the desirability and the durability of once and for all macro-social contracts. Instead, the market is seen as the meeting point of an owner of money (M) and an owner of commodities (C). M and C have reciprocal preferences: M prefers having the commodity over having the amount of money that is equivalent to the price of the commodity, and C has exactly the reverse preference. The exchange contract that occurs between them as a consequence results from each of the two actors' conscious intention to achieve his most preferred state. Economic theory teaches us how it happens that both sides of this market transaction give rise to further ones, thus generating an invisible hand type of unintended collective order. Collective and once for all times contract-making (solution 1) is thus unnecessary and replaced by individual and infinitely reiterated contract-making.

Solution (3) is based on a critique of the happy outcomes suggested by solution (2). The rational and intentional market interaction of individuals remains a mixed blessing – as long, that is, as it is not complemented and to an extent compromised by an authoritatively enforced and morally recognized institutional order which provides and protects 'status'. The rules providing such market-exempt status are not interest-driven, but will still serve the interests involved. This type of solution comes in many variants – Roman Catholic, social democratic, conservative and neocorporatist among them. Their shared claim is that market actors must first be located in the right places and endowed with the right kind of status rights and privilege before the market transaction can possibly lead to collectively beneficial and hence stable social order. Some 'sacred' ordering of status, based on tradition and the recognition of tradition or moral principles, must transcend the realm of what is interest-contingent and hence appropriately assigned to market transactions. It is this combination of 'order' and 'interest' that will eventually serve interests better than any arrangement driven by interest alone. To illustrate, it is argued by the theorists of the social democratic variant of this solution that granting the status right of a supply cartel to organized labor (in the form of unions with protected procedural rights in the process of collective wage determination) is not only mandated by *normative* considerations of social justice, but is equally justified on *consequentialist* grounds. For it is only a system with strong unions that will generate sufficient wage pressures to force employers and investors to pursue a dynamic strategy of efficiency-increasing innovation and competitiveness.

Such a hybrid combination of market forces (i.e. the free play of interests) and status order (i.e. the observance of durable status rights and regulatory norms) is seen to be preferable to a 'pure' market mechanism because of the desirable (if unintended) byproducts the latter is bound to generate. The basic intuition behind this solution is that if we restrain the operation of interest, interests will be served better. Within this approach, social order is conceptualized as a kind of *metabolism* between symbiotic elements rather than the intentional transaction between partners in *exchange*, the difference being that the mutually beneficial chain effects that operate within the former become visible only to the outside observer or in retrospect, whereas in the latter case of exchange the anticipated benefits are the sole motivation for action. Solution (3) in its many variants thus always advocates the preservation of a synthesis of the 'good' and the 'right', of institutions and interests, the sacred and the secular, status and contract, or principles and consequences, usually with an emphasis on each of the first elements within these conventional pairs of apparently opposite sociological concepts.

Solution (4) draws purposive-rational consequences from the discovery of the favorable latent function of some institutions. It restores the rational and intentional element of institution-building that we also find in solution (1). If we see in retrospect that adherence to 'sacred' institutions, status orderings and principles has not only not damaged the pursuit of individual and collective interests, but positively furthered it (at least in the long run), the rational consequence to draw from this insight is to 'design' institutions in ways that best serve given purposes and interests, thereby turning the hitherto 'latent' functions into 'manifest' ones. For instance, if we learn from comparative historical research that liberal democratic political institutions show significant correlations with high growth rates, or corporatist arrangements with a consistent location of the national Philips curve on the inward side, or certain forms of federalism with acceptable levels of public debt – it is certainly tempting to turn such analytical knowledge into so many blueprints for institutional engineering. In this perspective, much of the institutional setup of Western capitalist democracies is seen in the Central and East European countries as a model to be transplanted – not so much because its normative assumptions and guiding *principles* are shared, but because its economic *consequences* are so strongly desired. Similarly, the IMF often prescribes certain institutional reforms (leading again to Western-style liberal democracy) for Third World recipients of its loans because it is anticipated that the adoption of these reforms will generate the right institutional framework for healthy economic development.

These and other examples may help to illustrate the idea that there are not only 'games *under* rules', but also 'games *about* rules' which result in a designed, negotiated and intentionally chosen and adopted institutional order. Such institutional choices often take the form of transplanting arrangements that are believed to have been working successfully in one place (e.g. Sweden or Germany) to other places (such as the United States). There are, however, a number of conceivable faults with this mode of reasoning and its implications for institutional (or constitutional) choice.

First, simple quantitative correlations between certain institutional features and economic indicators may be misleading in that they causally attribute certain effects to one institutional pattern which in fact are the synergetic result of a whole network of institutions. As a consequence, it remains a matter of uncertainty and good luck whether or not an institutional arrangement will actually be able to perform the intended function. Second, the 'purposive' adoption of institutions for the sake of promoting some economic objective (rather than 'for their own sake') may well spoil their desired effect, as only the institutions as a formal set of rules and procedures, but not the cultural values, norms, shared meanings and moral underpinnings that generate compliance with those rules, are being transplanted. Third, the supportive beliefs and expectations may or may not be generated by the implantation of the rules themselves, but if they do, they are likely to emerge only after a time-consuming process in which people 'get used to' and begin to feel 'at home' in the new institutional framework. It remains always an open question whether the institutions can survive this period of transition (other than under the most fortunate of circumstances) during which the complementary attitudes, beliefs and practices must emerge and become accepted as 'normal'.[1] Alternatively, a sense of cynicism may emerge which would doom the whole operation to failure and which would also expose the efforts of its initiators as a case of consequentialist misunderstanding of the nature of institutions. Finally, if institutions consist mostly in procedural rules and extend status rights to the incumbents of certain positions, they seem to presume that the players of the game are already constituted, the only problem being that their interaction must now be regulated. In transferring 'successful' institutions to other places, we often see that it is by no means clear who qualifies as a player, and consequently that players (corporate actors, trade unions, political parties, professional associations, etc.) must first be constituted before they can play according to the newly designed rules. This logically prior problem of constituting players can, however, not be solved by copying institutional rules which presume this problem as one being solved already.

Four Positions in the Debate on Corporatist Arrangements

The role assigned to organized groups or associations in political
life (or, for that matter, of keeping certain issues and conflicts out of
political life) has always been at the center of designs for institutional
innovation, if sometimes (as in the Rousseauian tradition) in sharply
negative ways. This is so for two reasons. First, organized groups have
two great advantages over individual action. They pool individual
resources (such as membership dues) and thus accomplish enormous
scale effects. Second, they generate not only much improved means
of action, but affect the ends of action itself in desirable ways. This
happens as groups help to discover the 'true' preferences of individual
members – preferences that would easily be missed or distorted as
long as individuals have to rely on their own insights, experience and
communicative resources.

The second reason why intermediary associations have such a
central role in political theory and the practice of designing 'appropriate' institutions is a little more complicated. It has to do with the
fact that only a limited range of institutional mechanisms is available
if it comes to determine the best way of the intentional making of
collectively binding decisions.

In principle, there are three, and only three, modes of explicit collective decision-making: voting, commanding and bargaining. These
activities are performed, respectively, by the many, the individual
agent at the top and the few. One is the bottom-up aggregation of
individual preferences through voting and referendums, which is well
known to have many disadvantages. It relies on the primitive language
of yes/no or for/against communications; it tends to be future-blind
and beset by passions; and much of the outcome depends on the
questions being asked or candidates being proposed, which itself
cannot be done through voting or referendums. The Achilles' heel of
'polyarchic' decision-making is the problem of agenda-setting: the
people cannot answer the question, which question needs to be
answered? The second mode of collective decision-making is through
binding commands issued top-down by some supreme authority.
While this method involves some regard for the future (depending
on the length of the term of office and the statutory possibilities for
re-election), and while it also allows for qualitative variation (more/
less, this/that, sooner/later, etc.), there are also some major drawbacks,
the most significant of which are (1) doubts about the legitimacy of the
authority, and (2) the transaction costs of enforcement/implementation
of the orders given. Third, there is the 'lateral' method of bargaining

between collective actors. In terms of the rationality (by which I mean in the present context something like 'probability of retrospective approval' or 'non-regret') of collective decision-making, this method is superior to the other two methods in that (1) it is capable of filtering out passions, (2) its potential for qualitative variation, as well as flexibility in time and space, is greatest, as dimensions of demands and concessions can be discovered and utilized in the process of bargaining itself, and (3) as long-term considerations, even extending beyond a term of office, can easily emerge. This 'timespan capacity' of bargaining systems is one of their greatest functional advantages, as 'bargaining partners [share] a common institutional memory of past behavior and [their] relative stability lengthens the shadow of the future'. Another functional advantage of intergroup bargaining is commonly seen in the fact that such negotiations take place behind closed doors, a feature which minimizes the chances for mobilization and 'incompetent' interference of outsiders. Cohen and Rogers[2] quote approvingly authors who conclude 'that certain forms of group organization play a central role in resolving problems of successful governance, not in causing them'. They are consistently convinced of the virtues of the bargaining between properly designed groups (referred to as 'performance-enhancing group structures'), and of the cooperative gains resulting therefrom.

The great number of arguments concerning the political role of voluntary associations in general and of corporatist arrangements in particular that have been advanced in the 1970s and 1980s can conveniently be ordered along two axes. One axis measures the evaluation given by authors in the debate. This evaluation can be measured along the dimension of *favorable evaluation/explicit advocacy* of a strong role of functional representation through interest associations vs *critical assessment/explicit rejection* of such role as something dangerous or illegitimate. The other axis represents the kind of criteria that enter such evaluation. Here we find *normative* arguments (explicating the principles of a well-ordered democratic polity and the standards of its legitimacy) vs *functional* ones, which point to observable consequences of certain arrangements for the solution of public policy problems. To simplify the latter dimension, we can also say the 'normative' approach assumes the point of view of the *citizen* (and his or her supposed interest of being part of a legitimate and well-ordered democratic *polity*), whereas the 'functional' approach is much closer to the narrower concerns of *policy*-making elites confronted to given problems of steering, intervention, control, regulation and institutional reform.

Let us now look at the type of arguments that have emerged in the debate and locate them in the matrix defined by these two dimensions. Most participants in these debates would probably agree that the majority of arguments and insights derived from the extensive research on business and other associations conducted in the 1980s fall into the favorable/functional quadrant, which hence is the most densely populated of the four. Among these arguments, three stand out as particularly widely shared:

1. Contracting out policy-making functions to voluntary encompassing associations taps their expertise and unburdens governments from parts of their decision load and responsibilities, thereby enhancing the efficiency and effectiveness of governance.

2. Involving target groups of regulation in the formulation and implementation of regulatory standards and granting them a role in decision-making will facilitate enforcement of the policy.

3. Strengthening representative monopolies will provide them with authority over their constituency and put them in a position that allows them to play an active role in the shaping of preferences among the rank-and-file membership.

Next numerous are arguments that clearly belong in the opposite box, namely the negative/normative quadrant in which 'mischiefs of faction' or 'exploitative coalitions' types of argument are being revived. This set of objections to a strong role of interest associations in the making of public policies claims that corporatist arrangements will violate principles of popular sovereignty and/or market freedom which must be defended even though this may involve forgoing some functional advantages of corporatism. These objections come from two sides.

First, there is the objection from the democratic Left. Corporatism, it claims, even 'liberal' corporatism, interferes with fair and egalitarian methods of territorial representation through elections, parties, parliaments, legislation and the division of powers, ultimately also popular sovereignty. It assigns privileged, perhaps even monopolistic, representational and decision-making roles to certain collective actors representing key economic groups and discriminates against others. It invokes the *bourgeois*, as defined by his position in the societal division of labor, rather than the *citoyen* as the idealized locus of autonomous deliberation and judgment about public affairs. Cohen and Rogers summarize these concerns by saying that 'the system of organized interests will tend both to be highly particularistic, and to reflect inequalities in conditions favoring collective action across different populations and areas of concern' (pp. 23–4). Furthermore, the authors emphasize the important insight that the set of groups participating in inter-associational bargaining is almost by definition 'incomplete' and hence very likely to impose negative externalities on excluded third parties: 'A system of peak bargaining among encompassing groups plausibly requires the exclusion of some interests. For it is precisely the limits on the number of "social partners" that permits such groups to function effectively' (p. 94; cf. also the quotation from Schmitter on p. 105).

Second, there are objections from the market-liberal Right. From this political point of view, stable associational regimes are thought to interfere with the free market and competition and to lead to cartelization and the formation of exploitative coalitions. Proponents of this set of arguments cite the dangers of the 'autonomy' of collective bargaining, of rent-seeking, of captured agencies, as summarized on pp. 39ff. Even if it is granted that collectivist arrangements based on strong associations will produce the morally attractive benefit of comparatively greater distributive equity and 'decommodification' (pp. 94–5), it is still predicted that such arrangements will soon tend to strain the capacity for class solidarity by making the 'better-off' segments of both major classes aware of the opportunity costs they contribute to the arrangement – an awareness that will soon lead them, as decentralizing tendencies in the Swedish union federation LO in the 1980s serve to illustrate, to 'opt out' of solidaristic wage and labor market policies.

Both these normative objections to the distortions that group power can imply for both the democratic political process and the operation of market mechanisms must be weighed, however, against the plain fact that in 'post-liberal' or 'post-individualist' societies the joining of citizens into groups and associations is a sine qua non of popular sovereignty. People have 'voice' only to the extent that they merge their political resources into associative action, thereby overcoming a communicative condition of the mere 'noise' of unorganized interests, initiatives and opinions. Groups facilitate coordination among individuals with shared interests and thereby 'make a substantial contribution to the welfare of citizens' (p. 29). For this reason, and 'given the existence of associative liberties, groups will form to influence policy, and once formed, they will affect policy. They cannot be legislated out of existence' (p. 27). They may even have desirable retroactive effects on their constituent members, as they socialize them, draw them into deliberative processes and thus 'function as informal school of democracy and citizenship' (p. 29). Furthermore, the absence of organized groups would deprive governments and legislatures of indispensable sources of information.

The design problem of the political theorist is thus one of optimizing, that is to say, the problem of inventing an institutional framework that is capable of checking the democratically undesirable consequences of associative action, while preserving the features that contribute to the democratic quality of citizenship and governance.

Third, we have a sparsely populated category of negative functional arguments. Sometimes the Austrian example is used to demonstrate how extreme forms of 'social partnership' can lead to immobilism and stalemate, as well as to an inability to cope with problems of the international political economy.

Another set of arguments that seems to belong in the functional/ negative cell raises doubts about the transnational transferability of institutional arrangements. One could argue, for instance, that models of the political economy and the institutional rules governing whatever the functional superiority of such models may be *cannot* be designed in the spirit of a purposive-rational, problem-solving approach. For they 'evolve' out of centuries-old national traditions and the elite values inculcated by them. It is the very essence of 'institutions' (as opposed to 'organizations') that they are not amenable to rational change and design as they rely on ideas and a specific 'spirit' that transcends rational calculation. Similarly, non-corporatist elements of the institutional structure of the political economy, e.g. individualism and market liberalism, have sunk their roots so deeply into the everyday habits, practices, expectations and modes of thinking of investors, consumers, bureaucrats, banks, employees and commercial organizations that it is at best under conditions of extreme crisis that such inherited patterns will become replaceable by alternative modes of interaction. In the absence of such crisis, normal practices will assert themselves and will resist major institutional innovations.

Underlying these objections is the notion that institutional arrangements are ultimately based on cultural dispositions and national traditions that transcend the scope of what can be easily engineered or manipulated. After all, the politics of designing and implementing new institutions must take place in the context and under the shadow of the very institutional patterns that are to be replaced, and the expectations, habits and power relations generated by the old system of rules will combine to obstruct all but the most marginal alterations of the status quo. Thus the whole process resembles a bootstrapping act and is bound to frustrate the ambitions of rationalist-constructivist political theorists. At any rate, it might be only under conditions of extreme crisis[3] that a negotiated or otherwise agreed change of institutional rules can ever occur, and the path-dependent self-reproduction of an existing institutional regime can be interrupted.

While Cohen and Rogers, rightly in my view, emphasize the 'artifactuality' of associative action (p. 30), they also tend to equate this property with 'contingency', i.e. the property of institutional arrangements of being relatively easily tractable, elastic and alterable. It is not only students of, say, British industrial relations, or British union reform, or of the attempted abolition of large-scale state subsidies to German industry who will tend to take less sanguine views on this issue.[4]

Finally, we have the almost empty cell of arguments that are both favorable *and* based on normative considerations. Along with the work of the Austrian socialist Otto Bauer on 'functional democracy', written in the interwar period, the essay by Cohen and Rogers, together with a few recent contributions by Schmitter, Mansbridge and others, plays a pioneering role in this field. Their essay is dedicated to the effort to explore 'forms of group representation that stand less sharply in tension with the norms of democratic governance'. They believe that 'the artful design of secondary associations can strengthen democratic order' (p. 5) and that 'qualitative variation' (p. 36) and 'deliberate artifaction' (p. 37) can pave the way toward democratically more appropriate associative action.

A Digression on Institutional Designs

Let me consider for a moment, by way of a digression, what we can possibly mean by the activity of 'artfully designing' institutions. The act in question involves an actor who commands sufficient power or control to alter the given institutional setting and a standard of rationality or evaluation according to which a different set of institutional rules, viz. the one proposed, can be shown to be 'superior' to the ones that are currently in existence. In a nutshell, this means a situation in which *institutions* can be treated as if they were *organizations*, namely authoritatively imposed and relatively easily changed rules that are justified in an instrumental perspective as being the best available means to achieve a 'trans-institutional' set of objectives. For example, if you want to economize on interest payment and still ensure a continuous flow of deliveries, and if you also have sufficient power over the suppliers of parts, you can achieve an improvement of organizational rules by installing a JIT regime. Under these conditions, there is no relevant and sufficiently powerful motive to stick to the old rules if evidently 'better' ones are available.

But in most cases, institutions *cannot* be treated like organization. This is so because institutions do not serve an external purpose (against which they can be compared to other institutions), but they 'internalize' the purposes and values to which they contribute. That is to say, they select means and ends simultaneously, and they thus come to define and prescribe practices that are 'valuable in themselves'. Even if they can be shown to be grossly deficient in some conceivable instrumental respect, there are other aspects that still make them intrinsically valuable and are seen to compensate for those deficiencies by those who recognize the institution as valid. Moreover, institutions always have a dual function, instrumental and expressive: they select and prescribe certain ways of doing things, and they educate and socialize citizens into the value code they themselves incarnate. They generate a 'spirit' which in turn contributes to their continued operation.

After having reminded ourselves of these fairly conventional sociological preliminaries, we can now explore the problem of 'artful design'. To be sure, institutions are not 'natural', but artificial; but does that mean they are alterable at any point in time? And to the extent they are, are they tractable by rational design? The third of the four approaches to the problem of order I have distinguished before considers institutions contingent, but *not* 'designable'. If institutions change, this occurs in slow, evolutionary or quasi-biological ways which are immune from intentional manipulation – or so proponents of the third approach would argue. Somehow, and under unanticipated circumstances, certain institutions do not make sense any longer to those involved in them, or they break down under the burden of costs and inefficiencies that places them into a position of relative competitive disadvantage[5] vis-à-vis other institutions, or under the burden of revolutionary or military violence.

From these evolutionary models, the special and rather exceptional case must be distinguished in which 'new designs' are in fact conceivable and 'political choice' (p. 58) concerning institutional patterns can seriously be considered – the case, that is, which Cohen and Rogers seem to presume as the normal one. Let me claim here, without much further argument, that the features that set this case apart from both the 'path-dependent' and the 'evolutionary' case of institutional change are either (1) a built-in tension between the principles and structures of institutions, or (b) the coexistence of multiple, but potentially inconsistent principles within one institution.

1. Tensions between principles and structures: The values and principles built into an institutional structure are so highly abstract and reflexive that from the point of view of the actors, the institution in question is not the *only* structure that can implement these abstract principles, but the way toward improvements is itself kept open, and the rebuilding of institutional structures permitted, by the underlying principles. Operational rules and underlying principles are loosely coupled, and in order for the institution to remain consistent with the latter, the former must be continuously adjusted. As a consequence, the following apparent paradox can emerge: the institutionalized principles may *mandate* an alteration of (parts of) the institutional structure in which they are supposedly incarnated. To put the same notion differently, the institution that embodies the principles exposes itself to criticisms that are based on these principles and activates, through ongoing self-monitoring, the scrutiny of its own insufficiencies. In this case, the institutional rules that make up the social order allow themselves to be treated as intentionally contingent *organizational* rules, if only the design activity that leads to reform is guided by the principles established and sanctioned by the original institutional structure. 'Immanent self-transcendence' would be another way to capture the paradoxical quality of this kind of arrangement. It is to be found in institutions that contain a program of optional self-amelioration. Examples may be found in certain radical conceptions of democracy, but certainly not in others. Some constitutions regulate the process of constitutional change and at the same time specify the principles that are to remain immune from change, but rather guide it. The same applies in scientific institutions in which the pursuit of the core value of 'true knowledge' may enforce the reform of the institutional structure through which it is pursued. One might find other examples of this unlikely condition in some religious institutions.

Cohen and Rogers recognize this problem when they emphasize that a move toward 'associative democracy' cannot be driven by considerations of functional superiority alone but that 'active popular support is needed, and that it is unlikely to be forthcoming unless an associative democracy connects with deeper aspirations to democratic order' (p. 90). They fail, however, to point out which kind of reformist agents and political promoters of such popular support they have in mind, nor what the widely endorsed 'deeper aspirations' are that they consider a necessary catalyst in the process of institutional change. May we conclude from this symptomatic omission that 'associative democracy' is an arrangement of the greatest functional, but at the same time very limited normative appeal,[6] which for this very reason is quite unlikely to be adopted in contexts in which it does not already find favorable conditions due to historical antecedents? To say the least, the authors' 'background assumption that . . . some measure of refashioning of conditions of association is possible' (p. 99) bears some elaboration.

2. Conflict within an institution about the structure of the institution and the potential for intentional change may also emerge in institutions that base themselves on more than one basic value or principle. It might then become possible to utilize such latent inconsistencies and ambiguities for the purpose of intentional institutional innovation that alters the mix of already existing ingredients. The examples I think of are dual sovereignties in federal systems, the conflict between liberal and democratic principles in Western democracies, or the co-incidence of 'social' rights of workers and 'economic' rights of owners and managers which together shape the legal framework of labor and industrial relations.

The Dual 'Non-naturalness' of Interest Groups

The design problem as conceptualized by Cohen and Rogers focuses on just one of two problems of the role of groups in democratic governance. Central to the discussion of the authors is the question of how groups might be 'appropriately designed and related to one another and to the state' (p. 61). This focus assumes, in the tradition of liberal political theory and its problem of 'faction', that the *substance* of groups is already there, and that the problem is now to find an appropriate *form* for them, i.e. a model according to which they must be constituted and a procedural role they are to play in the political process. Logically prior to this latter question, on which the authors spend most of their imaginative and constructive discussion, however, is the question, what makes for the existence of groups, their substance, in the first place? Why should it be the case that individuals with their preferences and interests decide 'naturally' to join and to engage in associative action in order to defend and promote their common interests?

The conventional answer to this question is well known. The original endowment of individuals and the societal division of labor together determine a class structure which places individuals into types of positions from which their central interests will follow 'naturally'. Furthermore, as the advantages to be obtained through associative action are self-evident to individuals, as such action provides the opportunity to limit internal rivalry and to pool resources, they will equally 'naturally' tend to form some sort of organized groups (provided they can somehow overcome the collective action problems through the autonomous or external generation of either positive or negative selective incentives). As a consequence, we get those well-known organized blocks of interests as the owners of land and industrial capital, employers, unions, the self-employed, professions, civil servants, all subdivided by sector and region, all of which in turn form the raw material for constitutional or institutional designs of 'associative democracy'. Manifest groups, together with 'potential' or 'quasi-groups', are thus the natural substance of politics, or so the conventional wisdom of pluralist political theories tells us.

A number of doubts and objections can be raised against this conventional view and its validity for contemporary democratic capitalist societies.

First, the ease with which groups will crystallize and play a role in the process of governance depends not only on social structures, but also on the 'interventionist' vs. 'liberal' nature of the state. Briefly, if there is lots to win from the state through associative activity, there will be a correspondingly stronger incentive to undertake the efforts of group formation and pressure politics. The same holds true if the state provides resources supporting associational action or assigns functions to them (such as the binding definition of technical and safety standards). Inversely, governments that follow extreme market-liberal doctrines (such as Thatcherism) will not only be unresponsive to groups, but beyond that will actively try to disorganize intermediate groups. A number of groups exist which are constituted by the fact alone that they are the target population of some state policy, rather than some autonomously formed entity growing out of the division of labor or some cultural or social formation within civil society. The recipients of welfare transfers or university students are examples of such groups of 'policy-takers'.

Second, 'production cleavages' play a receding role. It is hard to determine whether this is true in an 'objective' sense. But it suffices to note here that it seems to be true on the reflexive level, given the prevalence of consumption cleavages and other lines of differentiation and stratification that cross-cut the cleavages that result from the class structure and the societal division of labor. The paradigm of consumption cleavages is illustrated by the intuition that there may be (however 'subjectively') more in common between two owners of a yacht, one of whom is a blue-collar worker, than between two blue-collar workers one of whom owns a yacht. More relevant is, of course, the cross-cutting cleavage of owner-occupancy vs. renting. A further reason that contributes to the relative obsolescence of production-related cleavages may be seen in the fact that the ideological and cultural distinctiveness of socioeconomic 'blocks' has largely evaporated under the impact of democratic mass politics and mass communication.

Third, socioeconomic categories are not easily coded as the bearers of homogeneous interest. Internal differentiation within these categories of individuals – by regional location, industrial sector, organizational status, skill-level, gender, age, ethnicity, household type, family status, mix of sources of household income, social security status, consumption status, cultural and political background, etc. – increases the difficulty to define the common denominator of a shared interest, and it also undermines the intensity with which this supposedly common interest is pursued. This applies to both labor and capital. The direct consequence of this differentiation and individualization, if not 'atomization', is a shrinking scope of interest generalization and increasing organizational costs to recruit and mobilize members. It is this feature of 'modern' societies and the vanishing of 'natural' blocks of interest that makes the basic idea of Schmitter's 'secondary political market' particularly attractive – an idea which renders the political weight of groups and the political resources at its disposal contingent not on a group's members, but on resources allocated to it through a voting process in which the citizenry as a whole is entitled to participate.

Fourth, interests and preferences that perhaps used to be best promoted through associative action can today often be satisfied through commercial alternatives, such as in the paradigm case of the athletics club being replaced by a commercial fitness center. Other alternatives include services provided for by the state administration or through privately purchased insurance packages, services of lawyers or consulting firms.

Fifth, sociopolitical movements, whether nationalist, populist or 'new', which receive only very scant attention by Cohen and Rogers, appear to offer an alternative mode of collective action and of aggregation of individual preferences that surpasses more conventional forms of collective action in terms of its dynamism and attractiveness. The issues on which such movements focus are typically such that they do not put one interest against some distinctive opposite interest (which then must in some way be respected as a partner in negotiation), but some claimed value or principle against some inferior holders of power. Also, communities sharing certain lifestyles, consumption preferences and habits are forming everywhere which

also differ from group politics in that they show a lesser degree of
formal organization and capability for strategic action. In the spirit of
political postmodernism, they tend to be – and express themselves as
being – 'different from' other communities and subcultures, without
being related to them through any kind of adversary or bargaining
relations. The core motive of associative action is 'identity', not
interest. Even if an 'opponent' is named and focused on (as 'patriarchy'
is in feminism), it is often not the case that this opponent is organized
(no National Association of Patriarchs exists), nor is it clear what
negotiations (should they ever start) would be 'about' (as it is clear in
the case of industrial conflict that union-management bargaining is
about wages, working conditions and perhaps union rights). Many
bearers of political preferences and interests have fuzzy social boundaries, amorphous opponents and uncertain substantive domains.

Sixth, it is the standard practice of large and well-organized interest
groups to present their own interests and preferences not as such, but
as the outcome of the prudent and impartial consideration of the
common good. Groups act as if they were not partial groups, but
detached experts. For example, farm associations will demand price
subsidies in order to maintain national autarchy in food supplies, and
teachers' unions strive for making possible the best possible education
for our children. This practice may be driven by tactical considerations
and attempts to disguise the interest-related component of the group's
demands. But chances are that this is not the case. If so, can we
still speak of 'group politics'? How and where do we draw the line
between 'groups' and the responsible agents and authentic advocates
of the public good? Strong power positions may make the difference
unrecognizable, as in the case where a single big employer so dominates the local or regional economy that if that company is allowed to
suffer, everyone else suffers even more severely. In these circumstances,
if the company's board claims to stand for the common good, it is not
easy to disagree. In such cases – which are by no means uncommon in
advanced capitalist economies – the very notion of group politics
seems to break down. For 'group politics' always connotes that where
there is a group, there must be an opposite and eventually 'counter-
vailing' group, or at least potential group, which is not the case under
such circumstances.

Finally, the question must be asked what the normative presump-
tions are that we employ if we speak of certain collective actors
as 'groups' or 'factions'. The clear assumption in all three of the
paradigms of political theory that the authors discuss – namely, liberal
constitutionalism, civic republicanism and egalitarian pluralism – is

that 'beyond' groups, there are – or ought to be – collective agents that are less afflicted with the ills of particularism and the narrow and selfish pursuit of interests. If, on the other hand, *all* kinds of collective actors were conceived of as groups, the concept would lose all of its critical implications. Thus the questions emerge: What is the anti-thetical notion to group politics, what is its institutional location and what evidence can we produce to the effect that legislative assem-blies, the executive branch of government, the public administration apparatus or the judiciary do in fact differ from 'groups', in that they are more deliberative, farsighted, unbiased, neutral and fair than any 'group'?

Hence the problem is not to design an appropriate form for already *existing* groups, regulate their interaction and curb their power and influence wherever it is deemed inappropriate, but to go one step beyond and design the structural conditions for the *formation* of groups – as opposed to individual action and to other forms of interest aggregation. How much group activity is possible and desirable from the point of view of democratic political theory and in the context of structural transformations that are going on in society? What forms of collective action should be encouraged, and their formation facilitated? What can and should the state do in order to make the instrumental uses of collective action, as well as its deliberative and preference-forming byproducts, more widely available to citizens? By answering questions such as these through legislation, the state would not only regulate the interaction among groups, but would 'create incentives to group formation and operation along certain lines' (p. 64).

Underlying this proposal, there is a complicated and certainly controversial logic which can be reconstructed in three steps. First, governance should be contingent on the empirical will of the people. Second, the task of governance is to design and implement institutions which will have a formative impact on the empirical will of the people. Third, this task is mandated, and its implementation legiti-mized, by the (hypothetical) will of the people to have not its *empirical* will of the many isolated individuals determine governance, but a refined, deliberated and 'laundered' set of preferences which are brought about through appropriate institutional arrangements. For this chain of arguments to become valid and plausible, two further assumptions must be introduced. First, the people do empirically dis-trust their own empirical will, being aware of its weakness, fallibility and susceptibility to passions, idiosyncratic interests, shortsightedness and other distortions, which might easily lead to an 'unwilled will' and subsequent regret. Second, the institutional arrangements that are being introduced and, as it were, self-imposed through the government are not perceived to manipulate, but to the contrary to enlighten and to make more reasonable, the will of the people.

In the absence of the first of these conditions, the second cannot be fulfilled. If people hold fast to the belief that their empirical will is to be trusted without any reservation, then they will resist any institutional change that is designed to influence the process of will formation, even if this is done in the indirect way of granting representation rights and other roles in the making of public policy to organized groups. But even if the people realize the fallibility of their empirical preferences, the arrangements that are being introduced in order to assist them in 'probing' their preferences (Lindblom) may still be experienced as rather doing violence to or distorting their interests. For instance, group practices in politics may be perceived not as enlightening and representation-enhancing, but as oligarchic and paternalistic. In order to avoid both these negative outcomes, the proposed arrangements would have to be of a strictly procedural and interest-neutral nature.

This discussion of the nature of groups – and the doubts concerning the 'naturalness' of their presence in political life – leads me to distinguish between two design problems. One concerns the instrumental aspect, or the best mode of operation of groups that are already in existence. The solution to this problem provides an answer to the question: How should groups be allowed and prescribed to operate in the process of democratic governance if we want them to bring their coordination capacities, as well as their problem-solving and rule-enforcement potential, to bear upon the making of public policy, but if we also want them not to interfere with the 'republican' premises of the rule of law, of political equality, popular sovereignty and territorial representation?

The other design problem concerns the micro-effects that collective action has upon the formation of cognitions and preferences of the members of an organization, and the provision of the political resource of 'voice' to them. Here the question is to be answered: How must groups be internally constituted in order to make and empower 'good citizens' by encouraging and spreading a 'deliberative' mode of approaching collective problems? In one of the most interesting, but perhaps also least compelling, sections of their paper, Cohen and Rogers claim that encompassing associations might contribute to 'civic consciousness' by promoting among their members an 'awareness of interdependence' and by 'creating something approximating a "public sphere"' (pp. 96–7). At least, it is an open question to what extent contemporary associations live up to the Tocquevillean notion of the cultivation of civic spirit through associative action. On this point, the overwhelming majority of political theorists (such as Bobbio) write in a deeply pessimistic tone.

Notes

1. As an East European observer has half-seriously hypothesized, the institutional system of the 'social market economy' must have been in place for least ten years before people get used to it and before it *therefore* can begin to unfold its beneficial effects. The question, however, is what helps it survive this critical period of adjustment and accommodation? To the extent the institutions in question are not adopted for the intrinsic *values and principles embodied in them*, but just for the *outcomes expected from them*, they enjoy much less of a counterfactual validity and will hence more easily fall victim to some empirical evidence of failure. This in turn will tend to shorten the lifespan credited to them, and it may even lead to their abolition at a point before their desired side-effects have had a chance to unfold. Institutions adopted for instrumental reasons are disappointment-sensitive.

2. References to Cohen and Rogers refer to the manuscript version of their 'Secondary Associations and Democratic Governance', *Politics and Society* 20 (1992), no. 4, pp. 394–471, reproduced in this volume pp. 7–98.

3. Even that may not be true. The current East Central European efforts at constitution-making and institution-building seem to provide ample evidence that, after the total breakdown of the old regime, too *few* uncontested routines, identities and widely shared values are in place which could serve as a reference point for renovating the institutional structure.

4. This line of reasoning is also useful, in my view, to expose the illusory and utopian nature of neoliberal proposals to abolish the pathological outcomes of a 'bargaining democracy' within the framework of a 'bargaining democracy' itself.

5. It is worth noting, however, that institutional patterns that are characteristic of certain countries, such as contribution vs. tax-financed social security schemes, 'make' vs. 'buy' patterns of industrial organizations, banks vs. brokerage firms as the major channels of the mediation of capital of share holders, or federalism vs. centralism, often do exist side by side within the international political economy without one of them (presumably the one less conducive to 'efficiency') succumbing to the competitive pressure generated by the other. In these cases at least, stubborn path-dependency seems to be stronger than quasi-biological mechanisms of selection.

6. As I have argued elsewhere about corporatism, it is a practice without a political theory.

4

A Deliberative Perspective on Neocorporatism

Jane Mansbridge

The political Left in the United States is suspicious of corporatist thought because of the strong historical links between corporatism and fascism. To moderate this view, I shall argue that bringing some private negotiations among interest groups under some form of state umbrella has two beneficial results. It can make power more equal between participants in the negotiation, and it can interject into the negotiation greater consideration of the public interest.

Politics consists of persuasion as well as power. Empirically, interest groups deliberate as well as apply pressure. They deliberate externally with elites from other interest groups in an effort to create common interests and define areas of conflict, and they deliberate internally in an effort to create common interests and define conflicts among their members. Their internal deliberations are both vertical – between elites and ordinary members – and horizontal – among members within different levels of information and authority. Normatively, any political deliberation ought to draw its participants closer to understanding their interests, regardless of whether those interests conflict or coincide. The quality of deliberation, external and internal, should be one of the major criteria on which to judge a system of interest representation.

Interest groups can also act as self-serving collectors of 'rent'. In the absence of governmental institutions designed to curb 'rent-seeking' they will often use power to seek benefits for themselves at the expense of others rather than contributing to the common good by enhancing productivity or justice. Attempts to improve systems of interest representation should therefore follow the advice: 'maximize the deliberative benefits; minimize the rent-seeking costs.'

Normative Considerations

Power[1] and persuasion[2] both play, empirically, an important role in

133

politics. Normatively, both also play an important role in democracy, as legitimate coercion and legitimate changes in preferences among political actors are the most effective means of solving collective action problems.[3] Democratic politics, including the politics of interest groups, must find ways through which the exercise of both power and persuasion can meet democratic norms.

What makes power and changed preferences legitimate? In brief, most democrats usually consider it legitimate, so long as individual rights are protected, to allow some people to coerce others (to threaten them with sanctions or use force against their interests) when the power that produces this coercion is divided equally . . . one person, one vote. We usually consider it legitimate to change preferences through persuasion when the new preferences are in the actor's interests (e.g. suggesting more effective means to a given end). Although it is never possible to achieve absolutely equal power on any decision and although what is in anyone's interests is always contestable, democratic institutions are usually designed to try to make power more equal than it otherwise would be and persuasion more likely to serve the interests of those persuaded.[4]

In the United States today, interest groups are designed in large part to make the votes of some count more heavily than those of others whenever possible. The resulting deviations from the ideal of one person, one vote are usually justified on three grounds: respecting freedom of association, registering intensity of preference and providing information for deliberation.

The first argument is the most powerful. The First Amendment to the Constitution guarantees freedom of assembly in a way that might seem to legitimate any resulting inequality of power. Yet an argument for pure *laissez-faire* works no better in the modern polity than in the modern economy. In the economy, monopolies and oligopolies are sometimes necessary, but their immense power must be regulated to limit intolerable distortions of the market. In today's polity, the most powerful organized interests look no more like the textbooks' citizen-initiated concerns than General Motors looks like a ma and pa store. The oligopolistic power of the biggest interests in the 'pressure group' system needs some regulation to prevent too great a distortion of the wishes of the citizens.

The second argument is that in a utilitarian calculus intensely felt preferences deserve greater weight than weakly held ones. This argument is debatable even within the utilitarian framework (in one view, everybody should 'count for one, nobody for more than one', regardless of intensity). But even if we accept the intensity argument, the relatively small deviations from equality that would recognize legitimate differences in individual intensity could never account for the large inequalities in political power that interest groups presently produce in US politics.[5]

The third argument justifies inequality through the increased information that unequally powerful groups provide. It fails as a justification, however, if groups more equal in power could provide as good or better information. Although one could argue that concentrating resources in a few hands enables more thorough investigations, spreading resources more equally produces more diverse information. At least in experimental small groups facing questions with a correct answer, procedures that empower the minority increase the chances that a group will discover the right answer. In addition, making power more equal among participants can, especially in dyadic confrontations, result in a balance of powers that reduces the effect of sanction and force in the deliberative process, giving arguments 'on the merits' greater weight. This aim of balance between forces may help explain why many deliberative groups are constituted with equal representation from the opposing sides (e.g. management and labor), even when this equality between sides fails to reflect proportionally the number of individuals each side represents.

Neocorporatism as a Means to More Equal Power

As Joshua Cohen and Joel Rogers point out, a *laissez-faire* market in interest representation gives different interests very unequal power in the negotiations that take place both in and out of the formal governmental arena. In the United States, huge disparities in political contributions affect the relative power of the rich and poor. Moreover, groups whose interests are intense and concentrated, like the potential beneficiaries of tariff protection, have far greater power than groups whose interests are dispersed, like consumers. Because the members of groups with concentrated interests get a greater individual payoff from organization, they are more likely to pay the costs of organizing in time, effort and money. Large groups, and groups whose members' needs are not easily quantifiable and negotiable, are much harder to organize.

Neocorporatism advances democracy when it requires the contest for power among interest groups to take place in conditions that redress to some extent the imbalances of the *laissez-faire* war of all against all. 'Neocorporatism' has three attributes. Like traditional corporatism, it values interest groups as ongoing institutional mechanisms for representing interests not easily represented in the territorial representative process. Again like traditional corporatism, it attempts to bring the *laissez-faire* system of interest representation partly under public control. Unlike traditional corporatism, however, it looks beyond traditional economic and sectoral interests for the interests that should be represented. As a system of interest representation becomes more directly involved with state law-making and law-enforcing processes, it more fully deserves the name of 'corporatist', and to the degree that it recognizes non-traditional interests, it more fully deserves the prefix 'neo'. Cohen and Rogers make a strong case for borrowing elements from European neocorporatism in order to make the power exercised by different interests in US politics more equal.

In the United States, administrative agencies in the executive branch have for a long time informally consulted groups whose interests they affect. As a result, interest groups often 'capture' the agencies that affect them. As these unofficial relations have become more formal, the agencies have been required, by their own codes and by the courts, to admit new and conflicting interests into the deliberative process. The new public requirements that come along with formal democratic recognition often specifically bring traditionally less well-represented groups into the process of consultation and take some account of the difficulties of organizing small, diffuse interests.

These developments, often incremental and judge-made, have gradually transformed administrative law in the United States. The new legal model, dubbed by some the 'model of interest representation', considers not only material but ideological interests. It requires 'participation rights' and 'adequate consideration' for the interested parties through the formal participation of interest groups in decisions by agencies in the executive branch.[6]

Such neocorporatist developments, which try to involve representatives of all affected groups in governmental decisions, do not, as some critics claim, assume 'that there is no ascertainable, transcendent "public interest", but only the distinct interests of various individuals and groups in the society.'[7] Any particular negotiation among competing interests may or may not involve the public interest. Often, however, negotiations among private interests will involve features that affect the nation as a whole or the public at large. To privilege the public interest in such negotiations usually requires devising forms of organization that moderate the exercise of raw power. It does not require eliminating or delegitimating all non-legislative forms of interest representation. In the US legislative arena, recent suggestions for restricting or eliminating political action committees, limiting political advertising and providing public funding for electoral campaigns all assume that the state must involve itself in some way in associative arrangements in order to reduce some of the inequalities that otherwise dominate the political market. Similar suggestions are reasonable for interest representation in the executive branch as well.

European corporatism, however, is still tied heavily to an era when only two great interests, capital and labor, dominated the interest agenda. To expand the numbers and kinds of interests represented in the system, today's neocorporatists need new institutions and theories. Philippe Schmitter proposes the strategy of establishing a semi-public status for interest associations, financing these associations through compulsory citizen contributions (e.g. taxes), and distributing these funds by means of citizen vouchers ('voted' for, perhaps, through check-offs and write-ins on the annual income tax form). The semi-public status of these interest associations would derive from their agreeing to a charter guaranteeing democratic rights for their members, the expectation that public policy affecting the interests of their members would be made in part with and through the association, and the funding of the association in part through Schmitter's system of obligatory contributions from citizens, allocated through vouchers that allowed those citizens to distribute their allotments in any proportion to as many or as few associations as desired. The voucher system is designed to be flexible, open to new interests and responsive to the variety of citizen preferences.[8]

Although no politically imaginable reform could eliminate the great and unequal power of business interests in any capitalist polity, neocorporatist institutions begin to suggest partial solutions to the existing problem of unequal representation of interests. A neo-corporatism appropriate to the United States would not duplicate that in Europe but would have to be tentative, experimental and incremental, and to blend associational intervention in the existing *laissez-faire* system of interest representation with pluralist concerns for openness, public accountability and the variety of potential interests.

Neocorporatism as a Means to Better Persuasion

Much of US political science has been written from within a primarily adversary political culture. Interest groups, consequently, have generally been conceived primarily as vehicles for pursuing greater power in a zero-sum conflict. This conception captures the primary

goal of many actual interest groups, which are deliberately organized
to act as rent-seekers, using the unequal power they derive from their
organization and funding to wrest from the public treasury – or,
through the state's police power, from private citizens – benefits or
'rent' for their officers, staff and members.[9] The rent-seeking account
of interest group activity is a transfer model, in which whatever I get
must be taken from you, rather than a productivity model, in which
you and I jointly produce extra gains through innovation or other
means. Yet the deliberation in which interest groups engage often
produces information, generates innovation and changes preferences,
creating gains that did not exist before the process began.

Negotiations among representatives of interests not easily
represented on a territorial basis can result in hard but fair decisions
which both sides honor. Unions and management provide one major
example, but so also do many smaller negotiations, such as those
between publishers and universities which resulted in the photocopy-
ing provisions of the 1978 copyright law.[10] Bringing such negotiations
under government auspices increases the chances that diffuse interests,
such as consumer interests, will be represented and that the decision
itself will reflect a larger public interest.

In 1984, Richard Freeman and James Medoff gave to their much
cited book on the efficiencies of unions the title *What Unions Do*.
Asking whether unions serve productive functions or act as pure
rent-seekers, they concluded that unions served the important function
of finding out what workers wanted. American unions, hardly
models of a developed deliberative ideal, still provide a forum in which
collective 'voice' can instruct employers on workers' needs more
efficiently than can worker 'exit', a traditional market mechanism.
Exit, or quitting the job, is usually more costly for both worker and
employer than collective voice. Moreover, voice can often produce
more complete information and more creative solutions than can
autonomous management decision-making. When their quantitative
research revealed that in the United States 'unions are associated with
greater efficiency in most settings',[11] Freeman and Medoff attributed
that result primarily to what I would call 'deliberative efficiencies'.
Interest groups perform deliberative functions similar to those
of unions. Yet social scientists have rarely studied those functions or
provided a theory for integrating the deliberation that takes place
among and within interest groups into a larger understanding of the
political system.

The standard textbook answer to the question 'What productive
activity do interest groups perform?' has been that they provide

information to legislators. This model does not require preference change among the interest group members. Nor do the groups involved have to be 'public interest' groups. As in the economic market, pure self-interest provides sufficient incentive for each interest to invest in collecting and disseminating information that best makes its case. Yet the model does require some public-spirited motivation among at least some of the policy-makers and public. Some group must act as the 'jury', using the information and arguments that interest groups provide to weigh the costs and benefits of a policy to the public as a whole. The model builds on the empirical fact that, at least on some issues, both citizens and their representatives can be influenced by arguments in the public interest.[12]

This simple adversary model cannot explain the actual functions of interest groups at the level of either the elites or the rank and file. At the elite level, political scientists have recently begun to look more carefully at processes of preference change, including the ways the mix of motivations among elites can begin to incorporate the public interest. In international relations, political scientists have noticed the effects on public policy of 'epistemic communities' – networks of experts in a given field whose professional self-definition is partially entwined with some conception of the public interest and whose members reinforce one another in these public goals.[13] In the United States, Hugh Heclo has concluded that public policy issues have tended increasingly to be refined, debated and framed by members of what he calls 'issue networks'.[14] For these policy elites, in his view, 'any direct material interest is often secondary to intellectual or emotional commitment', and they seek instead of power based on force or the threat of sanctions, 'influence commensurate with their understanding'.[15]

Some members of these elite issue networks are members of administrative agencies; some are staff to members of Congress or a congressional committee; some work for foundations; some are academics with a policy specialty. Some work for interest groups. Many influential members of the various issue networks are staff or officers of the burgeoning number of 'public interest' groups. But even within the 'private' interest groups, the staff, officers and membership can have some public-interested personal motivations. In the United States, for example, many lobbyists in state-level 'anti-Reaganomics' coalitions had jobs whose nominal goal was to increase benefits for their constituents, but almost all also had some personal commitment beyond their jobs to a larger progressive politics. Much of the activity of these groups can be explained as simple power politics or coalition-building: we will back your bill now if you will back ours next year. But some of the effort derives from a commitment among both members and elite of the various 'private' groups to some conception of the public good. If the members of the groups were more narrowly self-interested than the elites, we could say (borrowing a term from Joseph Kalt and Mark Zupan) that the elites sometimes engaged in 'ideological shirking' using for the public interest the time and effort that they were theoretically paid to use only in the narrow private interests of the members of their groups.[16]

Even in a *laissez-faire* system of interest representation, the incentive systems in these issue networks reward some forms of concern with the public interest. Any one individual's reputation in the network depends on the assessment of the other members, who often do not have similar structural positions. Each individual's desire for the respect of others in the network gives those others the power to reward and punish behavior.[17] Because the common language and object of study is ostensibly one or another version of the public interest, considerations of the public interest are likely to influence the participants' mutual assessments and consequently their self-image and behavior.

When the state enters relatively directly into negotiations among interest groups in the private sector, it necessarily gives power to state actors who have both their own private self-regarding interests and, often, other-regarding interests directed at increasing the authority of their own unit within the administration. Yet state structures can find ways to privilege the public interest in this situation through the construction of agendas and the selection of personnel. Some European forms of training for the civil service inculcate, among other motivations, a commitment to the public good. Arranging for negotiations between interests to take place under a state agenda and with the participation of state personnel often increases the space dedicated to considerations of the public good.

Most corporatist understandings of interest groups, however, do not require or stress preference change. Corporatist interest representation can remain in the 'conduit' or 'transmission belt' mode, in which representatives (in this case the interest group elites) simply carry into the policy arena their constituents' previously existing preferences. But in more recent deliberative models of corporatist representation, such as that of Cohen and Rogers, interest groups function to change preferences as well as to aggregate them.[18]

Corporatist deliberation includes 'negotiation', which stands between pure power and pure persuasion. In negotiation, the parties involved not only maneuver for advantageous positions but try to understand what the other really wants in order, for example, to offer what may be a cheaper satisfaction of wants than the other is demanding. The quest for understanding requires asking and listening. It requires understanding the other's language and putting oneself in the other's place. It requires making suggestions that the other may not have thought of and learning both from acceptance and refusal. When negotiators engage in this quest for understanding, they can use the understanding so gained to change the other's preferences. They can help the other discover what that other really wants. They can help create new preferences that better reflect the other's needs or values. They can even help the other develop new values. Successful negotiations in the real world rarely rely on mere jockeying for advantage in the conflict. Successful negotiators often find ways of meeting the other's real needs at less cost than seemed originally required.[19]

Understanding neocorporatist deliberation requires understanding both external and internal interaction and both negotiation and deliberation. Traditional corporatist models focus on external negotiation, in which the elites of groups formally established to represent their members' interests negotiate with one another to reach agreements that are then adopted by the state as law. More recent researchers add internal negotiation, in which elites negotiate with the members of their interest groups to reach agreements the members can accept as binding. Few have asked how the rank and file can deliberate within interest groups to reach new understandings of their interests that make sense in the light of their experience.

When political scientists do investigate the internal deliberative function of interest groups, they usually describe the process as 'aggregating' existing preferences, in a way that downplays the potential for preference change. Even scholars who argue that interest groups are more than simply 'interest articulators' add only that such groups 'reduce the range of alternatives on the legislative agenda', 'submerg[e] disagreement' and 'mobilize support for preferred political positions',[20] not that they play a role in helping their members, both rank and file and elite, change their preferences. Freeman and Medoff, for example, summarize the productive internal activities of unions with the static formula: 'Unions collect information about the preferences of all workers.'[21]

Interest groups not only collect information, mobilize support and submerge disagreement (presumably against the interests of those whose views are submerged); they also distill and order individual preferences by encouraging their members to think about, talk about and bring to the point of individual decision considerations on various sides of an issue. Unions and a few interest groups distill and order preferences collectively through internal democratic processes, as constituents choose the policies that most attract them through 'voice', voting on policies or leadership. Many groups distill and order more informally, through 'exit', as members join or send money to the organization that most appeals to them out of a range of competing organizations. Although the process of distillation and ordering does not produce fundamental preference change, it makes subsequent negotiation, and consequently legislation, more fruitful, as the interest group takes on the burden of letting the other parties in the negotiation know what its constituency in its present state of consciousness wants most.

Yet beyond distilling and ordering previously existing preferences, interest groups can serve as a forum for genuine preference change, including change so deep that it generates a change in personal identity. People who become active, especially in causes directed at some version of the public interest, sometimes find that they themselves have changed in the course of their activity. Wolfgang Streeck and Philippe Schmitter, applying to interest groups the ideas of Jürgen Habermas and others, consider interest associations 'transforming agents of individual interests' and argue that existing organizational theory fails to adopt 'a political concept of interest' in which interest groups are 'much more than passive recipients of preferences put forward by their constituents and clients'.

> Organized group interests are not given but emerge as a result of a multi-faceted interaction between social and organizational structure. . . . This interactive relationship is only partly described as one of organizational goal formation; at the same time it is one of collective identity formation . . . [in an] institutional context within which group interests and identities are defined and continuously revised.[22]

Empirical political scientists, however, including those in the volume that follow Streeck and Schmitter's introduction, have yet to investigate these postulated processes of identity change. Moreover, even Streeck and Schmitter focus on preference and identity changes among elites. They describe the internal functions of interest groups narrowly, as elites 'controlling the behavior of their members' and 'offering . . . to deliver the compliance of their members'. They conclude, indeed, that external negotiations among interest group elites must be kept 'informal and secretive in an effort to insulate them as much as possible from . . . dissidents within the associational ranks'.[23] In his voucher proposal, Schmitter again argues that neocorporatist arrangements often increase public spirit among polity elites. But here too he concludes that 'public-regardingness will be maximized if the leadership and staff of associations can be ensured some degree of autonomy from the immediate preferences of their members.'[24]

I would argue that elite deliberation must be supplemented with deliberation among the rank and file. Only citizens (or group members) themselves can know what outcomes they want, and better versions of this knowledge usually require deliberation. Elites can easily develop distorted understandings of the interests, including the public-regarding interests, of those they represent. The movement to incorporate the Equal Rights Amendment in the Constitution of the United States, for example, was highly decentralized. It also involved very largely public-spirited motivation. Yet even in this democratic and public-spirited movement, the elites never learned what the grass-roots activists would have formulated as good public policy if both elites and activists had taken part in a more extensive process of deliberation.[25]

When processes of accountability are functioning, a narrowly self-interested citizenry will eventually throw out its public-spirited representatives. But ordinary citizens are quite capable of committing themselves to public-spirited rather than self-interested action and are more likely to do so after deliberating with public-spirited others. Deliberative processes within interest associations can help create effective social cooperation as participants affirm or alter their social identifications, place limits on their own and others' options through agreed procedures and work out or reinforce their obligations to neighbors, colleagues, opponents and other participants in the political process.[26] When participants appeal to public values, deliberative forums within interest groups help create a larger public citizenship.

Conclusion

It is true that dangers to individual rights, efficiency and equity arise any time the state – with its great police power, its bureaucratic sluggishness and its own autonomous interests – gets involved in matters formerly reserved for private action. Sometimes, however, these costs are offset by benefits in equity and productivity. Cohen and Rogers conclude that, in Europe, corporatist arrangements have produced noticeable 'gains in productivity, productive equity, efficiency of state administration, and general social peace'. I have argued both logically and with the shreds of empirical information at my disposal that, in certain circumstances, bringing private negotiations under a state umbrella should make the power of competing groups more equal in their negotiations and promote concern for the common good.

At the moment, we have no idea in what contexts which elements of existing deliberative processes, including those of European corporatism, will actually increase productivity, equity, efficiency and public spirit. No political scientist has empirically investigated the deliberative functions of the system of interest representation, including groups outside, under, and partially under a state umbrella. A fully developed model of interest group deliberation would include the ways the deliberative process within interest groups can inform and change preferences and even identities. It would describe not only how representatives of interests influence one another outside their groups and how (if at all) the rank and file and their representatives engage in mutual influence, but also how (if at all) the rank and file influence one another within their groups. The present literature on negotiators' relations with their constituencies begins to model the actual and potential reciprocal relationships.[27]

Today, few interest associations in the United States or Europe institutionalize any formal deliberative processes among their membership, let alone deliberative processes designed to promote identification with the public good. A few public interest associations with historic links to the participatory movements of the 1960s, such as the Green Movement and the Democratic Socialists of America, continue to explore participatory formats with more or less success. A large opportunity for empirical and normative investigation lies in exploring the internal deliberation processes of both traditional and more participatory interest associations in the public and private sectors. We should judge any neocorporatist arrangements on the degree to which they facilitate all three levels of deliberation – among elites, between elites and rank and file, and among the rank and file – as well as on the degree to which they accomplish successfully the two goals of redressing the existing disadvantages of potential participants in the process and insisting that negotiations among interests include the broader good of the polity as a whole.

Acknowledgment

This essay derives from a longer treatment in 'A Deliberative Theory of Interest Representation', in *The Politics of Interests: Interest Groups Transformed*, ed. Mark P. Petracca (Boulder, CO: Westview

1992). I am grateful to the following for comments on an earlier draft: Christopher Jencks, Mark Petracca, Ken Kollman and participants in the Conference on the Political Economy of the Good Society at Yale University and the Conference on Competing Theories of Post-Liberal Democracy at the University of Texas at Austin. I thank the Russell Sage Foundation for support while writing this work.

Notes

1. By 'power' I mean A's preference causing B to do something that B would otherwise not do through force or the threat of sanction. This definition draws from Peter Bachrach and Morton Baratz, 'Decisions and Non-Decisions: An Analytical Framework', *American Political Science Review* 57 (1963) pp. 632–42; Jack H. Nagel, *The Descriptive Analysis of Power*, New Haven, CT: Yale University Press 1975; and Steven Lukes, *Power: A Radical View*, London: Macmillan 1974.

2. By 'persuasion' I mean A causing B to do something that B would otherwise not do through reason, new information and emotional appeals, along with shorthand cues to these means embodied in one form of authority, the capacity for reasoned persuasion. See Carl J. Friedrich, 'On Authority', in *Authority*, ed. Carl J. Friedrich, New York: Liberal Arts Press, 1959. I shall use persuasion here to mean only persuasion that is in the other's interests (Lukes, *Power*). Persuasion that is not in the other's interests, sometimes called 'manipulation' (Bachrach and Baratz, 'Decisions'), plays an important role in politics but is legitimate in very few normative understandings of democracy. For this reason, any normative critique of deliberation requires an account of underlying interests, as opposed to surface preferences. See Jane J. Mansbridge, *Beyond Adversary Democracy*, Chicago: University of Chicago Press 1983; Jürgen Habermas, *Legitimation Crisis*, trans. Thomas McCarthy, Boston: Beacon 1975, and *Communication and the Evolution of Society*, trans. Thomas McCarthy, Boston: Beacon 1979.

3. Jane J. Mansbridge, 'On the Relation of Altruism and Self-Interest', in Mansbridge, ed., *Beyond Self-Interest*, Chicago: University of Chicago Press 1990.

4. See Mansbridge, *Beyond Adversary Democracy* and Jane Mansbridge, 'Using Power/Fighting Power', *Constellations* (1994), pp. 53–73, for a more extended discussion.

5. Scholars disagree on how much power interest groups exert in the United States. This controversy derives in part from the difficulty of attributing cause both generally, and specifically in politics, power being a form of cause (Nagel, *Power*). Richard L Hall and Frank W. Wayman, 'Buying Time: Moneyed Interests and the Mobilization of Bias in Congressional Committees', *American Political Science Review* 84 (1990), pp. 797–820, summarize the literature failing to tie specific monetary contributions to specific votes but argue that 'political money alters members' patterns of legislative involvement' in ways that affect legislative outcomes. See also Thomas Ferguson, *Right Turn*, New York: Hill & Wang 1989; Gary C. Jacobson, *Money in Congressional Elections*, New Haven, CT: Yale University Press 1980; and Kay L. Schlozman and John T. Tierney, *Organized Interests and American Democracy*, New York: Harper Row 1986.

6. Richard B. Stewart, 'The Reformation of American Administrative Law', *Harvard Law Review* 88 (1975), pp. 1669–813.

7. Theodore Lowi, cited in Stewart, 'Reformation', at p. 1712. Cohen and Rogers provide an excellent criticism of Lowi's position.

8. 'Corporative Democracy' (paper presented at the Conference on Politische Institutionen und Interessenvermittlung, Konstanz 1988) and 'The Irony of Modern Democracy', this volume.

9. The concept of 'rent-seeking' is often used to discredit any departure from pure *laissez-faire*. This appellation is justified, in my view, only in so far as the departure from *laissez-faire* does not have a public purpose, such as producing justice, repairing past wrongs or creating a community that reflects the larger national diversity. Because much rent-seeking behavior pretends to have a public purpose, citizens and policymakers must always ask both whether they think the purpose is a genuinely public one, that is, whether it might reasonably be thought to benefit the polity as a whole in reasonable proportion to its costs, and whether the policy in question will further that public purpose.

10. See Jane J. Mansbridge, 'Motivating Deliberation in Congress', in *Constitutionalism in America*, vol. 2, ed. Sarah Baumgartner Thurow, New York: University Press of America 1988.

11. Richard B. Freeman and James L. Medoff, *What Unions Do*, New York: Basic Books 1984, p. 19.

12. For postwar pluralist writers arguing that there is no public interest, see Mansbridge, *Beyond Adversary Democracy* (esp. p. 340, n. 31) and Mansbridge, 'The Rise and Fall of Self-Interest in the Explanation of Political Life', in Mansbridge, ed., *Beyond Self-Interest*. For empirical evidence of citizens' and legislators' concerns for the public interest, see Mansbridge, 'Motivating Deliberation', and essays in Mansbridge, ed., *Beyond Self-Interest*.

13. Peter M. Haas, 'Do Regimes Matter? Epistemic Communities and Mediterranean Pollution Control', *International Organization* 43 (1989), pp. 377–403.

14. In 'Issue Networks and the Executive Establishment', in *The New American Political System*, ed. Anthony King, Washington, DC: American Enterprise Institute 1978, p. 103, Heclo defines an issue network as 'a shared-knowledge group having to do with some aspect (or, as defined by the network, some problem) of public policy'.

15. Heclo, 'Issue Networks', pp. 102–4.

16. Joseph Kalt and Mark A. Zupan, 'Capture and Ideology in the Economic Theory of Politics', *American Economic Review* 74 (1984), pp. 279–300, apply the term 'ideological shirking' to legislators.

17. Errol Meidinger, 'Regulatory Culture: A Theoretical Outline', *Law and Policy* 9 (1987), pp. 355–86.

18. See also Claus Offe and Helmut Wiesenthal, 'Two Logics of Collective Action: Theoretical Notes on Social Class and Organizational Form', in *Political Power and Social Theory*, vol. 1, ed. Maurice Zeitlin, Greenwich, CT: JAI 1980, pp. 67–115.

19. Paul J. Quirk, in 'The Cooperative Resolution of Policy Conflict', *American Political Science Review* 83 (1989), pp. 905–21, suggests that when negotiation can achieve joint gains, the forms of agreement possible are, in order of increasing difficulty, (1) compromise, where the factions make comparable, moderate concessions on each issue in dispute; (2) tradeoff, where they exchange large or even complete concessions on different issues; (3) compensation, where one faction concedes the original issue and the other makes up for it on unrelated matters; and (4) reorientation, where both factions abandon their initial positions to adopt a fundamentally new alternative. I would argue that some measure of reorientation is required in many negotiations.

20. W. Douglas Costain and Anne N. Costain, 'Interest Groups as Policy Aggregators in the Legislative Process', *Polity* 14 (1981), pp. 249–72, at pp. 251 and 257; see also pp. 255, 259, 260, and 271.

21. Freeman and Medoff, *What Unions Do*, p. 13, Table 1–1.

22. Wolfgang Streeck and Philippe Schmitter, 'Introduction', in *Private Interest Government*, ed. Streeck and Schmitter, Beverly Hills, CA: Sage 1985, pp. 16, 19.

23. Streeck and Schmitter, 'Introduction', pp. 11–13.

24. Schmitter, 'Corporative Democracy', p. 26; see also pp. 15, 27–9, 52–3 (but see suggestions at pp. 10, 18 and 45 that his scheme may also make the citizenry more public-spirited). Quirk, 'The Cooperative Resolution', also argues on the same grounds for insulating elites from the public.

25. Jane J. Mansbridge, *Why We Lost the ERA*, Chicago: University of Chicago Press 1986.

26. Schmitter, 'Corporative Democracy', pp. 10, 17–18, citing Claus Offe.

27. See James A. Wall, 'The Effects of Constituent Trust and Representative Bargaining Visibility on Intergroup Bargaining', *Organizational Behavior and Human Performance* 17 (1975), pp. 244–56; and Richard J. Klimoski and James A. Breaugh, 'When Performance Doesn't Count: A Constituency Looks at its Spokesman', *Organizational Behavior and Human Performance* 20 (1977), pp. 301–11.

5

Progress through Mischief:
The Social Movement Alternative to Secondary Associations

Andrew Szasz

The core idea advocated in Cohen and Rogers's essay – 'through politics, to secure an associative environment more conducive to democratic aims' – is certainly an attractive one. I am left, though, with two quite different concerns. First, how can such a thing be achieved? And second, what may be lost if it ever is achieved?

I was troubled, first, by the very great distance between what Cohen and Rogers advocate and the political process as it currently exists. How could we possibly get from here to there? That nettlesome question kept arising, insistently, as I admiringly followed the essay's argument. Cohen and Rogers chose to leave such considerations outside the frame of their essay. To me, though, the essay would have been immeasurably more powerful and persuasive had they discussed not only a desirable imaginary end-state but also something like a plausible transition scenario.

When I assumed, for the sake of argument, that such a reform of state/civil society relations can be achieved, concerns of a different order arose. If government busied itself deliberately crafting secondary associations that are well-behaved, not mischievous, and if secondary associations thenceforth knew their place, stayed in their place, dutifully played their assigned role and contributed responsibly to democratic governance, would we not lose some of the oppositional space from which the pressures for real change have always come?

For the past four years or so, I have been studying the politics of hazardous waste in the United States. The history of the hazardous waste issue is rich, dynamic, complex; a short comment must pass over many important features.[1] None the less, I had this history in mind as I read the Cohen and Rogers paper and felt that some features of the social movement part of the hazardous waste story speak directly to the second of my concerns.

148

The Hazardous Waste Movement

Local hazardous waste organizing began in the 1970s. It grew explosively after 1980, following extensive media coverage of the contamination of the Love Canal community near Niagara Falls, New York. Movement organizations, such as the Citizens' Clearinghouse on Hazardous Waste, claim to have worked with over five thousand local groups. Although these numbers may be somewhat inflated, government and industry spokesmen, who have no reason to exaggerate the extent of local organizing, a phenomenon they fervently wish wouldn't exist, depict the situation as totally out of control. Since 1980, *everyone* concerned – corporate waste generators, the waste industry itself, consultants, state and federal officials, lawyers, policy scientists – has agreed, without exception, that local opposition is the biggest impediment to facility siting. Waste industry surveys confirm that public opposition has made it practically impossible to build new off-site industrial waste facilities anywhere in the United States.

Two observations about local hazardous waste organizing appear to me especially relevant to thinking critically about the positions taken by Cohen and Rogers in their essay. First, the relationship between local hazardous waste or toxics groups and the state is very far from, in fact the diametric opposite of, the normalized, mutually constituting, corporatist arrangements envisioned in the essay. Local organizations do not act remotely like the well-behaved secondary associations Cohen and Rogers envision. Conversely, for the most part, the state has not responded well to these groups. Local organizing is feared and hated by both government and industry; the official political world has done everything in its power to try to reduce these groups' capacity to wield power in the policy process. Second, it is none the less true that, overall, local opposition movements have had a fundamentally positive impact on society, both in terms of *product*, in forcing stronger regulation and creating conditions that have forced a turn toward source reduction, and in terms of *process*, in fostering direct democratic action, increased participation and increased politicization of heretofore apolitical citizens.

Movement Ideology

The movement is often depicted as the latest manifestation of a larger phenomenon that has plagued the American polity for decades, namely, nimbyism, the Not In My Back Yard syndrome in which, in narrow self-interest, communities refuse to accept unattractive but socially necessary institutions or infrastructure (e.g. highways, prisons, low-income housing for the elderly).[2] The movement did indeed start out with a nimby consciousness. Even today, individuals or communities that are just becoming involved do so from the narrow perspective of 'anywhere but here'. But it is no longer accurate or fair to characterize the hazardous waste movement in this way. The movement has grown ideologically. It has a more sophisticated understanding of the roots of environmental crisis and a more global sense of what needs to be done. But that does not mean that the movement has moved from an ideology of opposition to one of participation. If anything, its growing political radicalization has only made its opposition to the state and to capital more thoroughgoing, more absolute.

Movement Tactics

The movement proudly rejects anything that smacks of cooperation or normalized participation. Hearings that were intended to provide the opportunity for formal public participation are turned into occasions for building oppositional solidarity:

> The standard mechanism for involving the public – the public hearing – routinely becomes a crowded, highly emotional exercise in mob psychology.[3]

> Emotional bias and soapbox oratory often become the order of the day.[4]

According to New Jersey Siting Commissioner Frank J. Dodd, hearings

> have turned into political rallies. . . . It was how many people can you get into an auditorium to boo the speakers you don't like and cheer for the ones you support.[5]

The movement does indeed shun normalized participation. It embraces, instead, the grassroots, oppositional politics of direct action. Its tactical vocabulary is a familiar one: demonstrations, militant confrontation, escalating occasionally even to threats of violence.[6]

Official Reaction is Hostile

It should hardly come as a surprise, then, that the official political world of regulators, industry spokespeople and policy scientists has not reacted well to these 'actually existing secondary associations'. Quite the opposite.

The people who oppose hazardous waste facilities have been depicted as traumatized, irrational, too scared to distinguish between the admittedly unsafe practices of the past and the safe practices of today:

The American public is traumatized.[7]

Buzzwords like dioxin inflame public fears.[8]

Public opinion [is] inflamed.[9]

In some cases [there is] near-hysteria.[10]

The public is ... unable or unwilling to distinguish between patently improper sites for hazardous waste disposal such as Love Canal, and properly managed disposal sites.[11]

Citizens are accused of being narrowly self-interested, unaware or unconcerned about the dire economic and even environmental consequences of their refusal, and hence fundamentally irresponsible and antisocial:

Without adequate facilities, needed goods and services simply cannot be produced.[12]

Hazardous waste management facilities are needed ... to assure the smooth functioning of the many industries generating hazardous wastes as a result of providing valuable products for the United States.[13]

Citizens groups ... fail also to accept ... the need for solutions. 'Put it in Texas' is a convenient argument for local use (unless you're in Texas), but it merely passes the buck and denies the fact that those who benefit from technological advancements must also share the burden of responsible management of its by-products.[14]

If new hazardous waste facilities cannot be sited, the waste must still go somewhere – to existing overburdened facilities, or often to organized-crime fronts, to midnight dumpers.[15]

Ironically, but sadly, this opposition [to new management facilities] may be leading to situations that could seriously threaten public health, including, for instance, illegal dumping of wastes on roadsides.[16]

People's intransigence threatened to bring siting to a halt. Something had to be done to neutralize these groups' power, to get rid of this bothersome upsurge of direct, democratic self-insertion in the implementation of policy, and to get back to that manageable situation in which siting would once again be firmly in the hands of industry and the regulator, engineer and expert.

The situation gave rise to a vast, rather desperate discourse. Various strategies were proposed. Some advocated avoiding local opposition by *siting in industrial zones* at some distance from any neighborhood or siting near *communities that are most powerless*, those least able or willing to organize an effective opposition (in effect, in communities of the poor and of people of color), siting strategies that had been implicitly practiced for decades. Others advocated a direct disempowerment through state *pre-emption* of local control over land use. Still others advocated various *compensation* schemes that would increase local acceptance of siting by altering host communities' cost/benefit calculations.

Some observers called for new forms of *enhanced participation*, giving people more information, involving the community fully at every stage of project development, accepting the need to negotiate and make real concessions in response to community concerns, compensating for impacts that could not be mitigated, and perhaps even institutionalizing a degree of continuing community control over how the facility would operate.[17]

Calls for enhanced participation constituted the left end of this discourse. At first glance, such proposals appear close to the state/ civil society relations envisioned by Cohen and Rogers. A close reading, however, suggests that, in the end, these proposals were still fundamentally co-optative in intent.[18]

Yet the Results are Overwhelmingly Positive

Although neither the groups nor government have been 'well behaved', in terms of the model advocated by Cohen and Rogers, it seems to me that the hazardous waste movement has accomplished much of what the authors would like to see accomplished.

Policy Impacts

At the level of formal policy-making, the movement (and the levels of public distress, dread, perception of risk that accompany it) drove policy-makers repeatedly to strengthen federal regulation of hazardous wastes. During the Reagan administration's eight years, all environmental legislation stalled on Capitol Hill *except* for the two laws that govern hazardous waste: the Resource Conservation and

Recovery Act (RCRA) and Superfund. Attempts to deregulate both the RCRA and Superfund provoked a major scandal, the so-called 'Sewergate' episode at the EPA in 1983. The two laws were subsequently reauthorized and greatly strengthened in 1984 and 1986. At the same time, the local action component of the movement forcefully inserted itself into the implementation process, notably in the form of siting opposition that brought facility siting to a virtual standstill. The interaction of siting opposition and stronger regulations has created a kind of scissor in which regulations force demand and the masses veto the supply. The result has been that the cost of legitimate disposal continues to go up, with the liability provisions of Superfund and RCRA creating heavy penalties for improper or illegal disposal. The documented result is that US industry is now beginning to explore seriously the waste reduction alternative. The situation should be contrasted with 1976, when a very broad coalition of corporate sectors convinced Congress to shun any idea of regulation-driven 'source reduction', and opt, instead, for the more traditional regulatory logic of 'disposal regulation'.[19]

Process Impacts: Activism, Politicization

We should not neglect political process impacts that do not appear as immediate policy effect but are just as important and perhaps more important in the long run. By the end of the 1980s, the movement consisted of a vast, multilayered and multiply interconnected network of organizations, which spanned the whole spectrum of social movement forms from local ad hoc groups to large, sophisticated national organizations. The existence of a movement infrastructure made possible a movement culture, collective memory, the ability to analyze and learn from experience. The movement, and individual organizations within it, may have started with a nimby consciousness, but ten years of practice and analysis have generated a sophisticated political ideology. We can discern three major ideological or conceptual developments over the brief life of the movement: (1) an increasingly comprehensive and sophisticated understanding of environmental problems – movement 'locals' now embrace a much larger set of concerns: solid waste landfills, nuclear waste, waste-to-energy incinerators, military toxics, infectious hospital wastes and industrial facilities that emit toxic pollutants; in its literature, the movement also embraces more global environmental issues, such as global warming and ozone depletion; (2) the conscious location of the movement within a history of US activism; and (3) the growing sense that grassroots waste and toxics environmentalism is the place where a broader movement for social justice can be reconstituted.

At the level of the individual, many thousands have been introduced to the experience of activism. Almost all movement participants became active initially for narrow, purely immediate – selfish, if you will – reasons. Many, certainly, never moved beyond that; reports from within the movement suggest that many others have come out of the experience with a significantly more developed social and political consciousness and a different, more public and more confident sense of self. Some, perhaps several hundred, have been totally transformed and have taken up lives as full-time organizers.[20]

In Praise of Mischief

I can now briefly restate my second concern about Cohen and Rogers's argument. My work on the hazardous waste movement suggests that there are circumstances where what could be construed, in the term of authors' discussion, as an egregious case of 'mischief of faction' produces rational policy outcomes as well as other political developments that all supporters of genuine democracy fervently hope for.

Cohen and Rogers rightly point to source reduction as the best approach to environmental pollution. I think they are also right in saying that the source reduction strategy necessarily requires local, case-by-case analysis and problem-solving and that secondary associations can involve both workers and consumers in the process. But the turn toward waste reduction may not have happened in a world of normalized cooperation between government and artfully constructed secondary associations. Such an arrangement would have made for easier facility siting. There would have been no threat of disposal capacity crisis. Costs would not have risen nearly as much as they have. The conditions that have put source reduction on both government's and industry's agenda either would not have existed or would have had less force than they do today. The hazardous waste movement did not invent the idea of source reduction; it was, however, the historical agent that created the conditions that finally forced that idea to the center of environmental policy.

Additionally, I have argued, the process of the movement has itself produced important results. We live in a moment where most 'citizens' are profoundly apolitical, inactive and disinterested in the larger world. To the degree that anything political has been going on in our society, conservatism is in command. Given that conjunctural context, the hazardous waste movement's capacity to mobilize and radicalize thousands of previously inactive people is to be praised and cherished. Day-to-day life in the movement *is* the stuff of popular, truly participatory democracy. The ideological/conceptual development has been remarkable. Artfully constructed secondary associations might have made the process of regulatory implementation more trouble-free in the short run; I cannot see how they could possibly have produced similar changes in political consciousness and behavior.

The authors are undoubtedly right to argue that the 'mischief of factions' infirms democratic governance. I would venture to respond, though, that disruptive mischief is also the motive force for all real forward movement in social history. If so, then even the best-intended attempts to rid society of the former risks diminishing, as well, the latter.

Notes

1. Andrew Szasz, *Ecopopulism: Toxic Waste and the Movement for Environmental Justice*, Minneapolis, MN: University of Minnesota Press 1994.
2. For information on locally unwanted land uses (LULUs), see Frank J. Popper, 'The Environmentalists and the LULU', and 'LP/HC and LULUs: The Political Uses of Risk Analysis in Land-Use Planning', in *Resolving Locational Conflict*, ed. Robert W. Lake, New Brunswick, NJ: Center for Urban Policy Research 1987, pp. 275–87.
3. US Environmental Protection Agency, 'Hazardous Waste Facility Siting: A Critical Problem', Report no. SW–865, Washington, DC: US Environmental Protection Agency 1980.
4. James E. McGuire, 'The Dilemma of Public Participation in Facility Siting Decisions and the Mediation Alternative', *Seton Hall Legislative Journal* 9, no. 2 (1986), pp. 467–73.
5. Peter M. Sandman, 'Getting to Maybe: Some Communications Aspects of Siting Hazardous Waste Facilities', in *Resolving Locational Conflict*, pp. 322–44.
6. The hazardous waste movement is analyzed in Szasz, *Ecopopulism*, ch. 4.
7. Alvin Alm, 'Opening Address in ABA Standing Committee on Environmental Law: Siting of Hazardous Waste Facilities and Transport of Hazardous Substances', Washington, DC: American Bar Association, Public Services Division 1984, pp. 1–4.
8. Editor, 'Editorial', *Hazardous Waste and Hazardous Materials*, 5, no. 1 (1988), p. ix.
9. William L. West, 'Hazardous Waste Management – An Industry Perspective', in *Management of Toxic and Hazardous Wastes*, ed. Bhatt, Sykes and Sweeney, Chelsea, MI: Lewis 1985, pp. 35–400.
10. Richard L. Hanneman, 'A Service Industry Perspective', in *Hazardous Waste Management for the 80s*, ed. Sweeney, Bhatt, Sykes and Sproul, Ann Arbor, MI: Ann Arbor Science Publishers 1982, pp. 1–12.
11. J. A. Duberg, M. L. Frankel and C. M. Niemczewski, 'Siting of Hazardous Waste Management Facilities and Public Opposition', *Environmental Impact Assessment Review*, 1 (1, 1982), pp. 84–8.
12. Chemical Manufacturers Association, *A Statute for the Siting, Construction, and Financing of Hazardous Waste Treatment Disposal and Storage Facilities*, Washington, DC: Chemical Manufacturers Association n.d.

13. Robert W. Craig and Terry R. Lash, 'Siting Nonradioactive Hazardous Waste Facilities', in *Hazardous Waste Management: In Whose Backyard?*, ed. Michalann Harthill, Boulder, CO: Westview 1984, p. 100. Craig and Lash are representatives of the Keystone Institute.

14. Peggy Vince, 'The Hazardous Waste Management Triangle', in *Hazardous Waste Management for the 80s*, pp. 17–25.

15. Frank J. Popper, 'The Environmentalists and the LULU', in *Resolving Locational Conflict*, pp. 1–13.

16. Craig and Lash, 'Siting Nonradioactive Hazardous Waste Facilities', p. 104.

17. For more detail, see Szasz, *Ecopopulism*, ch. 5.

18. Information has to be packaged carefully: 'Factual materials ... must be presented in a manner best suited to the needs and backgrounds of the recipients'. See Keystone Center, 'Siting Nonradioactive Hazardous Waste Facilities: An Overview', in *Final Report of the First Keystone Workshop on Managing Non-radioactive Hazardous Waste*, Keystone, CO: Keystone Center 1980.

The community leaders and opinion-makers who will serve on advisory councils must be selected carefully so that they will be seen as legitimately representing local concerns but will not truly represent, in the sense of being selected by and accountable to, a community constituency. See Richard L. Robbins, 'Methods to Gain Community Support for a Hazardous Waste Facility or a Superfund Cleanup', in *Hazardous Waste Management for the 80s*, pp. 514–15. See also Eleanor W. Windsor, 'Public Participation: The Missing Ingredient for Success in Hazardous Waste Siting', in *Industrial Waste: Proceedings of the Thirteenth Mid-Atlantic Conference*, ed. C. P. Huang, Ann Arbor, MI: Ann Arbor Science Publishers 1981 p. 523. The bottom line is that the local advisory board should represent community concerns, but it should also, and above all else, serve 'to diffuse a confrontational siting dispute'. See A. D. Tarlock, 'Siting New or Expanded Treatment, Storage, or Disposal Facilities: The Pigs in the Parlors of the 1980s', *Natural Resources Lawyer*, 17 (1984), p. 456.

Expanded participation is most likely to produce results if the ultimate trump card of state override looms over the siting process, pressuring the community to reach some sort of negotiated agreement to accept the siting. See Craig and Lash, 'Siting Nonradioactive Hazardous Waste Facilities', p. 108. In Habermas's terms, expanding participation is a form of communicative action that intends *success*, not *understanding*. See Jürgen Habermas, *The Theory of Communicative Action*, trans. Thomas McCarthy, Boston: Beacon 1985.

19. For more on these developments, see Szasz, *Ecopopulism*, chs 6 and 7.

20. For more detail, see ibid., chs 4 and 8.

6

Democratic Corporatism and/versus Socialism

Andrew Levine

It is remarkable that, in the current period, radicalism has virtually disappeared from political life, and socialism has come to seem increasingly irrelevant even to those who still identify with the historical Left.[1] No doubt, the fall of Communism is partly responsible, especially for socialism's apparent demise – even though capitalist property relations were abolished in all the formerly Communist countries without the requisite material conditions in place, and the economic structures that replaced them were maintained under the superintendence of states that violated virtually every norm traditionally embraced by the Left. Social democracy's decline too has undermined socialism's standing, despite the fact that, for many decades, social democrats, almost without exception, have sought to reform capitalism, not to transform it. It is also plain that the relatively good performance of capitalist economies throughout the world have turned capitalism into a positive ideal in the minds of many of its former detractors. But these are only fragments of an explanation. It must remain for future historians to explain why the political and economic institutions of Western liberal democracies seem, for the time being, to have overcome what was only recently believed to be a significant 'legitimation crisis' and why, correspondingly, liberalism has come to exercise an unprecedented hegemony over contemporary intellectual life. It is most unlikely that the current situation is the product of a rational consensus. For one thing remains clear: the old economic and political order is as guilty as ever of the charges socialists traditionally leveled against it. Indeed, inequality and immiseration have become worse in all the advanced capitalist countries and throughout the world capitalist system. I would therefore venture that the impulse that motivated anti-capitalist fervor in the past continues, even as the appeal of socialism, ostensibly capitalism's historical rival, is temporarily or permanently suspended.

It is, in any case, deeply ironic that in the present conjuncture intellectuals of the Left have become unabashed liberals, transforming what was once considered a justifying theory for the inequalities generated by capitalist property relations into a vehicle for waging the struggle for equality associated historically with socialism. Less remarkable, in view of the longstanding connections joining many strains of socialist theory with democracy, but no less characteristic of progressive political theory in recent years, is a tendency to transfer the emancipatory faith that socialists used to invest in the transformation of property relations to democracy itself. In retrospect, Cohen and Rogers's first joint venture in political theory, *On Democracy*,[2] can be seen as an early attempt to derive conclusions consonant with the spirit that motivated generations of socialist militants from liberal and democratic premises. 'Secondary Associations and Democratic Governance' continues this project, though, as befits the times, without explicitly identifying with socialist aspirations. Whether liberalism and democracy alone can adequately ground the emancipatory project socialists have historically assumed is, I believe, the central question for intellectuals of the Left today. It would be worthwhile to examine Cohen and Rogers's contribution to democratic theory from this perspective. However in the space allotted here I shall be able only to register certain hesitations about their recent project. To this end, I shall briefly turn the larger question I just posed on its head. After voicing some doubts about whether the institutional arrangements Cohen and Rogers envision can be expected to move society toward the ends they are intended to achieve, I shall ask whether these institutions themselves can be implemented without socialism – that is, without socializing the regime of private property that prevails in Western liberal democracies. Since the issues involved in assessing the feasibility of Cohen and Rogers's proposals are ultimately empirical, it will not be possible to conclude anything definitively. I will nevertheless indicate why, provisionally and with due awareness of the need for further investigation, I strongly suspect that the democratic corporatism Cohen and Rogers envision, whatever its merits, is no substitute for socialism and is probably not even feasible without socialism.

First, however, a comment on Cohen and Rogers's use of the term 'democracy'.

Historically, 'democracy' meant rule by the *demos*, the people, the popular masses in contrast to elites. By the time, roughly the mid-nineteenth century, that democrats and liberals forged an uneasy peace (overwhelmingly to the detriment of democratic values), democracy had lost its class content to become rule by the (undifferentiated) people, supplemented perhaps by public deliberation and debate. Thus we might say that a polity is democratic to the extent that its collective choices are determined by (all relevant) individuals' choices for alternative outcomes in contention, each individual counting equally. However, real-world liberal democrats advocate representative, not direct, democracy. Thus in democracies, as conceived today, the citizenry determines only who their representatives shall be – and then only through a variety of mediating institutions of which the party system is probably the least offensive to democratic values. This is not the place to reflect on rationales for representative institutions or to elaborate on the respects in which the theory and practice of representative government diverges from direct democracy. But it is important to note that, whatever their differences, the two are of one mind in rejecting the original, class-centric understanding of rule by the popular masses.

Today, as Cohen and Rogers acknowledged in *On Democracy*, there is much to gain – politically and theoretically – by bringing back the class content of 'democracy'. There is also much to gain, I think, by understanding 'democracy' more as a process than as a state of affairs. I would suggest, in other words, that it would be well for democratic theorists to shift their focus from 'democracy' to 'democratization' – to popular empowerment, 'power to the people'. However, in 'Secondary Associations and Democratic Governance', democratization is seldom at issue, and 'popular sovereignty' and 'political equality' are only two of six conditions stipulated for 'the abstract democratic ideal'. 'Distributive equity', which is evidently something short of full equality, is another condition, along with 'civic consciousness, good economic performance and state competence'. Thus by 'democracy' Cohen and Rogers seem to have in mind something like 'good government' or, more precisely, what people of generally democratic and egalitarian sensibilities take good government to be. It is hard to quarrel with any of these features: better that states be competent than not, and that they superintend flourishing economies without severe inequalities and with lots of civic consciousness. But by bringing so many good things together and calling them 'democracy', a certain ambiguity enters into Cohen and Rogers's central claim. Is democracy an end in itself? Or is it a means to some larger end? Cohen and Rogers seem mainly to argue for the latter, less contentious, claim, though much of what they say suggests the former. If they consider democracy to be an intrinsic good, as I suspect they do, they ought to explain why. On the other hand, if they view democracy instrumentally, they ought to explain more clearly than they do exactly what larger ends it serves. I have suggested that the most that can be inferred from what they write is that democracy serves 'good governance' under existing historical conditions. But this objective seems even more plainly instrumental than democracy itself.

This ambiguity carries over into Cohen and Rogers's account of secondary associations. Secondary associations are corporatist institutions, democratically run, on which at least some traditional state functions devolve. Are they worth implementing in their own right or for their effects? It is not possible to say unequivocally. But even if we take the less controversial instrumentalist understanding, and even if we consider good governance in the vague sense Cohen and Rogers articulate to be the larger end that these institutions serve, we might ask whether they can in fact be expected to do what Cohen and Rogers intend. Presumably, it is internal democratic governance, guaranteed perhaps by the state or by the legal system, that should underwrite confidence in these institutions. But however beneficial internal democracy and democratic participation may be, there are reasons to be skeptical that these factors will suffice to assure beneficial outcomes.

There is, first, a difficulty that Cohen and Rogers's proposal shares to its detriment with the political theory assumed in the past by writers who identified explicitly with the socialist tradition: that is, a readiness to assign a role to the state that risks violating liberal safeguards against intrusion by public institutions into individuals' lives and matters of 'private' conscience. For unless the state actually favors particular secondary associations and proscribes others, unless it exercises a licensing function in evident violation of liberal 'neutrality', there is reason to expect that secondary associations will form that actually diminish democracy overall. Let us concede, for example, that democracy, on Cohen and Rogers's understanding of the term, is advanced by assuring reproductive rights to women, and that prohibitions on abortion violate reproductive rights. What, except illiberal legal proscription, could prevent the development of secondary associations by groups opposed to abortion? So long as these associations assume state functions – organizing adoptions, for example, or providing obstetrical care – they would be secondary associations according to Cohen and Rogers's criteria. Yet they would effectively disempower female citizens and otherwise work to the detriment of democratic values. The requirement that the internal organization of 'pro-life' secondary associations be democratic hardly contravenes this expectation.

The apparent incompatibility of Cohen and Rogers's proposals with liberal restrictions on activist states is ironic in so far as their intent is to contrive institutional arrangements that advance progressive objectives while remaining feasible and stable in political cultures shaped by liberal values. The erstwhile Communist states suffered from a profound insensitivity to liberal concerns. I have argued elsewhere that a failure to appreciate the importance of liberal safeguards is perhaps the central failing of Marxist politics as it has developed historically, but that Marxist political theory can be revised to incorporate liberal concerns.[3] It would be odd indeed if institutions designed to retain continuity with existing, liberal arrangements – and not to revolutionize them, as Marx prescribed – turn out to be less capable of addressing liberal concerns than Marxism is.

There are also reasons to question whether the secondary associations Cohen and Rogers envision will work to empower the disempowered. Since secondary associations are corporatist by design, they will tend, as corporatist institutions usually have, to benefit differentially the stronger parties within the corporate entity. It would be unfair, of course, to associate Cohen and Rogers's democratic corporatism with the expressly anti-democratic and anti-liberal corporatisms of recent history. Nevertheless, it is worth recalling that corporatist strategies were adopted with some success by European fascists intent on undoing insurgent labor movements after World War I. Corporatism lends itself to such uses; indeed, its point is to mitigate antagonisms by drawing potential antagonists together in common projects. Whether or not this effect is beneficial from a generally progressive standpoint depends on circumstances. The gun lobby in the United States is wont to declare that people kill people, not guns. There is a sense in which this slogan, however disingenuous, is beyond dispute. But guns do escalate the level of violence and therefore make killing more likely. Corporatism too is an instrument, which is neither good nor bad in itself. But just as guns tend to augment the level of violence, corporatism tends to enhance social cohesiveness by drawing otherwise antagonistic political forces into common projects. My own intuitions run counter to those of Cohen and Rogers. But I concede that it is not implausible to believe, as they do, that in the present conjuncture cooperation with capital may be advantageous for labor in ways that would have been unthinkable just a few years ago. It is at least arguable, therefore, that Cohen and Rogers have contrived a progressive strategy for what remains of the labor movement, and not only the labor movement. For they envision secondary associations at all the principal interstices of social life, not just in the workplace.

Theirs is a pluralist corporatism, attuned to the heterogeneous social divisions that characterize contemporary social formations. Moreover, theirs is a self-consciously 'realistic' corporatism. They aim to push society in a broadly democratic and egalitarian direction at a time when the desire to change the world fundamentally strikes most people, including many who once entertained aspirations more radical than those Cohen and Rogers propose, as dangerously utopian. I will not try to counter this sensibility here, although I cannot forbear from registering the opinion that it is needlessly pessimistic. But I would point out that the old question about corporatism's consequences for advancing a broadly progressive agenda remains pertinent, even if the prospects for abrupt and momentous changes seem remote. What will prevent the more powerful forces within corporatist entities from taking advantage of their position to reinforce existing power structures and systems of domination? I worry that nothing will.

Needless to say, there is no reason, in principle, why all parties to corporatist arrangements cannot benefit from them. There may even be circumstances in which the weaker or less well-off benefit more than the better-off do. If nothing else, in a corporatist system, the weak are 'incorporated'. Arguably, therefore, they stand to lose less than they might in more antagonistic forms of social interaction – in traditional collective bargaining arrangements, for example. But they also stand to gain less when their antagonists are also their partners. It is fruitless to speculate on these issues a priori. Outcomes will depend on the conditions under which corporatist entities exist and on the aims, skills and capacities of the agents involved in them. The point is just that there is no systemic reason to expect favorable outcomes. If anything, the contrary is true. For corporatist institutions to advance progressive agendas, the tendency of the strong to take advantage of their strength must somehow be countervailed.

Let us suppose, however, that the skepticism I have voiced is unwarranted. The question I want finally to raise is whether this design for society can be implemented, to a degree sufficient to change society fundamentally, without putting capitalist property relations in question. Can radical democrats be soft on capitalism in the way that Cohen and Rogers are?

Associative institutions need resources. Can they obtain them when society's principal productive assets are privately owned? Can secondary associations deploy resources effectively in the face of threats of disinvestment or underinvestment? In the United States, where the principal political parties are unusually subservient to 'the business community', even by the standards that prevail in other advanced capitalist countries, there is hardly any data on which to base speculations. It is fair to maintain, however, especially for the United States, that far-reaching changes are unlikely to come onto the political agenda without a drastic political realignment consequent on a reinvigorated class struggle in which capital suffers genuine defeats. Cohen and Rogers, like so many others today, focus on social unity, not class struggle; nevertheless, I suspect they would agree that a change in the balance of class forces in favor of workers and other *demotic* constituencies is desirable and probably indispensable for associative democracy. But I question whether they take this exigency seriously enough. Despite their efforts to propose institutional arrangements consonant with real-world political forces, I fear that they underestimate the difficulties involved in putting the changes they envision onto the political agenda.

Small moves toward associative democracy surely are feasible here and now. If they could be made to succeed, it would perhaps be a small gain for democratic governance. In a political culture in which less than half of the citizenry participates at all, in which political participation consists mainly in voting periodically for lesser evils, and in which the available choices become ever worse and more alike, even a slight improvement is not to be despised. But what Cohen and Rogers have in mind is more momentous. The institutions they envision are supposed to secure a profound democratization of the political culture – a non-socialist path to some (if not all) the objectives that, historically, socialists sought to bring about through socialism. My worry is that the path they propose cannot be traversed; that radical democrats cannot dispense with socialism after all.

Capitalism is plainly incompatible with *economic* democracy; if productive assets are privately owned, they cannot be democratically controlled. But capitalism constrains *political* democratization too. The problem is not just that capitalists' wealth buys political influence. So long as they are (somewhat) accountable to public opinion, public officials in regimes with capitalist economies must to some extent accommodate to the interests of those who own society's principal means of production. Otherwise, capitalists will withdraw or under-employ their assets, and political leaders will be held incapable of 'delivering the goods'. Then their own positions will be at risk and the legitimacy of the regime itself will ultimately be put in jeopardy. In this way, capitalism *limits* democratization. Of course, in particular circumstances, general tendencies may be successfully countervailed. My suggestion, however, is that in anything like the circumstances that actually obtain, the democratizing proposals Cohen and Rogers propose would fall outside the limits of feasibility. To be sure, this suggestion cannot be established a priori, and it is pointless to speculate in general about structural constraints and conjunctural impedances to democratic transformations. To assess the prospects for Cohen and Rogers's associative democracy properly, it would be necessary to consider detailed institutional proposals in the context of concrete situations. With due regard, therefore, to the tentativeness of any opinions registered at this level of abstraction from real-world politics, I would nevertheless adduce one consideration that supports my hesitations about the prospects for *any* democratic but non-socialist route to significant social amelioration.

Historically, capitalism has proved adept at accommodating democratic transformations to a degree that confounded widely shared expectations. Thus it survived the extension of the franchise to voters without property, the principal objective of a number of ostensibly anti-capitalist, nineteenth-century social movements. But the extension of the franchise was accompanied by the emergence of institutions – the party system, above all – that severely mitigated the extent to which 'democratic' institutions implement governance 'of, by and for the people'. Arguably, the extension of the franchise to the property-less, though undeniably 'progressive', mainly served to legitimate the existing political regime without jeopardizing established economic interests. There is some chance that a similar phenomenon might result from the implementation of Cohen and Rogers's design for society, should their democratic corporatism ever become a compelling political ideal. Thus at a time when 'global competitiveness' has become a consensus value across the entire (but very constricted) political spectrum, corporatist schemes for enhancing 'human capital' might well seem eminently desirable. I do not doubt that workers' retraining programs, for example, or other educational measures could be contrived that would be helpful to popular constituencies. But just as the extension of the franchise to propertyless workers delivered less than it promised, so I suspect would even the most progressive corporatist schemes mobilized 'to grow the economy'. For along with some increased likelihood of employment as well-paying jobs diminish, the diminution of workers' power in the long run and the decapacitation of the *demos* for more radical social transformations must also be taken into account in any balanced assessment. Thus the question is not just whether capitalism can accommodate associative democratic institutions – an unlikely enough prospect; the more important question is whether it can do so in a way that will result in anything like the far-reaching changes for the better that Cohen and Rogers evidently intend. Their proposed 'new social partnership' will be instrumental for fundamental social amelioration only if capital is sufficiently interested in cooperation to accede to genuine demo-cratization; in other words, if the popular movement is in a position to make the owners of society's principal means of production offers they cannot refuse. The *demos* must be able, as it were, to co-opt economic elites. But if the nineteenth-century battle over the franchise is exemplary, as I believe it is, historical precedents point in the opposite direction. Indeed, it is fair to say that since the advent of capitalism, whenever capitalists have acceded to the demands of the *demos*, even when the outcome has been overwhelmingly for the better, it is the popular movements that have been co-opted.

Following Marx, many Left militants used to describe themselves as 'scientific' socialists because they sought to ground the political struggles they waged in genuine historical possibilities. The contrast was with 'utopian' socialists who proposed visions of ideal arrange-ments in disregard of real-world economic, social and political processes. Cohen and Rogers too seek to avoid utopianism, even as they assume the mantle of social engineers. But their plea for a new social contract joining everyone regardless of their class position in a common democratic project suggests that utopianism has gained the upper hand after all. In the older, justly discredited corporatisms of the early twentieth century, it was the nation that united the people with their rulers. For Cohen and Rogers, it is an interest in democracy that assumes this role. My claim is that this interest is illusory; that the owners of society's principal means of production may be able to adapt to formal democratization, but must remain unalterably opposed to its substance. And I further claim that the balance of class forces in almost all likely circumstances is overwhelmingly stacked against the genuine democratizers. Cohen and Rogers's asso-ciative democracy, therefore, flies in the face of the social divisions that structure capitalist societies. Paradoxically, their pragmatic and 'realistic' design for society is, if anything, more utopian than socialism is. Despite their best efforts to the contrary, they are 'utopian democrats'.

In recent years, as faith in socialism has declined, it has become less clear than was once assumed what the socialist alternative to capital-ism involves. But this is not a reason to retract longstanding socialist commitments altogether. It is instead a challenge to develop a more adequate socialist vision. Nor do we need to have that vision fully in hand to assert that 'scientific democrats' must be socialists too. We are entitled to draw this conclusion, albeit provisionally, first, because it is likely that socialism is indispensable for realizing the objectives progressives of all descriptions ultimately want to achieve; and second, because it is almost certainly the case that support for capitalism today, even if only in the course of promoting benignly demo- cratic corporatist ventures, is ultimately detrimental to virtually any progressive agenda.

According to a slogan of the 1974 revolution that overthrew fascism in Portugal: 'Socialism is the soil, democracy the seed, liberty the flower.' It would be well for those of us who want to reconstruct a genuine Left in these darkest of times to take this slogan to heart. Cohen and Rogers may be right in this time and place to focus on democracy, liberty's seed. But they have selected the wrong soil for democracy to develop. The Portuguese slogan asserts that socialism is indispensable if democracy is to issue in liberty. It is difficult these days to be confident of any prescription for changing the world radi- cally for the better. But there is less reason, I believe, to be wary of this proposition than of Cohen and Rogers's acquiescence in an indefinitely prolonged capitalist future.

Notes

1. The only significant exceptions are minority currents within social movements like feminism or environmentalism. But even radical feminists and environmentalists tend to share the disinterest in fundamental alternatives to social and political arrange- ments characteristic of the larger movements of which they are a part.

2. Joshua Cohen and Joel Rogers, *On Democracy: Toward a Transformation of American Society*, New York: Penguin Books 1983.

3. Cf. Andrew Levine, *The General Will*, Cambridge: Cambridge University Press 1993.

The Irony of Modern Democracy and the Viability of Efforts to Reform its Practice

Philippe C. Schmitter

Consider the irony: On the one hand, many countries on the world's periphery and semi-periphery have recently liberated themselves from various forms of autocracy and are desperately seeking to acquire the institutions of already established democracies; on the other, those advanced capitalist societies which have been practicing this form of political domination for some time are experiencing widespread disaffection with these very same institutions. The East and South want nothing more than an imitation of existing practices; the North and West are bored and disillusioned with them.

In both cases, normative democratic theory has been largely excluded from the process of deliberation and choice. Joshua Cohen and Joel Rogers revive this venerable tradition of critical thought and apply it to the (re-)design of democratic institutions – not by attempting to affect the nascent practices of South/Eastern democracies where one might expect that the uncertainties of the regime transition to provide the greatest window of opportunity, but by addressing the entrenched habits of North/Western democracies where one has every reason to suspect greater resistance to change. After all, it is 'we' who have won the Cold War and squelched obstreperous demands for a New International Economic Order. The 'end of history' beckons and 'they' must conform to our tried and proven formulas of economic and political liberalism! *N'est-ce pas?*

The Dilemmas of Reform

Institutional (re-)design is not an easy reform strategy to advocate or implement. It tends to be 'lumpy' and slow to produce its effects.

Unlike piecemeal improvements, its sheer ambitiousness provokes an almost instinctive negative reaction from the status quo – especially when its ethical justification or instrumental rationale has been extracted from a 'foreign' source and hence, by definition, must be antithetical to the 'domestic' culture. Most of all, it presumes that the existing arrangement it would replace is amenable to change. Those benefiting and victimized by it must somehow be willing to learn that there is another, better way of doing things and to accept the risk of paying the transaction and transformation costs for getting there. Revolutionaries (presumably) do not bother to make such petty calculations, given the magnitude of the anticipated benefits, but institutional reformists (prudently) should.

Independent of the merits of their proposal, Cohen and Rogers stand a reasonable chance of gaining a hearing for two reasons: one general, the other more specific to the polity that mainly concerns them. The very victory of capitalism/democracy over its opponents has not only eliminated all 'systemic' alternatives for the foreseeable future (I shall leave aside Islamic or other fundamentalisms on the grounds that they are only 'locally' plausible), but it has also shifted the grounds for evaluation. It will no longer be possible to justify practices by extrinsic criteria, i.e. isn't it true that our system works manifestly better than theirs? It will be increasingly necessary to satisfy internal criteria, i.e. does our system fulfil the expectations that its own citizens have about capitalism and democracy? The standards are likely to be much more demanding and the dissatisfactions correspondingly greater. Moreover, when compared to its (less) liberal capitalist-democratic brethren, the United States is a relatively poor performer. Mass communications, tourism, the balance of trade, the decline of the dollar, the quality of products, the stagnation of real wages – all of these are likely to drive home the message that Americans, despite their superior size and resource endowment, are doing worse than their North/Western neighbors. Whether the combination of these two factors will be sufficient to create an atmosphere of crisis that will make them willing to consider their long-entrenched practices amenable to institutional (re-)design is, I admit, problematic, but the moment seems more favorable for considering what a 'post-liberal democracy' might look like than at any time since the early 1930s.

The Merits of Cohen and Rogers's Proposal

Now to the merits of what Cohen and Rogers propose. They have chosen an unusual Archimedean point from which to lever change: the system of organized interests. Most reform movements in the past have focused on more public and apparently tractable institutions: electoral laws, party statutes, constituency size, apportionment criteria, legislative committee structure, executive prerogatives, civil service autonomy, etc. Interest associations are much less obvious components of modern democracy. They are more numerous and secretive, have evolved in complex historical trajectories, adopt a great variety of legal forms and perform an even greater variety of functions for their members. It is no accident that attempts to regulate 'lobbies' have been notoriously unsuccessful. In short, it is much harder to get a 'policy grip' on them – something I fear Cohen and Rogers have occasionally overlooked.

Which is not to say that I reject the notion that interest associations should be the focus of deliberate reform effort. Quite the contrary. I have argued at length (but not yet published) that there are very significant net gains to be made from improving what de Tocqueville called 'the art of association' – both from the normative perspective of democratic theory and for instrumental reasons of productivity and competitiveness.[1] So, by and large I accept those parts of their paper that stress the advantages of a well-designed system of interest associations, with some reservations about the transferability of lessons from European neocorporatism to the United States. Where I find myself in fairly strong disagreement is with the means they propose to accomplish these ends.

1. If I understand their proposal correctly (and there is some ambiguity on this crucial point), 'the state' would deliberate, certify what the appropriate interest system should be for each policy arena and put together an attractive package of incentives for each participating association. Not only does this presume an existing capacity for judicious consideration and neutral choice for which there is no evidence in the United States (and much rhetoric in their paper to the contrary), but the sheer complexity of making such decisions is mind-boggling. Leaving aside how policy arenas would be defined (and what would be done about those that are intersectoral or cross-cutting), the necessary information about the literally tens of thousands of potentially eligible associations would completely overload the legislature. Even if 'the final authority continues to rest with the more traditional, encompassing, territorially based systems of representation', there is no way that making such a volume of detailed choices could be described as 'a deliberative collective decision' embodying popular sovereignty.

Moreover, once the arenas had been set, the participants chosen and the state subsidies/exemptions allocated, there would be a powerful tendency toward 'locking in' the solution. How would new claimants be processed? What would be necessary to have a new policy arena declared? And how would derelict arenas be closed down? The necessary monitoring of these publicly vested interests would be considerable – and perhaps even more subject to oligarchic influences than the original choices. Cohen and Rogers mention briefly at one point the problem of sclerosis, but do nothing subsequently to allay my fears. All existing corporatisms, state and societal, have had to face serious difficulties with the fixity of their interest categories and the vestedness of their constituent organizations.

2. Cohen and Rogers barely mention what is the most important emerging property of Western interest systems, namely, the explosion of activity on the part of organizations that claim to represent 'causes' and 'rights': feminism, consumerism, environmentalism, pacificism, vegetarianism, animal protectionism, ethnicism (and sometimes, racism), familism, communitarianism, speciesism, and so forth. Presumably, some of these organizations might make it through the certification process, but they are not likely to be represented on all the issue arenas they would prefer. How are partisan/territorial representatives (whose election depends on the votes of these aroused people) going to justify refusing them access?

Moreover, it is not clear (to me) whether one can apply to them the same evaluative criteria of 'encompassingness', 'scope of responsibility', 'formality' and 'integrative capacity' that would be used to discriminate in favor of associations based on class/professional/sectoral interests. They are bringing to the political process a measure of 'other-regardingness' and 'principled conviction' that cannot be weighed (or bargained away) in the same fashion.

According to my reading, Cohen and Rogers are trying to ensure that class – capital and labor in their most encompassing organizational form – will continue to occupy a predominant role in the policy process, at the expense of more diversified sectoral and professional cleavages and against the rising tide of less 'productively' defined interests. I believe that the democratic political process has no normative grounds for imposing and, thereby, reifying a particular set of cleavages – unless and only as long as it is freely chosen by the citizenry. Whatever one thinks about the past (and future) role of class and class conflict in capitalist societies, most people would agree that to legislate its centrality is likely to be futile.

3. Which brings me to my third major objection. At various points in the essay, especially in the last section on 'Reforming a Liberal

Polity', Cohen and Rogers are manifestly less concerned with improving the quality of associability in the United States than with accomplishing specific policy objectives. To put it bluntly, they are trying to bring social democracy to the United States by the back door, when it has been unable to pass through the front (i.e. the electoral) door. Leaving aside my own personal preferences on the matter (which hardly differ from theirs), I believe that this is a major strategic error for any project of institutional (re-)design. No reform of this magnitude is likely to pass muster unless the citizenry is convinced (1) that the measures will produce a major net benefit, if possible for everyone; and (2) that they will not upset the existing distribution of power in ways that can prejudice future decisions. The Cohen and Rogers proposal makes some effort to overcome the first test, but fails the second. Defective as they may be, the US party system and electoral process have not produced a majority that supports such substantive policies, much less the class empowerment that would subsequently emerge from them. Given the entrenched nature of existing institutions, only a reform project that is more convincingly 'neutral' (but still significant) in its impact stands a chance of being enacted.

An Alternative Proposal for Reform

To all three of these objections, I have a proposed solution.[2] Cohen and Rogers must be aware of them since they had in hand, and cite, an unpublished article of mine on 'Corporative Democracy'.[3] First, let me stress the contrast between my proposal and theirs:

1. The obvious way to rid the state and the legislative process of the enormous burden of crafting the details of a reformed associative system is to hand it over to the people. An appropriate means for doing this would be to create a system of 'secondary citizenship', in which individuals would be issued vouchers at regular intervals for the support of associations and allowed to distribute them according to their own, self-assessed interests.[4] These vouchers would be exchangeable for public funds from the general budget. Only organizations accepting certain restrictions, e.g. internal democratic selection of leaders, transparency of finances, nonprofit-making activity, etc., would be eligible to receive vouchers and by so doing would be accorded the status of 'civic' or 'semi-public' institutions. This relatively simple measure would have the effect of channeling substantially greater resources into associations of all types and would also greatly reduce (but not completely eliminate) the existing inequalities in the

capacity for collective actions across social groups. The sum total of this distribution would automatically and indirectly 'redesign' the system of interest representation – without the need for detailed state intervention.[5]

2. My proposed voucher system would be open without discrimination to all existing and potential interests (provided they accept the limitations of semi-public status). It would not ensure the predominance of any specific line of cleavage – just equalize the conditions for associability across categories differing in initial resources, numbers, intensities, locations, etc. Citizens would choose which interests concerned them the most and which associations best represented them. Depending on the periodicity with which the vouchers were distributed, the whole system would be reasonably flexible, rewarding those that succeeded in identifying new concerns and punishing those that held on too long to outdated ones. Competition between voucher-seekers would be lively, which should improve the flow of communications about the pros and cons of rival associations and could even encourage a fair amount of increased deliberation and debate among citizens.

3. I believe the voucher system could convincingly be described as 'institutionally neutral' in that it is not manifestly intended to benefit any interest or cause. It certainly cannot be accused of being social democratic. No doubt, it would give some presently under-represented groups a better chance at self-organization, but no one can know for sure how citizens would distribute their vouchers until the experiment has actually been performed. Public opinion polls and, certainly, elections are not reliable guides. Initially, one can anticipate a certain amount of 'gaming' as individuals will hope to free-ride on others to cover their basic and more prosaic interests, but after several iterations a pattern should set in which will be a reliable indicator of what people are really concerned about. Frankly, I cannot assure the reader that such a scheme would generate all the productivity and competitiveness benefits claimed by Cohen and Rogers – although the general increase in the capacity of associations and their greater availability (and autonomy) for taking on publicly mandated tasks suggest this might be the case – but I am sure that such an institutional (re-)design would be more democratic for the citizenry and less burdensome for the political process.[6]

More Specifics about an Alternative Reform

The core of what I propose consists of three, closely intertwined, general reforms:

1. the establishment of a semi-public status for interest associations;

2. the financing of these associations through compulsory contributions; and

3. the distribution of these funds by means of citizen vouchers.

Before going into further details, let me stress that the proposed arrangement is not intended to be exclusive. Interest associations and social movements that wish to constitute themselves in ways proscribed by the rules of 'semi-publicness' or to finance themselves purely on the basis of voluntary payments by members would be free to opt out and yet remain active in the political system. They would not be allowed to receive the voucher-distributed contributions, however, unless they agreed to abide by certain public constraints on their procedures and behavior. Individuals could continue to join and to contribute to 'uncertified' and 'purely private' associations in whatever way and amount they preferred, although everyone (or, more accurately, all taxpayers) would have to pay a fixed amount for interest representation in general. All citizen-taxpayers could distribute their vouchers in varying proportions, but only to the semi-public associations of their choice.

In many continental European polities, the Chamber system for the representation of industrial, commercial, artisanal and/or agricultural interests has established a legal precedent for this form of associability, even if – as will be developed below – what is being proposed here differs from it in important ways. These compulsory arrangements for sectoral representation offer a good example of measures that were deliberately instigated – beginning in the Napoleonic period and later expanded and strengthened toward the end of the nineteenth century – to serve the dual purpose of overcoming intrinsic deficiencies in the 'art of association' for certain socioeconomic groups, and of fulfilling specific public policy goals. One could quarrel over whether it was democratic to establish these systems so selectively or whether their subsequent performance did meet public expectations – but the arrangements have persisted and not proven antithetical to other democratic institutions.

In the contemporary period, the most obviously analogous reforms have been the provision of public funding for political parties and the extension of guarantees that accused persons will be provided with adequate legal counsel. Vouchers, of course, have been proposed by a wide variety of advocates as a means for introducing competition and accountability into the provision of public service, and some experiments with them have already been carried out and evaluated. To my knowledge, however, this is the first suggestion that vouchers be used for the purpose of choosing and funding interest representatives.

Semi-public Status

Modern interest associations already perform a variety of public functions in the dual sense that they affect the public with their actions and that they carry out policies at the command (and sometimes, under the subsidization) of public authorities, but rarely are they required to operate under a specific public charter which specifies their rights and obligations. Chambers, of course, are the exception, but the liberal laws of the nineteenth and early twentieth centuries deliberately made it easy to form and register an association and, thereby, to acquire a 'juridical personality' in most Western polities. Trade unions, however, were a frequent exception and have been subjected to elaborate rules and procedures for attaining the coveted status of 'most representative' or 'exclusive bargaining agent'. In state corporatist systems, this reaches the extreme where the very categories of class or sectoral interest are pre-established by these authorities, who then licence only a single organization to occupy that space. The system proposed here would deliberately avoid the specification of any fixed category of representation based on class, status, sector or profession, but would leave the organizational boundaries surrounding these semi-public bodies to the initiative of interest entrepreneurs, the self-determination of social groups and the subsequent competition for vouchers from individual citizens.

The central idea behind the development of a semi-public status is to encourage associations to become better citizens, i.e. to treat each other on a more equal basis and to respect the interests of the public as a whole. This effort would involve nothing less than an attempt to establish a 'Charter of Rights and Obligations' for interest associations, which would, thereby, be recognized as 'secondary (organizational) citizens' – alongside the usual individual variety. It would be naive to suppose that merely imposing certain forms and rules would eo ipso make them into more 'fact-regarding, other-regarding and future-regarding'[7] actors. The legislation of most Western democracies is strewn with unsuccessful attempts to regulate lobbies and pressure groups. What is distinctive about this approach is the coupling of respect for certain conditions of self-organization and management with quite concrete incentives for support and a competitive process of allocation.

It would be presumptuous of me to specify here all the rights and obligations that might be included in such a Charter. This would require a great deal of comparative research into existing legislation, for much of what would be involved is probably already on the books in one way or another. The purpose served by bringing it together in one formalized 'status' and asking individual interest associations whether they would agree to abide by that specific package of rights and obligations would be to clarify ambiguities and jurisdictions – and to place eventual enforcement under a single, standard authority.

For purposes of illustration only, I could imagine the following general provisions:

1. A special registration procedure and title for all associations operating under the Charter that engage in the activity of interest representation/intermediation.

2. An assurance of access to public authorities concerning all deliberations relevant to legislation and implementation in their respective interest domains (*Vernehmlassungsverfahren* is the inimitable Swiss-German expression).

3. A guarantee of democratic procedures for the election of all executive officers and their accountability to the full membership, with provisions for the protection of minority rights.

4. A commitment to accept as members all individuals, firms, families, etc. whose interests fall within the association's self-defined domain of representation, without regard for partisan affiliation, gender, race, nationality, etc.

5. A prohibition against the advocacy of violence, racism and other forms of criminal behavior.

6. A commitment to full public disclosure of associational revenues and expenditures.

7. A prohibition against engaging in profit-making activities.

8. A prohibition against contributing to the financing of political parties, social movements or other interest associations (except those which are their members).

9. An assurance of capacity to participate directly in the implementation of public policies – even a presumption that relevant policies will be administered to the maximum feasible extent through associational channels.

10. A guarantee that public authorities will not intervene in the internal deliberations and choices of semi-public associations, except to ensure compliance with the above provisions of their status and the applicable sections of the civil and criminal codes.

11. Finally, permission to receive public funds, raised by obligatory contributions from citizens and distributed by voucher, in addition to funds raised voluntarily from members.

In my opinion, this list does not represent a massive set of new entitlements or constraints, but more a formalization and condensation of existing norms contained either in public legislation or in the private constitutions of most associations.

Obligatory Contributions

No one advocates the creation of a new tax lightly – especially in the face of neoliberal diatribes against fiscal obligations which are supposed to be already too high. But this proposal rests squarely on the need to develop a new method for financing interest intermediation which is independent of the ability and willingness of individual citizens to pay – and that means extracting resources involuntarily from all those who ultimately will benefit. It may be disguised under some other label: 'an associative contribution' or 'a representative donation', but it would still have to be a coercive levy.[8]

The contribution/tax should be extracted from everyone resident in a given territory, but not from firms or corporations, since they would be forced to pay twice and could, therefore, exert more influence over the resultant distribution of revenues (and would, in any case, pass on the cost to their consumers). Anyone who so wished could also give voluntarily to various causes, but this would not exempt them from the general 'representative donation'. Note that, by tolerating such a freedom, small and compact 'privileged groups' would still be more likely to attract disproportionate resources, since their members would continue to have greater incentives to give voluntarily in addition to the general levy. Nevertheless, given the large numbers involved, a very considerable evening out of resources across interest categories and passionate causes would be likely.

The most feasible manner for doing this would be to attach the obligation (and the voucher system) to the annual filing of income taxes – at least, in those countries where virtually all adult residents are required to file, if not to pay, such taxes. Indeed, in the interest of equity, those with such low revenue that it exempts them from paying income taxes could also be exempted from the representation levy, but they would still be empowered to distribute vouchers which would count toward determining which specific associations received money from the common fund.

Even if the amounts involved are quite small, it will not be easy to generate consent for such a measure. For example, if each taxpayer in the United States were required to contribute a modest $25, the tidy sum of almost $2.5 billion would be raised. That would fund a lot of associative action and, depending on how citizens 'spend' their vouchers, it could go a long way to rectifying existing inequities in organizational resources and systemic under-representation. What is important is to retain the low level of individual payments in order not to scare away potential supporters of the reform, but make the aggregate level of resources provided sufficient to compensate for persistent inequalities between interests. It is also essential to convince the public that such an arrangement would constitute an important extension of democratic rights – analogous to the previous extension of the franchise. This is where the voucher notion comes in.

Choice by Voucher

What pulls the entire scheme together is the mechanism of vouchers. These specially designated, non-transferable units of account could only be assigned to interest associations with a semi-public status, in proportions chosen by the individual citizen/taxpayer. Their value would be established by public policy at some uniform level ($25 per person in the above example) and there would be no way of avoiding paying for them, but the only cost to spending them would be the time and effort in getting acquainted with alternative recipients, plus the few moments it would take to check off boxes or fill in blanks.

There are many attractive features of vouchers in the domain of interest representation:

1. They would permit a relatively free expression of the multiplicity of each citizen's preferences, rather than confine them to one party list or a single candidate as do most territorially-based voting systems.

2. They allow for an easy resolution of the 'intensity problem' which has long plagued democratic theory, since their proportional distribution by individuals across associations should reflect how strongly each person feels about various interests.

3. They equalize the amount and sever the decision to contribute from the disparate command over resources that is intrinsic to the property system.

4. They offer no rational motive for waste or corruption since they cannot provide a direct or tangible benefit to the donor and can only be spent by certified associations for designated purposes.

5. In fact, they provide a very important incentive for reflection on the nature of one's interests and, as they are repeated over time, a virtually unique opportunity to evaluate the consequences of one's past choices.

6. They would, therefore, become a powerful mechanism for enforcing the accountability of existing associations since, if the behavior of their leaders differs too markedly from the preferences of those who spent their vouchers on them, citizens could transfer their vouchers elsewhere.

7. They make it relatively easy, not just to switch among existing rival conceptions of one's interest, but also to bring into existence previously latent groups that presently cannot make it over the initial organizational threshold.

8. Finally, they offer a means of extending the citizenship principle and the competitive core of democracy,[9] which neither makes immediate and strong demands on individuals, nor directly threatens the entrenched position of elites.

All of the above represent significant improvements over the present practices of electoral democracy and pluralist intermediation, in my judgment. What is perhaps not so clear is how the voucher system would dramatically improve the performance of the more corporatist systems. Most centrally, it eliminates the favorable and fixed designation accorded to class, sectoral or professional categories. With vouchers, all categories of interest and passion represented by associations with semi-public status stand the same hypothetical chance of attracting support, and no single organization would be granted a permanent monopoly over any specific domain. Granted some will receive more vouchers than others and that there are good arguments (to be explored below) in favor of encouraging the chances of more encompassing categories and more monopolistic associations, but even this degree of intentional rigging of the outcome could be upset if citizens persist in spending their vouchers elsewhere. Moreover, under the voucher system, contributors would not automatically become members. They would vote their vouchers and neither be compelled to join or to obey the association they had chosen. Granted that with the increased resources and salience that are likely to flow to them, associations will become more attractive sites for individual participation. The competition among organizations for vouchers may lead them to invest substantial amounts in convincing potential supporters, not just to spend their voucher on them, but to become regular members with a say in how the money from those vouchers will be spent.

As with many reform proposals, their eventual impact may hinge more on seemingly insignificant details than on their general conception. Space and a lack of familiarity with the implementation of previous voucher schemes in other areas leave me incapable of specifying thoroughly their *mode d'emploi* in this case, but I shall advance a few suggestions:

1. Vouchers would be administered jointly with the income tax, and would probably take the form of a set of questions and an accompanying brochure listing the eligible 'semi-public' associations.

2. Citizens could distribute their support among a limited number of associations (say, five) and small fractional distributions (say, less than 20 percent) would be discouraged for simplicity of accounting (and in an indirect effort to discourage the fragmentation of support).

3. Citizens would check off their preferred contributions from a list of semi-public associations. This list could be structured in such a way that organizations with larger memberships and more comprehensive interest domains would be listed first and perhaps in a special 'favored' section. More specialized and localized groups would be encouraged to join these encompassing and national groups – and, thereby, to receive their financial support indirectly from them, rather than by competing with them. Associations below a certain size in proven membership would be ineligible for inclusion in the national voucher system, although smaller thresholds could be established for regional or local systems (where the tax system is articulated in that fashion).

4. In the initial iterations of the scheme, existing associations which accepted semi-public status would naturally be at a considerable advantage. Their names and symbols are better known and they could expect a considerable loyalty from the membership they have already acquired. In one sense, this is desirable since it may lead these organizations to support the scheme in the first place; in another sense, it could have the undesirable effect of perpetuating organizations that are no longer representative. Eventually, the logic of competitive appeals for vouchers would have the effect of either revivifying moribund groups or displacing them by more authentic others.

5. Given the advantages of monopolistic (or highly oligopolistic) representation stressed in the corporatist literature, it is preferable that these be 'certified' and 'ratified' by the voucher mechanism. Other than the modest 'favors' accorded large and comprehensive associations that were sketched out in (3) above, no measures should be imposed to insure this outcome *à la* Mussolini and the *Carta del Lavoro*. If

overlapping and multiplicity within an interest category is established or emerges, there should be no authoritative fixing to correct it. What vouchers do permit is for bystanders, i.e. non-members but potential contributors, to have a say in whether such fragmentation is to persist. If they swing their voucher votes around in ways that differ from the entrenched behavior of militants, then the organizational structure may change and differences over the perception of interests and the pursuit of strategies will be worked out within associations rather than between them.

6. Citizens could also write in unlisted associations which, however, would receive the earmarked funds only if they accepted the conditions of semi-publicness and only if the write-ins exceeded some minimal amount, similar to the 5 percent threshold in the electoral laws of some countries.

7. Citizens/taxpayers who chose not to indicate a specific *déstinataire* or *déstinataires* would have their contributions distributed according to the distribution of preferences of the citizenry as a whole.

8. Non-citizens who pay taxes would also receive vouchers which they could offer to associations representing their interests. In distributing them, they would be exercising rights of citizenship that are currently denied them in the party, electoral and legislative arena.

9. The voucher funds would be distributed by the state tax collection agency automatically to all eligible associations every year, but the voucher selection system would only function every other year – partly to reduce the burden on individuals, but mainly to allow associations a sufficient time-horizon to adjust their policies and programs to changing group preferences and to protect them against momentary surges of enthusiasm or unpopularity.

10. Associations would be prohibited from 'bribing' citizens by simply offering to return to them some proportion of their vouchers in cash or direct services.

The Probable Advantages

I am convinced that, if implemented, this proposal with its three closely intertwined components of a semi-public status for associations, a compulsory mode of financing and a voucher system for distributing resources would represent a significant improvement over either pluralism or corporatism in the governance of modern democracies. Its implementation should lead to a dynamic and self-disciplining solution to the problem of resolving interest conflicts that would not require constant monitoring and intervention by the state, and that would not leave citizens at the mercy of an erratic and unjust marketplace. Central to that conception of a future stable and consensual order is the notion that it will depend on the continuous negotiation of a social contract – not one based on a class compromise among individuals signed by an invisible hand only, but one comprising a multitude of cleavages between groups, negotiated and implemented by visible and accountable organizations.

I have been deliberately silent on the substantive changes that would ensue from such a restructuring of interest politics. That there would be significant differences in *cui bono*, I am fully convinced, but I am not at all sure what they would be. In major part, this is because it is fundamentally 'unknowable' how citizens would express the scope and intensity of their true preferences if given the opportunity to do so at such a low cost and with such ease. Moreover, it is equally difficult to envisage how the other institutions of democracy – parties, movements, legislatures, local governments, etc. – would react to a more equal distribution of the organizational weapon in the hands of associations representing interests and passions. Hopefully, this ambiguity with regard to policy outputs and substantive outcomes will facilitate the implementation of the reforms – if only because many groups will see in it an attractive solution to their existing deficiencies and future aspirations, even if in the long run these solutions in the aggregate prove to be incompatible.

I am also aware that the appeal is 'unheroic'.[10] It advocates not 'strong' democracy, but 'weak' democracy. It makes no claim to return to a glorious past of direct and individual participation in public deliberations. It promises no future with civic-minded citizens exercising eternal vigilance over the public interest. Implicitly, it denies both these historical quests of democratic theory. It empowers organizations, not individuals; it initiates a process, not an end-state. It accepts the ubiquity of partial and private interests in modern society and rejects the possibility of an overriding general and public interest. In so doing, it affirms that 'only self-interests can counter self-interests', not nobler passions or an enlightened vanguard.[11]

Within these limitations, the proposed reforms focus on removing much (but not all) of the inequalities rooted in wealth, property and status that systematically discriminate between interest in our present democracies – not by eliminating them outright – but by controlling their effects. They would recognize and exploit persistent cleavages, and attempt to transform these differences in interest intensity into equivalences in organizational capacity. They would not attempt to extract more or better participation from the citizenry, but to make it easier for it to express its preferences. They would not seek harmony and concord 'beyond adversary democracy',[12] but establish a more equitable modus vivendi within it.

Notes

1. 'Corporative Democracy: Oxymoronic? Just Plain Moronic? or A Promising Way Out of the Present Impasse?', mimeo, Stanford University 1988.
2. I have several other objections, for which I have no constructive solutions of my own to propose. I will simply list them cryptically:

1. Cohen and Rogers seem oblivious to the international component of contemporary interest representation, despite their laudable sensitivity to the rising pressure of international competition;
2. Cohen and Rogers offer no reflections on how their proposed reforms would likely affect the existing party system and legislative process, the assumption being (I suppose) that both would remain unchanged;
3. Cohen and Rogers do not indicate how they would propose dealing with the demands for participation of, say, religious sects or patriotic groups on the grounds that they have an overriding ethical concern with virtually all substantive issue areas;
4. Cohen and Rogers, in their emphasis on 'artifactuality' (which I have also stressed in my work), do not indicate what its limits are and, therefore, what should be the extent to which existing 'natural' associations can be ignored and new ones should be encouraged and subsidized through public policy;
5. Cohen and Rogers do not address the critical 'agency question' and it is, therefore, difficult to imagine who would be sufficiently concerned to invest time and money in such a venture and what concrete steps and appeals would be necessary to bring about such a redesign of American democracy.

3. They did not, apparently, have my self-rejoinder in which I respond to my critics, some real and some anticipated: 'Some Second Thoughts about Corporative Democracy: Oxymoronic or Moronic, Promising or Problematic?', paper presented at the Conference on Competing Theories of Post-Liberal Democracy, University of Texas, Austin, 8–10 February 1991.
4. On reflection, it occurs to me that the Cohen and Rogers proposal does not once mention the concept of citizenship – a rather astonishing lapsus in a work of normative democratic theory. I am convinced that any viable institutional (re-)design should be aimed at expanding this crucial property intrinsic to all types of democracy. Not only would this engender a properly generic sense of empowerment, but it just might encourage individuals to utilize whatever powers are accorded to them in a more civic or other-regarding way.
5. Needless to say, by manipulating the details of such a reform – raising the threshold, giving premiums to more encompassing organizations, insisting on meeting more 'public' criteria, etc. – it would be possible to steer the system in different directions. Setting these criteria is what would be left to the collective deliberation of 'traditional' partisan-cum-territorial representatives in each specific polity. NB: This reform would be relatively easy to operate at different levels of aggregation: municipality, county, state, nation; whereas, the complexity of choice in the Cohen and Rogers one would increase exponentially if it were so implemented.
6. Readers who would like additional information about this proposal are invited

to write to me c/o Department of Political Science, Stanford University, Stanford, California 94305–2044.

7. For this 'trilogy' of types of regardingness I am indebted to Claus Offe.

8. The tax would be novel, but the amounts of revenue transferred to interest associations might not be. Since first presenting this idea in Norway several years ago, I have become increasingly aware of the very substantial sums that some Continental European governments provide as subsidies to specific organizations – ostensibly because they are accomplishing some public purpose. Norway, Spain and France are three cases in point, even if the amounts involved are rarely publicized. In my view, this subsidization of civil society is much less democratic than the one that I propose since the criteria used to determine eligibility are secret, bureaucratic and non-competitive; whereas, under a voucher-based scheme, this would all take place publicly and accountably, and would be accompanied by specific binding obligations to behave as 'secondary citizens'. If the countries that are presently subsidizing associations by clandestine means would agree to stop these practices, they might be able to switch to a better arrangement at virtually no cost!

9. Cf. my earlier essay, 'Democratic Theory and Neo-Corporatist Practice', *Social Research*, vol. 50, no. 4 (Winter 1983), pp. 885–928, where the role of competitiveness is evaluated along with such other normative standards for democracy as participation, access, responsiveness and accountability.

10. Terry Karl put it more exactly and brutally in our discussions: 'It lacks sex appeal.'

11. The discerning reader will see the hand of Bernard Barber behind these remarks. It was my critical reading of his *Strong Democracy: Participatory Politics for a New Age* (Berkeley: University of California Press 1984) that got me started and I have considered his provocative book as a useful foil throughout my subsequent musings.

12. With apologies to my former colleague, Jane Mansbridge, and her *Beyond Adversary Democracy*, New York: Basic Books 1980.

8

Inclusion and Secession:
Questions on the Boundaries of Associative Democracy
Wolfgang Streeck

Undoubtedly, associative democracy, or democratic corporatism, is about collective political rights. But it involves also, and arguably more importantly, the utilization of publicly regulated self-governance of groups for the creation and enforcement of *collective obligations*. Obligations, collective just as individual, are relations to and within a *community* that can lay claim to the loyalty and resources of its 'members'; indeed their effective presence constitutes the most important evidence for the existence of a socially integrated society. The project of associative democracy may therefore be properly characterized as one of *political reconstruction of community*, and it is primarily for this reason – not simply because it assigns a privileged place to organized collective action – that it can rightly regard itself as an attempt to transcend the limits of liberalism.

Social groups, or 'factions', in an associative democracy are cajoled into accepting collective obligations by institutional arrangements that permit them to pursue particularistic interests at the risk of finding them transformed in the process, as a result of carefully designed constraints for participating groups to expose their initial interest definitions to inter- and intragroup deliberation. For example, associative democracies place a premium on the construction by interest groups of strong 'private interest governments'[1] that have an incentive to sort out 'errant' interest perceptions and ensure predictable and cooperative behavior of their constituents, thereby stabilizing the expectations of interlocutor groups. Such arrangements, however, can work only if a number of conditions are met. Among the most important is that the groups in question be *both able and willing* to make use of the opportunities offered to them by associative democracy and, in the act, accept the constraints it imposes on them – if not as welcome assistance in a collective search for a more rational definition

of self-interest, then at least as an inevitable price to be paid for the
benefits of participation.

It appears to me that Cohen and Rogers are quite attentive to
the requirement for associative democracy of strong and balanced
capacities of groups to act collectively; this subject they address in their
discussion of group 'artifaction'. But at least as important is the need
for groups *being willing* to subject their initial preferences, with uncertain outcomes, to the kind of institutional laundering that the
authors have in mind for them and that may result in an 'enlightened'
definition of interest which includes collective obligations in addition
to collective rights. This latter theme appears undeveloped, and
surprisingly so, given its obvious relevance to democratic theory.[2]
What happens if a social interest refuses to organize as a group interest
and set up a private interest government, thereby avoiding the laundry
process which associative democracy holds in store for it? The
practical importance of this question is illustrated by the strange fact,
sometimes remarked on in the neocorporatist literature on 'political
exchange' and incomes policy, that employers may *draw political
strength from organizational weakness* – that is, from narrowly
limiting the capacity of their interest organizations to negotiate collective understandings on their behalf that would override 'market
forces'.[3] Related problems concern how associative democracy deals
with interests that extend beyond its territorial or functional domain;
that refuse to identify with the community that such democracy
intends to construct; or that prefer to organize themselves into a larger,
more encompassing identity, which is less likely to generate burdensome obligations.

In a sense, what is at issue here is *exit from collective citizenship*,
where the matter at stake is *not rights lost, but obligations avoided*.
Centrally important this becomes if and to the extent that some groups
find it easier than others to exit and do without collective voice.
Negotiating collective obligations with groups that can afford, or even
have an incentive, to leave the political community is bound to be
difficult; at the very least, the outcome is likely to be biased against less
mobile groups, whose interest in a successful political reconstruction
of community is bound to be much more intense.

It can easily be seen what this ultimately implies: that in order to
have associative democracy at all, exit from collective citizenship must
be foreclosed in particular for groups commanding resources that are
crucial for building a successful community. Associative democracy
presupposes a *boundary* around the society in and with which it is to
be built – in the same way in which it presupposes internal boundaries

between collectively acting groups. Critical collectivities are likely to be willing to organize and participate only to the extent that they have reason to perceive themselves as members of a 'community of fate' that they cannot leave and that they must improve if they want to improve themselves. *Democratic inclusion, that is, may require an effective prohibition on voluntary self-exclusion.* How can such a prohibition be enforced? How can it be legitimated, if at all, in democratic theory? Most fundamentally, what is the relevant community, or the 'society', within which the project of an associative democracy expects to create effective and legitimate collective obligations and from which exit would have to be made difficult for powerful social groups?

Cohen and Rogers, I am afraid, implicitly answer the latter question by referring us to the nation-state. Their essay, while pathbreaking in many other respects, is remarkably conventional here, adhering, together with the mainstream of today's sociology and political science, to the nineteenth-century tradition of conceiving of 'the society' as of a nation bounded by a national state.[4] In my view, this raises at least two problems, one concerning democracy and the other the capacity of modern political communities to govern their citizens under conditions of interdependence and internationalization. As to the former, if the background model of an associative-democratic political community is indeed the nation-state, then it is clear that its boundaries cannot themselves be drawn democratically. Nation-states have always claimed a right to force some of their citizens to remain just that, if need be against their express desire – see, for example, the American Civil War. The national state offers participation, if at all, to a citizenry that is territorially and functionally captive – in fact, often precisely in compensation for a strong, powerfully enforced prohibition on secession. The question 'faction of what?' must be settled before any faction can be democratically accommodated or incorporated.

Decisions on inclusion in or self-exclusion from a polity raise moral puzzles that democratic theory appears unable to address. The example of the referendum in Denmark on the Maastricht Treaty to deepen the European Community is instructive. Interestingly enough, the negative Danish vote can be seen as both a decision to secede (from a European Community that is advancing toward 'political union') and a refusal to join (the expanded Community). Either way, it may be interpreted as a refusal to pay for the benefits of Community membership by surrendering formal national 'sovereignty' to a strengthened supranational polity, endowing it with a capacity to make its richer members contribute to more equitable conditions for the poorer ones. What for the Danes may have been a legitimate

exercise of democratic self-determination is therefore likely to appear
to the Greeks and the Portuguese as a selfish attempt to free-ride on the
benefits of integration and seek protection from democratically
imposed collective obligations. What democracy is, in other words,
and where it is in place, depends on where one draws the boundaries.
Once that is done, democratic theory can go to work and debate questions like who is entitled to become a citizen; indeed, as we have
pointed out, this is a subject that liberals cherish. On how to draw the
boundaries, however, and on how one can be legitimately *required* to
become or remain a citizen *even if one does not want to*, and on what
grounds, modern theories of democracy seem to offer little guidance.

Before I go on to apply this line of reasoning to associative democracy in particular, I would like to elaborate a little on the democratic
significance of boundaries, narrow and encompassing, drawing
again on Europe and the changing position of nation-states within it.
Taken by itself, a country like Sweden is a highly successful political
community that has learned during the twentieth century to impose
effective obligations on its stronger members to assist the weak,
making it probably the most egalitarian industrial society on earth. But
what if, for whatever reason, the *relevant society* for Swedes today
was Europe as a whole and if this was to force their country, as it
seems to at present, to join the European Community? The moment
it joined, Sweden would turn into one of the most privileged regions
in a political-territorial entity whose regional inequalities by far
exceed those of the United States. Indeed, Swedish accession to
the Community would increase those inequalities further, making
it highly likely that Swedish foreign policy will face strong pressure
for higher Community taxes on rich member countries and large
transfers from rich to poor members. Like other rich countries in
the Community, Sweden may then come to favor constitutionalized
rules of the European political game which strictly limit the capacity of
Community institutions for redistributive politics.

Moreover, for various reasons, inequality within Sweden can also
be expected to rise as a result of accession, if only because privileged
domestic groups will have more opportunities for exit from national
obligations or will be able to transfer their interests to the weaker
polity of Europe as a whole; in a perspective, that is, in which the
relevant society is Sweden, accession would undermine democracy. On
the other hand, if the frame of reference is Europe, Swedish accession is
essential for a democratic redistributive politics to be possible, and not
joining would be selfish and particularistic, even though the domestic
'bite' of European democratic institutions will for long remain weaker

than that of Swedish institutions. My point here is that democratic theory is unable to adjudicate between these positions because it assumes that societal boundaries and social identities are settled, essentially in the form of the nation-state. Where the latter loses its plausibility, so, it seems, does democratic theory.

As to associative democracy specifically, not only can it not escape the old question of who 'belongs to' the political community and to what extent, but it is faced with a more demanding, radicalized version of it: how can groups of citizens be *required to organize and bargain in good faith* even though exit or non-entry may offer them a higher payoff? What social groups and what areas of social life can associative democracy mandate to be 'corporatized'? The problem as such is certainly not new, ultimately referring back to the relationship between democracy on the one hand, and the constitutional protection of liberty, privacy and property on the other. But whereas in the past this could essentially be framed as a *normative* question, in the context of constructing associative democracy today it seems to turn primarily into a *technical* problem, given the declining capacities of governments under permeable national boundaries to prevent crucial groups or functions from exiting from national domains and jurisdictions. This is the second question I mentioned above and to which I now turn.

Associative democracy is about socially responsible self-governance of functional groups. But underlying this idea is an image of 'complete' sets of social functions nested into national states, of coterminous territorial and functional boundaries, and of boundaries that are difficult to cross. There are many indications that assumptions like these are outdated and that a more adequate imagery would be one of a 'variable geometry' of social systems and subsystems – national, international and supranational – with different functional areas organized at different levels and with a variety of frames of reference between which social actors may freely switch in pursuit of their objectives and interests.[5] In such a world, nations cease to be communities of fate for important groups of citizens and for the performance of essential socioeconomic functions, and the political capacities of democracy, including democratic control over the forms of organized expression of group interests, are no longer ensured by coterminacy of functional domains. Domestic orders that lose their functional autarky can no longer freely organize and reorganize themselves democratically: in important respects, they will be shaped by forces outside of them and beyond the reach of their constitutional machinery for collective deliberation of interests. As the internal structures of political communities are increasingly conditioned by the emigration, or the possibility of emigration, of vital functions and functional groups to larger systems, the fundamental compact underlying associative democracy – the provision of collective political status to groups in exchange for their acceptance of a socially sustainable re-definition of their interests – becomes less and less possible or more and more biased toward those that can afford to move out.

To be sure, this is not just speculation. In an internationally integrated and, on this account, deregulated capital market, countries may attract investment capital by offering money-holders conditions exceeding those offered by other countries. But this is quite different from binding capital into negotiated national economies, in tripartite bargaining arrangements involving an associationally organized, 'corporatized' investment function constituted, like labor, as a 'faction' of a national society. For capital to be interested in exercising voice in this way at the national level, it must in some important respect be confined inside national economies – if not by exchange and capital controls enforced by the police and the courts, then by cultural and logistical barriers, high transaction costs in international markets, absence of suitable instruments for international investment, and so forth. These conditions, however, ended forever with the various 'big bangs' in world financial markets in the late 1970s and early 1980s, and it is not by accident that this coincided with the demise of the systems of 'political exchange', neocorporatist concertation and Keynesian labor-inclusive macroeconomic management, which had grown up in many developed industrial countries in the postwar era.

With capital benefiting from unbounded opportunities to expatriate its interests into the larger, less socially integrated and politically regulated circuit of the world economy – or to countries like the United States whose financial markets offered it higher and safer returns than industrial investment elsewhere – the very substance of political-economic bargaining in the 'bargained economies' of the West changed fundamentally. What in the past resulted, at least sometimes, in an imposition of social obligations on capital in exchange for labor and state cooperation with the requirements of accumulation, now began to generate obligations for the less mobile to behave in line with the need to attract and attach capital interests to their respective national economy. What came to be known as 'supply side policies' in the 1980s in effect replaced obligations for capital with incentives and substituted the voluntarism of the market for political regulation. With capital able and ready to leave, and with governments having lost the capacity to tax capital for full employment through a 'going rate' of inflation, monetary stability became the foremost economic objective even in the 'bargained economies' of Western Europe.

By and large, what we witnessed in the 1980s was the failure of ambitious attempts to impose collective self-discipline on capital as a socially organized functional group and the emigration of capital from national politics, from the nationally based bargained economy, into larger systems reigned by 'market forces'. Might this have been otherwise? The French socialist government between 1981 and 1983 tried to stop the emigration of French capital by deploying the historically accumulated enforcement capacity of what is arguably the most sophisticated bureaucratic state apparatus – with disastrous effect. Indeed, tendencies toward exit from democratic politics appear to be widespread and can be observed among many factions and functions other than capital, sometimes in response to and modeled on the emigration of the investment function, and reinforcing it. Often, exit takes the form of *domestic secession*, or *internal emigration*, triggered, or at least ideologically supported, by highly calculative, economistic, 'neoclassical' perceptions of a group's 'rational' interest: Italy, for example, where the prosperous regions of the North are increasingly less willing to support a redistributive politics that subsidizes the South; or, of course, the United States, where the suburbs refuse to pay for the inner cities, the pensioners for the schools, the healthy for the sick, and so on and so forth.

What we seem to observe here is a tendency toward *subnational fragmentation* of identities and interest definitions, with basically the same effects on the policy as internationalization: refusal of groups to participate in democratic politics as long as it may impose obligations on them, often enough in the name of democracy defined as a basic human right to the free use of one's resources and as an entitlement to a voluntaristic construction of society where social constraints are replaced with rational choices. How can one, in the face of this, be other than deeply pessimistic about the prospects of a move toward an associative version of democracy? How can a society that aspires to become such a democracy hope to rein in the new particularisms, international and subnational, and into what? How can it force its 'factional' interests to participate in collective democracy if the community that such democracy is to build is not perceived by them as theirs? If nationalism in its various forms, from acceptance of the 'necessary sacrifices' in wartime to simple tribal sympathy for people who are 'our kind', is increasingly less available as a vehicle for identification and acceptance of social responsibility, what can take its place? Can associative democracy restore a functionally complete political community with a boundary around it, which could stop the exodus from democratic politics and collective social obligations? Or does it not rather presuppose the existence of such a community is at its end if that presupposition is found not to be borne out by the real world?

To add to the problem, it is not just emigration, external or internal, that may frustrate associative democracy but also, and importantly, *immigration*. Open societies in a world of high mobility tend to be abandoned at the top and adopted at the bottom. Either way, loss of control by the state over a society's borders will tend to move the political economy away from collective negotiations and toward the market. As the effective supply of poor immigrants and cheap labor becomes indefinite, collective organization and participation will tend to turn into a tool for the indigenous citizenry to defend what will then have become particularistic economic privileges; as a consequence, associative democracy will cease to be democratic. Often, it may become de facto limited to the 'primary sector' of an economy and will otherwise be abandoned in favor of a more 'flexible' market order, thus preventing its being used by 'outsiders' to exploit the indigenous community by imposing social obligations on it to take care of mobile strangers. Once this has happened, a 'free market' will begin to look attractive.

Associative democracy, it would appear, can deal with diversity as long as it is held together by a sense of common fate, of inescapable and fundamentally involuntary mutuality – as long, in other words, as it is *diversity within the same society*. Associative democracy cannot, however, overcome the suspicion among the less mobile, the 'locals', that those who freely choose to join them are attracted, not by a sense of 'belonging' and a willingness to accept the long-term commitments that define a common civil society, but by the material benefits – for example, social assistance or a high minimum wage and publicly sub-sidized opportunities for human capital formation – the community has obliged itself to provide to its less fortunate members. *Nota bene*, its *members*. No community, and *especially not* a democratic one, can afford – for both economic and political reasons – to treat more than a few non-members as though they were members. Instead of collective obligations, life chances in a society without borders are, and can only be determined by the market – which treats citizens as though they were non-citizens, and in this sense offers equal treatment to both. No other order can do this. Without stable borders, which by itself it will find hard to supply, associative democracy cannot be stable.

Notes

1. See W. Streeck and P. C. Schmitter, 'Community, Market, State – and Associations? The Prospective Contribution of Interest Governance to Social Order', *European Sociological Review* 1 (1985), pp. 119–38.

2. Of course, since the first problem deals with enabling groups to fight for collective rights, it is the more comfortable of the two and easier to treat in a conventional democratic theory discourse. The second problem, addressing primarily the generation of obligations, is by far the trickier one.

3. See W. Streeck, 'Interest Heterogeneity and Organizing Capacity: Two Class Logics of Collective Action?' in *Political Choice: Institutions, Rules, and the Limits of Rationality*, ed. R. M. Czada and A. Windhoff-Heretier, Boulder, CO: Westview 1991, pp. 161–98. See also W. Streeck and P. C. Schmitter, 'From National Corporatism to Transnational Pluralism: Organized Interests in the Single European Market', *Politics & Society* 19 (1991), pp. 133–64. Both in W. Streeck, *Social Institutions and Economic Performance: Studies of Industrial Relations in Advanced Capitalist Economies*, London and Newbury Park, CA: Sage 1992.

4. For an early, highly perceptive insight in the limitations of this view, see E. Durkheim, *The Division of Labor in Society*, New York: Free Press 1984, where he explains what he sees an increasing respect for international law in Europe by the fact that European nations have become 'much less independent of one another. This is because in certain respects they are all part of the same society, still incohesive, it is true, but one becoming increasingly conscious of itself' (pp. 76f.)

5. The concept of 'variable geometry' was first used, not surprisingly, to characterize the territorially and functionally uneven progress of European integration, with a set of 'excentric', functionally specific arrangements with differing national participation increasingly superseding the original project of a concentric, consolidated, functionally diffuse European superstate.

9

On Architectural Syncretism

Ira Katznelson

'Secondary Associations and Democratic Governance' is a work of many virtues of analysis and advocacy, not least its marriage of institutionalism and (analytical and normative) democratic theory. At a time when academic political studies and the craft of political practice are impoverished by the absence of robust ties connecting politics, theory and policy, Cohen and Rogers's insistence that they must be joined is immensely welcome. Their text audaciously combines political and policy analysis, doctrinal invention and a willingness to traverse ordinarily distinct disciplines and political impulses while suggesting how to build alliances for meaningful political change. Further, they keenly understand that not just the rate of political participation, but its modes and densities are vital for both a healthy democratic politics and for the resurgence of the Left at a time of disillusion, disappointment and defeat.

It is important that we appreciate not only the content of Cohen and Rogers's arguments, but the distinctive qualities of their discourse. Normative political theory, as they note, since *A Theory of Justice* burst on the scene has been obsessed with questions of doctrine without betraying much interest at all in the institutional requirements or feasibility of their clusters of propositions and ideas about how to conduct political life. Reciprocally, students of comparative and US politics rarely take the work of political theorists seriously. Cohen and Rogers point us, instead, toward an engagement of theory and institutions, on the understanding that any meaningful vision of democracy requires democratic institutions devoted to negotiation, compromise, arbitration and provisional outcomes. Attention to institutions, of course, requires a shift in priority from principles to history, context and arrangements to imperfectly manage and adjudicate both the passions and the interests. In a democracy that realizes democratic ideals, all citizens, they underscore, must have access to these institutions and processes for the representation of interests.

Precisely because I believe these themes to be so fundamental, I should like to highlight qualities of opacity in the essay as a way of drawing attention to steps too hastily taken, to arguments left unclarified and to provocative silences. By inquiring about the kind of project entailed by the essay's proposals, as well as aspects of the current situation to which its design speaks, I should like to advance their project by extending the range of issues with which they deal.

Cohen and Rogers adopt the role of institutional architects; their building materials are drawn from both liberalism and socialism – especially the social democratic variant. Architects know, of course, that syncretism may produce beauty or ugliness, sturdy or flimsy structures, depending on both the quality of the blueprints and the decisions taken about how to make them work together. Cohen and Rogers know that we cannot hope to rebuild the Left without utilizing both liberalism and socialism to set goals, find means and leave room for situational adjustments. Whether the blueprints and materials they utilize produce beautiful and sturdy structures, however, depends on the manner in which they are to be used, sensitivity to intrinsic difficulties in their deployment and the mechanisms adopted to secure their joining.

I

Cohen and Rogers propose instruments with which to build a liberal regime with less institutional bias against a (refurbished) social democratic project than has existed within postwar US interest group pluralism, various European corporatisms and, even more certainly, non-liberal and non-democratic regimes. They do so by proposing to utilize public authority to provide incentives for a more robust and democratic associational sector with characteristics 'less sharply in tension with the norms of democratic governance'. The essay's commitments are to democratic processes and more egalitarian outcomes: quite obviously, the selection of the concrete examples of active labor markets, an incomes policy and environmental initiatives is not randomly drawn. Cohen and Rogers advance this attractive program at the juncture of liberalism and social democracy at a time when, not only but especially in the United States, the union and party institutions, as well as underlying ideas and persuasions, which have sustained the social democratic impulse within liberal democracies since World War II, are in very deep trouble. In these circumstances, their program gains urgency from the growing class bias of interest representation and from an understanding that the renewal of the Left depends on whether it is possible to navigate the site where liberalism and socialism meet.

The difficulties faced in joining liberalism and social democracy, however, are not limited to current events, and they must not be gainsaid. Not just Cohen and Rogers, of course, but a host of others, including John Stuart Mill, John Dewey, Bertrand Russell, Carlo Rosselli, Noberto Bobbio, Michael Walzer and Jorge Castaneda, have sought to marry liberalism and socialism (albeit on different terms) but, alas for those of us who are persuaded this liaison is the only possible basis we possess for a decent politics and society, it cannot really be said that their efforts have managed persuasively to weaken the tough-minded judgment of critics of this enterprise of varying ideological hues, including Perry Anderson, that 'liberal socialism reveals itself to be an unstable compound: the two elements of liberalism and socialism, after seeming to attract one another, end by separating out, and in the same chemical process the liberalism moves toward conservatism.'[1] Claims made for liberal socialism, in the main, have been more appealing for their social and political values than successful in their staying power or their capacity to fashion secure bulwarks against far less appealing options. Moreover, to the extent that liberalism is relatively thin, procedural, individualist, simply libertarian and indifferent to class structure; and to the extent that social democracy shares in the thick socialism of a Marxism that is consequentialist in its political morality, monistic in its understanding of interests and human nature and utopian in its expectations for the elimination of scarcity, liberalism and social democracy are incompatible. Not surprisingly, to this day the ordinary language of party competition in many Western countries treats liberals and social democrats as actors with incongruous values and aspirations.

Dating from the late nineteenth and early twentieth centuries the English 'new liberalism' of T. H. Green, Hobhouse and Hobson, and from decisions by social democrats to participate, however provisionally, in normal bourgeois politics, liberalism (having been made social) and social democracy (having been inserted within liberal premises) have been able to work out various forms of accommodation. These have been based on the domestication of class conflict, its canalization within unions and parties through the involvement of working-class actors, and the institutional creativity of welfare states which have incorporated and transcended class outlooks and have been legitimated on the basis of both liberal and social democratic world-views. This modus vivendi was most fully accomplished in the various 'postwar settlements', which are in such trouble today.

By their focus on democracy, Cohen and Rogers recognize that an attractive joining of liberalism and socialism must nestle the objectives and practices of the latter within a hierarchy dominated by the former. In this sense they are liberal socialists rather than social liberals. It is worth underscoring that while this kind of marriage of liberalism and social democracy may be desirable normatively, and while instrumentally it may be the only game in town, the thin imperatives of liberalism and the thick temptations of strong socialism have not disappeared. Thus, the relationship between liberalism and social democracy always hovers between mutual constitution and mutual threat.

II

Cohen and Rogers sidestep these questions by focusing on organizational engineering and by stretching 'democracy' to cover them over in an effort to fix the institutions of the US regime to make more possible the emergence of social democracy as a roughly coequal partner for liberalism. The authors suggest there may be topics, such as property rights, which they have chosen not to address, and which they think are intrinsically more important and more consequential for the realization of their objectives than those that focus on group life and political participation. Well and good, but at least two consequences follow from this. A resolution of the tension in the relationship between liberalism and social democracy appears more amenable to a relatively frictionless institutional invention than it possibly can be. Even more important, the essay gives the misleading impression that in the process of institutional design, all the relevant actors – whom they treat in terms of civil society as a whole – share a common ranking of goals, values and ideals, at least with respect to what might be called constitutional questions. Class and other markers of difference disappear into their discourse of democracy. This implicit tone and claim of consensus is not credible within the field of play defined by the complex relationship of liberalism and social democracy, let alone if we take any account of other political proclivities and their supporters. Democracy as a set of norms and practices thus manages to render tenebrous important bases of contest and conflict.

The essay's opaque treatment of state capacity is a case in point. The authors make 'competent government' one of the six conditions of democracy because the means to efficient performance are 'needed to maintain public confidence in the democratic process'. This is a remarkably bland discussion of a subject that has sharply divided the liberal and social democratic traditions. Liberals, of course, fear a despotic state (whether or not controlled by majorities) and act to limit its hubris; social democrats have sought to use the state as a counterweight to the powers of capital. Controversy about the advantages and dangers of capable states in the space between the minimum required for order and the regularity of transactions on the one side, and totalistic conceptions on the other, is as fundamental as property-centered questions to the tensions between liberalism and social democracy, yet here it is enfolded in an implicit consensualism about values. Just as Cohen and Rogers elide the hard issues about property rights and distributions, so they avoid taking a position on the key qualities of modern states and apprehensions about them.

The essay's audience appears to be scholars and activists who share the authors' goals, but with regard to the basic doctrinal and practical themes of property and sovereignty, these are equivocal. Further, the essay is written as if everyone not only should share its values, but do. It manages this feat by approaching democracy in terms narrower than often obtain on the Left (by its silences about capitalism and production-based limits to political democracy), but broader than the usual liberal minimum (by its stress on distributive equity). In the absence of a sustained discussion of the choices entailed by the position they take, the status of the definition of the six conditions of democracy enumerated by Cohen and Rogers is not clear. Is this precisely the program the authors would prefer in relatively unconstrained circumstances, what they think is the best available set of goals within the constraints of US political development and discourse, or something in between?

The status of the US case within the larger Western universe of capitalist democracies, moreover, is a tandem unaddressed subject. Do the authors seek to define a democracy of strengthened secondary associations for all these countries or just for the United States? Would they prefer to see what might be called the pluralist-corporatism they propose supplant more conventional tripartite corporatism (because it is limited by a narrow definition of interests and confers monopoly privileges on a tiny number of associational possibilities) even in circumstances where such arrangements have favored the Left? Or is the scheme one we have to accept, because none better is available within the realistic limits established in countries without corporatism and with weak, or virtually nonexistent, social democratic party and union institutions, with the United States being the lead-case of this kind? Put another way, what is the balance between the normative and instrumental torques of the paper? While the movement between democratic theory and US case illustrations provides a most welcome, and unusual, combination, it also obscures precisely these issues. The sui generis treatment of the United States necessarily leaves these questions open; but the failure to grapple with them is more than a problem for the clarity of the argument because it also impedes the potential political appeal of the program.

Not unrelated is the puzzle of how Cohen and Rogers view the status of the labor movement and, with it, orthodox conceptions of the significance, and signification, of class. Can there be any doubt that one of the main motivations for their essay is the erosion of labor strength – whether measured in terms of scale, scope or power – in the West generally and in the United States in particular (where today, about the same proportion of the active labor force belongs to unions as on the eve of the passage of the Wagner Act)? Yet there is a tension (even a contradiction?) in the essay between the way its proposals aim at the resurrection of organized labor – this is especially clear in the illustrations of associational democracy in practice with respect to economic regulation – and the manner in which its discussion significantly seeks to broaden the definition and bases of groups that are structured into political life as mediating locales between civil society and the state. Old Left, old-fashioned pluralist, new social movement and postmodern conceptions vie uneasily. Can we ride these horses simultaneously? Which types of group outcome, consistent with which of these formulations, should state-based incentives promote? More narrowly, what is the status of labor with respect to other potential bases of association? Does the resolution of such matters depend on a tacit or explicit model of social structure and interests, whether based on a single axis or multidimensional axes of domination and inequality, or will the free play of the associational market decide them? These, of course, are some of the most contentious questions within social science and social theory today as well as for political practice. Does it really make sense for policy engineering to skirt them? Won't these conundrums catch up with us later?

Even at the essay's most expansive moments with regard to the range of associations it would seek to promote, it is limited to instrumental groupings contesting divisible issues. In this respect, the paper reproduces a weakness shared by both the liberal and social democratic traditions, which might be characterized either as the inability or unwillingness to deal with nondivisible issues, which concern culture, communities and incommensurable moral dilemmas.

At a time when, for better or worse, cultural politics frequently overwhelms more economy- and distribution-centered issues, how would the prescribed associational democracy deal with matters of fragmented and heterogeneous culture and morality? It simply will not do in an age of feminist, ethnic and nationalist assertion to limit the scope of our politics to the kinds of themes the 'old' Left found most congenial. Does not associational life bear on the more multiple bases of identity and interest the Left has come, not without difficulty, to recognize and credit?

Put differently, the suggestive centerpiece of 'Secondary Associations and Democratic Governance' is the notion that the current organization of interests in US society is far too skewed and limited to make democracy substantive and robust for all citizens. The state is invoked not as an actor with interests or biases of its own, but as an agent of the rectification of these unequal resources. Yet, from another angle of vision, the more vibrant nexus of organizations and interest groups Cohen and Rogers propose would have the effect of both narrowing and privileging some forms of political identity over others. Such is the case in part because any system of interest representation – whether a non-hierarchical, non-compulsory pluralism or a hierarchical, compulsory corporatism, or the scheme of associative democracy they advance – necessarily privileges some groups and preferences over others and in part because the specific vehicles for interest representation they suggest demonstrate substantive (not just procedural) preferences. The result appears to be a narrowing of politics in the name of an extension of procedural democracy.

Finally, there is a worrying lack of precision about how Cohen and Rogers think the appealing institutional design they wish to construct could, would or should come into existence under popular democratic auspices. If the associational democracy they covet in fact is grounded in a broad democratic consensus, as they seem to imply, its instantiation should only be a matter of the dissemination of information and a process of persuasion. But if Cohen and Rogers's proposals do entail a radical redistribution of individual and group capacities, as in fact they do, then how, under current conditions of bias, do they expect that the transitional leap could be accomplished by democratic means? If their goals require the use of public authority to restructure the organization of civil society for political ends, then how can the divisions between constitutional and ideological issues, and between durable structures and situational majorities, be identified, defended and maintained? And who is to do the judging, as in 'if it were judged to be desirable for unions to be more encompassing . . . '?

Note

1. Perry Anderson, 'The Affinities of Noberto Bobbio', *New Left Review* 170 (July/August 1988), p. 36.

An Institutional Critique of Associative Democracy

Ellen M. Immergut

Joshua Cohen and Joel Rogers articulate a vision of associative democracy that aims to fuse democracy and group representation. They hope to overcome current problems of political malaise and policy ineffectiveness by drawing on the strengths of these forms of representation without succumbing to their weaknesses. These comments focus on two issues which I believe to be central to their program: the role of political institutions in creating a framework for associative democracy and the dilemmas inherent in setting limits to the scope of representation.

Associative Democracy and Territorial Political Representation

As Cohen and Rogers recognize, territorial political representation is critical to the process and outcome of interest representation. But in enumerating the artifactual aspects of groups, their essay could further develop the implications of links between interest group organizations, the process of interest group negotiation and what one could call the more 'standard' political system – that is, representative institutions and the ways in which they function in practice.

As I understand the argument, Cohen and Rogers view arenas of political deliberation and interest group negotiation as complementary. The party system is to provide constraints on associative democracy by constituting an alternative channel of participation that citizens can use to protest any excesses of associations – a substitute for pluralism's 'potential interests'. In addition, deliberative institutions are to be used to discuss explicitly the rules of the game for the associative negotiations – the groups that are to be included in the associative system, the accountability of the leadership of the groups, the policies that are to be delegated to associations – and to evaluate the substantive results of associative policy-making and implementation. The essay also notes the more indirect and less explicit impact of political institutions and policy choices on the structure and organization of groups, as the conditions for group formation 'are themselves in part a product of opportunities and incentives that are induced by the structure of political institutions and the substance of political choices, and so can be changed through public policy'.

Thus the political system is to exercise three separate functions in their scheme: it serves as a counterbalance to the interest group system; it sets the conditions for group representation and evaluates the results of group negotiation; and it subtly shapes the background conditions for the organization of interests and their expression in politics. This third aspect – the ways in which political institutions and policy choices shape associational life – indicates interaction rather than complementarity, however. These interactions should be explored in more depth because they could inadvertently undermine associative democracy in practice. The implicit effects of political institutions could even countermand the explicit decisions taken within those same institutions.

Political institutions are important not just for establishing the contours of associational representation, but they also affect the behavior of associations during negotiation processes. The willingness of association leaders to cooperate and their ability to impose compromises on their membership (more broadly, the ability of both leaders and members to see the interdependence of their interests on those of others) depend on the availability of alternative channels of political influence that can be used to overturn the decisions made by association negotiations. That is, if interest groups can veto the results of negotiations at a different point in the system, they will not be predisposed to cooperate during the negotiations. Moreover, as the results of negotiations will not be final, the negotiation process itself will lose credibility.

For example, in the United States the courts provide this kind of veto opportunity. This is one of the factors that has hampered the effectiveness of the Occupational Safety and Health Administration (OSHA), to name but one example. Legal recourse has slowed the process of setting standards, has considerably raised the requirements of scientific proof necessary to establish a standard and has exacerbated the effects of US adversarial industrial relations. Because neither employers nor unions have faith that regulation is imminent or will be enforced, neither is particularly cooperative during the negotiations and hearings that are already part of the OSHA standard-setting process.[1] Given that cooperative negotiation requires association leaders to impose significant costs on their members, increasing associative democracy in this area will not work unless territorial or other political institutions (1) provide positive pressure to ensure that agreements are reached (such as a time-limit on negotiation, after which an arbitrary standard will be used), and (2) do not provide associations with the hope of later veto of the negotiated outcome.

The impact of political institutions on associative democracy is not uniform across issue areas, however. For instance, although the courts have constrained OSHA, they have broadened environmental protections, thereby aiding the work of the Environmental Protection Agency (EPA). Moreover, even within the area of occupational health and safety, the threat of legal action on the part of employees has undoubtedly improved workplace conditions independently of OSHA.

Thus the exact effects of political institutions on associative democracy are complicated. Nevertheless, the point here is that the institutions cannot be put to the side for the moment because they may determine the extent to which associative democracy will bring positive results.

In working out the necessary institutional conditions for associative democracy, two subsidiary points should be kept in mind. (Both are standard criticisms of civic republicanism.) First, in the essay a great deal of weight is given to the party system. It is equally important to consider the interrelationships among and between different political arenas and different levels of government. The party system means very different things at the local, state and federal levels, and the impact of political parties is constrained by interactions among the executive, legislative and judicial branches. Second, as the party system is riddled with interest group influence, supervision of associational life by the party system may reinforce rather than provide a counterweight to the problems of faction. The same considerations apply to the other political institutions that various advocates of civic republicanism stress as the locus of deliberative decision-making, such as the Congress or the courts.

Inclusiveness of the Group System and Conditions for Cooperation

The impact of political institutions on associational democracy is one aspect of the more general problem of how to combine democratic systems with effective decision-making. Institutions that guarantee access to decision-making protect citizens from injustice, and notably, they protect minorities from domination by majorities, but they may also create policy stalemate. Similarly, broad access to group negotiation may conflict with the effectiveness of these negotiations. Thus the conditions for effective/efficient policies pose problems for the democratic/participatory aspects of associative democracy.

Most basically, associative democracy strives to forge effective policies through the cooperation of groups. Cooperation in turn depends on ruling out the ability of any one group to veto policy outcomes unilaterally. From this proposition, one could set out three conditions for successful (in terms of solving policy problems) associative democracy: (1) there must be a lack of alternative arenas for vetoing proposals; (2) the number of groups must be sufficient to allow groups to balance one another, yet not so large so as to produce a 'joint decision trap'; and (3) negotiations must be ongoing and repeated (iterative).[2]

These conditions, however, imply some limits on the inclusiveness of associative democracy – both in terms of the number and range of groups that are included and in terms of the scope of the issues that such negotiations can consider. Although Cohen and Rogers provide evidence from democratic corporatist systems to show that the tradeoff between the policy aims of associational negotiation and democratic norms can be overcome, these systems also illustrate some of the difficulties that associative democracy might encounter.

In my view, democratic corporatist systems owe at least part of their success to their exclusion of some interests. Not necessarily because of associational monopoly but by working with a restricted number of interests, the political agenda has been reduced to a more manageable number of problems, and interests not willing to go along with the overall consensus have been ignored or defeated. The Swedish example is a case in point. During the entire post-World War II period, the input of certain interests was minimized: small businesses, craft unions and professional organizations were under-represented in a system of representation that emphasized the three main producer organizations (LO, TCO and SAF). Policy-making contained in executive procedures with little scope for parliamentary changes allowed social democratic politicians to impose policies agreed on by the three main organizations on more recalcitrant groups. In health policy, for example, fee controls could be imposed on the medical profession, and the medical association was often not even represented on government health insurance commissions. Recently, however, there has been a kind of 'return of the repressed', with small business, professional and consumer mobilization against the emphasis on class-based representation.

More generally, arrival at consensus on the public good means that some interests may not be accommodated. What can be done about those interests? Cohen and Rogers suggest several mechanisms by which associative democracy might integrate opposed interests, thereby encouraging members of particular groups to view their interests as interdependent on the well-being of others. Relying on overarching groups and engaging a broad variety of groups in ongoing negotiations would facilitate relations of trust, compromise and reconciliation.

But each step toward integration is difficult. The larger and more encompassing the representative association, the less sensitive will be the leadership to demands from particular subconstituencies. Consequently, particular interests may resist representation by broader associations. Ethnic minorities will not necessarily feel adequately represented by wage-earner associations; doctors would most probably not want to be represented by a general union of health workers; members of particular trades or industries may prefer their trade association to a general employers' association. Thus the freedom of individuals to choose their own representatives may hamper effective negotiation.

In addition, leaders of organizations are often more ready to acquiesce than their members, yet democratic norms eschew oligarchy. Officials engaged in ongoing negotiations are more likely to think in terms of policy packages (the interdependence of interests) than are their members, but when decisions go back to the rank and file (just as when they go to alternative political arenas), the policy issues can become unbundled again. In the recent catastrophic health insurance debate in the United States, for instance, organizations representing the aged were willing to finance better health insurance coverage through income-based contributions paid by retired persons. These representatives accepted the congressional logic that as social security had been relatively sheltered from budget cuts, new benefits should be financed by the beneficiaries themselves. By contrast, individual, relatively wealthier older persons did not accept this package and protested directly to their congressional representatives, which ultimately led to the recall of the bill.

There is also the problem of 'maverick' groups. The relative lack of interest, information and expertise of the majority of associations in particular areas – typically agriculture, for example – tends to leave a few associations isolated and ruthless in their demands. There would be a strong temptation to silence these groups by agreeing to give them free rein over their own domain if they stay out of the bargaining in other areas. Yet such deals would undermine the balancing effects of broad representation.

Moreover, even the representation of a wide variety of groups is problematic. Aside from the obvious risk that the more people you include, the harder it is to reach agreement, the inclusion of too many groups may overburden the negotiations by widening the agenda to include conflicts that are extremely difficult to reconcile. Representation of agricultural and social welfare groups in negotiations over employment, incomes policies and social wages would invite discussion of the large socioeconomic inequalities between urban and rural workers, the employed and unemployed, as well as inequalities of race and gender. While this is precisely the point of associative democracy, consensus bridging such a broad issue space will be difficult to achieve. Resolution of conflicts of religion, language or ethnicity – the identities that have been termed cultural cleavages – pose an even greater challenge to associative democracy than do distributional issues. Certainly, corporatist bargaining institutions do not attempt to span such divides.

To conclude, the idea of using political means 'to secure an associative environment more conducive to democratic aims' holds promise for addressing a number of policy problems and increasing meaningful and responsible political participation. Involvement of associations in productive decision-making could even rejuvenate groups that are losing their constituencies by updating their mandates to engage in new issues that directly concern their potential members, thus encouraging a more deliberative form of public participation than electronic democracy. However, attention needs to be paid to the impact of the larger political and institutional framework on these procedures for interest negotiation and to the difficulties of balancing democratic concerns for broad representation with pragmatic considerations about effective negotiation.

Notes

1. See Steven Kelman, *Regulating Sweden, Regulating America: A Comparative Study of Occupational Safety and Health Policy*, Cambridge, MA: MIT Press, 1981.

2. On the problems of joint decision-making, see Fritz W. Scharpf, 'The Joint-Decision Trap: Lessons from German Federalism and European Integration', *Public Administration* 66 (1988), pp. 239–78.

11

Social Groups in Associative Democracy

Iris Marion Young

The collapse of Communism in Eastern Europe and the end of the Cold War and other worldwide economic and political changes have made an important opening and need to reform and experiment with political and economic institutions. This historical opportunity for trying new things, unfortunately, has not been accompanied by any significant institutional imagination, especially in the United States, where leaders consider its current political and economic institutions to be the Promised Land toward which reformers in other parts of the world should aim. Thus Cohen and Rogers's proposal for alternative political institutions in the United States is greatly needed. Some people will and should disagree with aspects of either their theoretical framework or their practical model. But at least the essay is imaginative and can shake up our political and institutional complacency. Cohen and Rogers's model of associative democracy offers political theorists and activists in any part of the world where there now exist liberties of association, assembly, movement and free expression something substantial to chew on. In so far as it puts forward both a framework of normative principles of democracy and draws a fairly detailed picture of some practical means for how reformed political institutions in the United States might better instantiate those norms, the essay can serve as a model for how to fuel the institutional imagination.

Alternative institutions cannot be made out of air. Both imagining and enacting alternative institutions must begin with some elements of existing social life; as Marx said, the new society comes out of the womb of the old. Theorists of more democratic alternative political institutions thus should look around our societies to find undervalued or underused democratic forms, which we propose to deepen, extend and radicalize. I interpret Cohen and Rogers's model of associative democracy as doing just this. It excites my imagination to see new possibilities in the civic and political associations that proliferate in our society as well as in institutions like coalitions, hearings, commissions and regulatory agencies.

Oddly enough, however, Cohen and Rogers do not seek to build on and deepen existing social forms in the United States. They acknowledge in passing that the United States has myriad forms of associative democracy and, indeed, some forms of associative governance. But their proposals for associative reform in the United States do not in any way draw on current associative forms.

This is a serious weakness in their view. My mail is flooded weekly with requests for money sent by various local and national associations, most of them civic-minded or politically oriented, and my mailbox is not unusual. Americans are compulsive joiners – of clubs, discussion groups, nonprofit organizations and their boards of directors, task forces, political committees and lobbying organizations, and community arts and theater groups, both at local and national levels. In Pittsburgh we have a progressive political coalition with forty-one member organizations, a minute portion of the civic and political associations in the region.

What could lead Cohen and Rogers to ignore these efforts and in effect to look outside the United States for an institutional starting point for their model? The basic reason is that they are not looking for the kinds of association that exist, but rather for class-based associations like unions and strong relatively encompassing constituency-defined political parties. They are looking for large, nationally-based labor unions, whose members together number a large majority of the workforce, and for strong, class-related political parties, whose political programs are comprehensive, clear and different. They fail to focus on the forms of association that are here because they are looking for those they find elsewhere. This failure is symptomatic of a more general bias of omission in the whole essay. Their model assumes economic class as the primary social group division and proposes issues of economic output and distribution as the primary issues that groups struggle about through democratic processes. This bias leads them to devalue the political importance of other major social group divisions, both in the United States and elsewhere, and the economic, social and cultural issues about which they struggle through political institutions.

I see the model of associative democracy as a means of linking state policy formation and implementation more strongly with the needs and interests expressed in civil society. Though such linkage risks sacrificing the autonomy of groups and movements in civil society, the model of associative democracy, as I read it, aims to preserve that autonomy. In the United States, as elsewhere, associations are primarily civil – they arise from below, out of the immediate affinities that people find they have in their everyday lives, in their neighborhoods, religious congregations, occupations, consumer interests, cultural expressions and orientations and in their values and political commitments. They are tenant groups, civil rights groups, neighborhood organizations responding to hate crimes, coalitions to expand affordable housing options, gay male cultural collectives that help organize gay and lesbian pride day, groups supporting the struggles of people in other parts of the world, groups providing services and support to old people, people with disabilities and victims of battering or sexual assault, and groups that organize against the siting of a toxic waste plant. Significantly for my argument, in the United States today and for some time past, civic groups more often than not are organized along lines of gender, race, religion, ethnicity or sexual orientation, even when they have not explicitly aimed to do so. Civic associations of this sort often promote grassroots participation and deliberation, provide their members with a sense of belonging and opportunities to develop skills of speaking and organizing, and frequently have a purpose oriented on what they take as a wider public good; often they do not regard themselves as merely working for the collective self-interest of their members.[1] Indeed, many civic associations of the sort I have listed may be more civic-minded in this sense than are many labor unions today.

As I imagine it, associative democracy would develop structures to link the opinions and activities of these groups more strongly to the policy-making process at both national and local levels. Some political practices already exist in the United States which could be built on and expanded as forms of citizen participation and representation in policy-making and implementation. Think, for example, of the process of public hearings. Especially in the last twenty-five years, in the United States many economic development, welfare and social service, and regulatory programs have been accompanied by mandates that legislative or executive officials hold hearings on policy proposals or proposed actions at which citizens may come and testify. During this same period, many of the sorts of associations I have cited above have participated in these processes at local, state and national levels. Presently such hearing processes have many flaws from the point of view of democracy. Rarely are the public officials who hold the hearings in any way bound to formulate their policies to accord with what they hear, and there are usually no mechanisms by which citizens can hold decision-makers accountable. Some kinds of groups

and associations have more direct access to information about when
hearings will be held and greater resources to prepare for and attend
them than others. As I understand the model of associative democracy,
it would remedy these and other flaws in representation and influence
in current, quasi-participatory processes.

Cohen and Rogers never specify what they mean by a group, but
as their discussion proceeds it appears that they have in mind an interest group formed for the purposes of influencing policy. Such an
understanding of group is too vague, narrow and instrumentalist. The
sorts of civic groups that I have cited above, which I take to be seeds
for the possible growth of associative democracy, usually have a
wider orientation than influencing policy. They have ongoing social
or cultural interests which lead them also and importantly to be interested in influencing policy.

Furthermore, as I have mentioned, such civic groups are often gender, race, class, age, ethnicity or sexuality specified. While Cohen and
Rogers do acknowledge that there are social groups with oppressions
or disadvantages of a form different from class oppression, they do
not incorporate this recognition systematically into their model. I
think this is partly because they fail to specify the meaning of 'group'
enough and to distinguish kinds and levels of groups.

In another place I have argued that we cannot understand
contemporary fractures of privileges and oppression and the new
social movements that resist these oppressions without a conceptual
distinction between an association and a social group.[2] An association is a formally organized institution, such as a club, corporation,
political party, church, college or union. Cohen and Rogers's model
recognizes only such formally organized institutions as groups.
They rightly insist that associational activity is 'artifactual', that is,
not natural and therefore subject to change and manipulation by
institutional designers seeking to expand democracy.

Social groups, as I understand them, on the other hand, are more
'natural' in the society; while socially produced and changeable, they
are not constituted by explicit decisions. Social groups emerge in
ongoing social processes of the division of labor, affinity formation
and the differentiation of communal identities from one another. A
social group is a collective of persons differentiated from at least one
other group by cultural forms, practices or way of life. Members of
a group have a specific affinity with one another because of their similar experience or way of life, which prompts them to associate with
one another more than with those not identified with the group or in
a different way. Groups often interact with relations of exclusion,

exploitation or dominance, and such relations historically have caused the development of some social groups.

In the United States, economic class locates one important kind of social group in this sense. But just as important are gender, race, ethnicity, religion, age, disability or sexual orientation for defining social group identity. The political importance of social groups arises, at least partly, from the fact that in all societies today some social group differences in addition to class privilege some groups and oppress others. Relations of privilege and oppression, however, are not necessary to the formation and relationships of social groups, and a multiculturalist politics aims for a group-differentiated society of inclusion and equality. Many actual and potential civic and political associations have members of these oppressed social groups as their primary constituencies, and aim to express the interests and perspectives of those social groups in public life.

I have proposed that one step, but only one, that political institutions can take to undermine social group oppression is to provide mechanisms for the special representation of oppressed or disadvantaged social groups in political agenda setting and policy formation. Since privileged groups tend already to be well represented in positions of power and influence in political and economic institutions, the promotion of procedural fairness and the voicing of diverse needs, interests and perspectives requires balancing that privilege with the special representation of, for example, women, African-Americans, American Indians, gay men and lesbians, and disabled people. Besides allowing the expression of diverse needs and interests, such group representation would promote greater orientation toward a public good beyond the expression of interests because it provides a greater check than now exists on dominant groups expressing their own interests as a general good. Distinct forms of representation for oppressed groups furthers political practical wisdom because it maximizes the sharing of social knowledge. Because members of different groups have different social perspectives, they are sometimes in a better position than members of other groups to anticipate the probable social consequences of implementing particular social policies. Thus the fair representation of all group perspectives can maximize the chances for making just and wise decisions.[3]

I think that Cohen and Rogers's proposal for associative democracy can be interpreted as one way to apply this principle of special representation for oppressed and disadvantaged groups. Interpreting it this way does, I think, require some adjustment in their model. Most importantly, their implicit assumption that most associations involved in an associative democratic scheme are either capitalist or worker interests must give way to a more plural understanding of the fractures of privilege and oppression along which there is political conflict. Further, where their model appears to allow for a rough equality of representation for any associations, to undermine oppression I would call for mechanisms of differential resource allocation and organizing capacity to associations arising from oppressed or disadvantaged social groups. It appears generally compatible with Cohen and Rogers's model that the state could decide to promote the self-organization of members of oppressed groups where such organization is weak, or to provide greater resources to existing associations representing oppressed or disadvantaged groups, and to create compensatory political forms to ensure that such groups have an equal voice in agenda setting and policy formation.

Once we go beyond class division to understand the fractures of political conflict as also involving gender, race, ethnicity, age, sexuality, and so on, it becomes clear that issues of economic performance and state efficiency are not necessarily the most central areas of conflict. It is certainly arguable that US legislation, law and official executive policy have been as much occupied with cultural and social issues – sexual and reproductive issues, affirmative action and other issues of the relations among groups, questions of religion and its relation to public life, free speech in art and media – as it has been occupied with classical political economic issues of state efficiency, economic regulation and the distribution of the fruits of production.

Cohen and Rogers's model appears to ignore non-economic issues of cultural meaning or social relations or even to argue that they cannot be dealt with in a political system. They say, for example, that matters of principle are not amenable to political negotiation. This would appear to exclude from the region of democratic policy formation those issues and conflicts not amenable to distributive divisions. 'All or nothing' issues – such as whether state agencies may fund artworks that express gay sexuality – must be excluded from the associative democratic agenda. Contemporary new social movements, and the issues of cultural and social oppression additional to economic oppression that they raise, show why such a distinction between substantive ends and distributive means can no longer be sustained as a political distinction. In addition to social group-based movements, I would include environmentalism as a movement that politicizes cultural, lifestyle and social issues along with economic issues. Of course, a democratic polity must promote fair distribution of the burdens and benefits of economic cooperation and just organization of economic institutions. But as events from Prague to Los Angeles remind us, just as important is the organization of democratic institutions so that social groups can deliberate about the policy conditions for promoting sexual, cultural, and social freedom and respect for difference.

Notes

1. Behind my identification of civic associations in the United States is the theoretical concept of 'civil society' being developed by some political theorists as a social arena not well conceptualized by either traditional liberalism or Marxism. For a recent comprehensive statement of this concept, see Andrew Arato and Jean Cohen, *Civil Society and Political Theory*, Cambridge, MA: MIT Press 1992.

2. Iris Marion Young, *Justice and the Politics of Difference*, Princeton, NJ: Princeton University Press 1990, ch. 2.

3. Ibid., pp. 183–91; see also Iris Marion Young, 'Justice and Communicative Democracy', in Roger Gottlieb, ed., *Tradition, Counter-Tradition and Critique: Essays in Radical Philosophy in Honor of Richard Schmit*, Albany: State University of New York Press 1992.

12

Extending Democracy in
South Africa
Heinz Klug

Introduction

Instead of responding directly to Cohen and Rogers's paper I shall
attempt to explore the significance of this discussion for debates among
participants in South Africa's transition to democracy. For this reason
I have tried to locate the debate within the context of the continuing
political transition and those aspects of recent political and social struggles which impact on the growing pressures for participation.

When F. W. de Klerk publicly launched South Africa's democratic
transition, by announcing the unbanning of the liberation movements
in February 1990, there was no agreement either on the specifics or
on the extent of this process of democratization. At that time de
Klerk's National Party was proposing a fifteen-year transitional period
with a new constitution providing for a multi-party executive, a
revolving presidency and a regionally elected upper house – with equal
representation for any party receiving over 10 percent of the vote per
region – wielding absolute veto powers. The democratic movement, on
the other hand, began demanding an interim government and a democratically elected constituent assembly to draft a new constitution.
Activists within the democratic movement, critical of 'bourgeois'
democracy, began debating associational socialism, participatory
democracy and the role of civil society.

I shall attempt to place these debates, focusing on issues of associative and participatory democracy, within the context of the process of
continuing transition and of constitutional mechanisms which may
promote the emergence and consolidation of democratic participation
in South Africa. First, I shall describe briefly the historical context of
these debates in South Africa and then begin to explore various suggestions for encouraging a process of sustained democratic participation
in a future constitutional order.

In the Context of a Democratic Transition

With the convening of the Conference for a Democratic South Africa (Codesa) on 20 December 1991, South Africa entered into a process of formal negotiations expected to extend political rights to all the country's citizens. Although the major parties – the African National Congress and the ruling National Party – agreed in principle on a multi-party democracy based on a system of proportional representation with a justiciable constitution containing a Bill of Rights, they were diametrically opposed in their understandings of the transitional process and the parameters of future governance. While the National Party sought to weaken the state by proposing a minimalist government based on the Thatcherite model, the ANC saw a future government playing a central role in the post-apartheid reconstruction of the country.

The assassination of South African Communist Party and ANC leader Chris Hani, and the mass outpouring of grief and anger which his death precipitated, galvanized the negotiating process. This event, after the collapse of the first round of negotiations, provided a glimpse of the consequences of a continuing failure to reach agreement. Having agreed to reopen multi-party negotiations at a multi-party planning conference on 5 and 6 March 1993, the parties refused to allow the right-wing assassins to achieve their aim of shattering the already brittle negotiations process and instead appealed in the name of Hani for heightened efforts to achieve a settlement.

Within weeks of his death formal negotiations reopened in the form of a Multi-Party Negotiations Process at the World Trade Centre outside Johannesburg. Unlike the failed Codesa talks, in which negotiations were conducted between party representatives in the different working groups, the new process provided for a negotiating council to discuss and decide on reports from seven technical committees whose role it would be to clarify and present alternatives and issues for negotiation. In addition a ten-person planning committee would be responsible for keeping the process on track by structuring the debates and dealing with grievances.

Dominated by academics and lawyers, the technical committees facilitated the emergence of clear alternatives. However, a range of participants and parties from within and outside the multi-party talks remained suspicious of the 'professionalization' of an essentially political process. Despite often harsh criticism of the initial proposals of some of the technical committees, and active intervention through the negotiating council and public debate, the process, focused as it was on the production of written proposals, gained in momentum. Although sent back to rework and reconsider their 'technical' inputs, the series of reports that flowed from the committees slowly crystallized the position of the negotiating council.

The adoption in December 1993 of an interim constitution requiring power-sharing in a government of national unity for five years after the first democratic elections facilitated the democratic transition but merely extended the debate over future democratic structures and procedures. Both the formal debate over a new constitutional order and the debates and struggles for a wider process of democratization in the society have continued since the elections. The most dynamic aspect of the democratization process has now shifted away from the negotiating process to the newly elected provincial and national legislatures, to the trade unions and civic organizations, within the ranks of the ANC and among non-government organizations. In these forums there is a dynamic debate about the nature of the democracy which should be cultivated in this transitional period and enshrined in the next constitution. Unlike the process of negotiations between the old and new orders which produced the 1993 Constitution, these debates, experiments and struggles are of vital importance to the democratic transition, as they will provide the immediate conditions within which the constitutional assembly, dominated by the ANC, will write the new constitution.[1]

Organic Precedents for Associational and Participatory Democracy

Despite the importance of intellectual debates and democratic advocacy, it is the experience of democratic participation during the struggle against apartheid which provides the foundation for the extension of democracy. For most activists and communities this exposure to active political participation came in the trade unions, United Democratic Front affiliates, civic associations (voluntary organizations which took up community issues such as the high cost or lack of municipal services, including rents, electricity, water and transport costs) or local community structures – street committees and people's courts – which carried forward popular resistance to apartheid from the early 1970s until the states of emergency which dominated the late 1980s.

Central to this process was the role of the trade union movement, and in particular the Congress of South African Trade Unions

(Cosatu), which has repeatedly called for the participation of organized representatives of the working class in the political process, and
for the incorporation of trade unions and management in the formulation and development of national economic policies. As the most
structurally organized element of the democratic movement, Cosatu's
centrality in the present debate is enhanced by its position as an arm
of the tripartite alliance of the ANC, South African Communist Party
and Cosatu.

The influence of the trade union movement is reflected in the
ANC's proposed Bill of Rights, which will form an important source
of guidance for members of the constitutional assembly. Workers'
and union rights are enumerated in detail compared to the rights of
other elements of the democratic movement such as civic associations
and youth and student movements, which are not explicitly eluci-
dated. This disparity is partly the result of the trade union movement's organizational resources, but is also due to the direct
repression suffered by the democratic movement under the state of
emergency: organized labor was able to protect its organizational
capacity by exploiting differences between the state and business
interests. These relative capacities of different sections of the democratic movement may best be understood by briefly examining the
development of mass organizations and participation during the
struggle against apartheid over the last two decades.

Grounded in the trade union movement which re-emerged in the
1970s and the development of community-based organizations in the
late 1970s and early 1980s, the United Democratic Front (UDF) was
launched in 1983. Unifying over six hundred organizations, the UDF
was established to oppose a new, undemocratic constitution, through
which the apartheid state attempted to divide the black community
by extending political rights to members of the Indian and Colored
communities while continuing to exclude the African majority from
political participation. Although it was made up of women's, youth,
sporting and other community-based organizations, civic associations
formed the backbone of the UDF.

Despite the exclusion of Africans at the national level, the regime's
1983 reforms did include participation for urban African communities in powerless local government structures or community councils.
It was the attempt by these councils to raise rents and other municipal service charges in late 1984, coinciding with the implementation
of the 1983 Constitution, which sparked off the urban revolt that
shook South Africa from 1984 to 1987.

Although of uneven strength and character, many black townships experienced different forms of mass participatory organization during the uprising as the ANC called on activists to make the country ungovernable. Street Committees and People's Courts functioned with varying degrees of success; at times they provided models of direct mass participation, while in some instances they degenerated into individual fiefdoms and coercive ad hoc kangaroo courts for one faction or another.

By the time the state of emergency was lifted following the unbanning of the ANC and other political organizations in February 1990, the trade union movement and various non-governmental service organizations – including public interest legal institutions – were the only parts of the mass democratic movement that had not suffered nearly total disruption as a result of state repression. However, as the ANC began to establish legal organizational structures and a mass-based membership from mid-1990 so the civic and other organizations which made up the mass democratic movement also began to re-emerge in the townships. Having failed to break township rent boycotts and other forms of local resistance the state now attempted to begin local negotiations with the civic organizations in order to strike separate deals and to preclude local socioeconomic struggles – housing, services, education – from the national negotiations agenda.

Although the mass struggles of the 1980s seem to have prepared the ground for the extension of democratic participation in South Africa and even for the possibility of establishing some forms of associational democracy, there was a number of developments which militated against the emergence of democratic alternatives. Most dramatic was the violence – both communal and state-sponsored – which was directed at both the disruption of political organization and at destabilizing the black townships with random attacks on black civilians, creating a climate of fear and instability. This fueled a tendency to political intolerance and was itself exacerbated by the consequences of political intolerance. The most direct effect of the violence – random attacks on civilians and the public slaughter of people wearing politically partisan colors – was to inhibit public political participation. Although ANC membership continued to grow, the early blossoming of ANC colors, sweatshirts and other garments gave way to ordinary members concealing their membership cards and avoiding being identified in public as ANC members.

In an attempt to reduce the violence, the major parties, including the ANC, Inkatha and the government, backed a business-church initiative which led to the adoption of a National Peace Accord on 14

September 1991. The Accord included detailed codes of conduct for political organizations and the security forces, as well as mechanisms for dispute resolution in areas of violent conflict. A significant aspect of the Accord was its inclusion of parties other than government in managing the transition process.[2] This set an important precedent for the involvement of non-government organizations and political parties in the monitoring of state institutions as it included multi-party monitoring of the South African police and multi-party participation in commissions of inquiry into violations of the Accord. However, it must be noted that the Peace Accord's police board was merely an advisory structure and fitted with the police force's own strategy of 'depoliticizing' the police force. Similarly, the establishment of police-community liaison structures and special police investigation units to investigate police misconduct was consistent with the South African Police's own agenda to build police credibility.[3]

Despite these criticisms the implementation of the Peace Accord at the local level took on wide significance. Even short-term failure of the peace process would affect community attitudes toward participatory structures such as the police-community liaison committees, police reporting officers and civilian police management boards. The result of such failure in the long term would be to delegitimate community control of policing both within the community and within the police force itself.[4]

Political intolerance is the product of both apartheid's historical repression of free political activity and, to a lesser extent, the polarization of communities during the struggle against apartheid. On the one hand, communities often rejected and expelled those who collaborated with the apartheid state while on the other, activists – in their attempts to mobilize communities – often advocated a simplistic division of all members of the community into those who were for or against 'the system'. All too often this leads activists to characterize those with whom they have political differences as the enemy.

The consequences of this political intolerance was felt within civic associations. Even when an attempt was made to define the civic association as representative of the community and not part of a particular political formation, there were conflicts over which political formation was ultimately in control of a particular civic association. As a result, there was internal confusion over the future political role of the civics. On the one hand, some ANC members accused others who were active in the civics of prematurely distancing the civics from the ANC. On the other, members of the Pan-Africanist Congress (PAC) and the Azanian People's Organization (Azapo) charged that because

220 ASSOCIATIONS AND DEMOCRACY

the very same civics refused to distance themselves from the ANC, they were therefore aligned with the ANC and not independent community organizations.[5]

New Opportunities to Participate?

Despite these difficulties there is a continuing debate on democratization within the democratic movement. Discussions range from different ways of promoting democratic participation, to the building of civil society and how to increase the role of existing popular organizations, such as the trade unions and civic organizations, in public policy formulation and implementation. The call to expand democratic participation since the elections also has been taken up by newly elected Members of Parliament and in the newly established provincial legislatures.

The trade unions' demand for a macroeconomic negotiating forum, asserted in the 1991 anti-VAT campaign, is an important indication of the relevance these discussions have for associational democracy. The anti-VAT campaign had two central focuses: first, it articulated a general political challenge to the government's legitimacy, demanding there be no taxation without representation; and second, it demanded a macroeconomic negotiating forum.[6]

The general strike on 5 and 6 November 1991, in which about 3.5 million people, or 90 percent of the black workforce, participated, was a dramatic assertion by the trade union movement that it could not be excluded from the process of economic policy formulation. Organized to protest against the government's imposition of VAT, the issues underlying the strike went far beyond the tax; Jay Naidoo, then Cosatu general secretary, described it as 'a referendum which demonstrated a vote of no confidence in the government'.[7]

Stimulated by the experience of the trade unions in negotiating the Cosatu-Saccola-Nactu[8] accord on the Labor Relations Act in 1990 – a bilateral agreement between the trade unions and business, which forced the state to withdraw unacceptable labor legislation – the debate on the role of the trade unions in a post-apartheid South Africa ranges from the notion of a multilateral 'reconstruction accord' to arguments for a new social contract founded on bilateralism or even the more established European model of trilateralism.[9] At first the debate focused on the distinction between a proposal developed within the National Union of Metalworkers for a union-led national development strategy to be based on a 'reconstruction accord' negotiated between the unions and other mass-based organizations, including progressive political parties,[10] and a bipartite approach which envisions unions exerting their influence on society through collective bargaining with employers,[11] such as the Cosatu-Saccola-Nactu accord.

Trade union practice seems, however, to involve a complex array of strategies including exchanges of views between Cosatu and ANC economists on the one hand, and continuing bilateral negotiations with organized business, and assertions of the need for trade union independence from a future government, on the other. Central to the discussion of trade union independence has been the process of preparing a Workers' Charter to supplement the proposed Bill of Rights in a post-apartheid constitution. As a result, discussion has increasingly turned to the question of whether the trade unions are moving toward support for the idea of a social contract or partnership.[12]

Complicating any analysis of this debate, however, is the fact that different strategies will be required for different aspects and stages of the transitional process now underway. Cosatu's general secretary, now Minister of Reconstruction and Development, Jay Naidoo, emphasized both the centrality of the 'organizations of civil society' to the strength of the democratic movement and the need to ensure that, although only political parties take part in political negotiations through the 'All-Party Conference, the interim government and the constituent assembly', this does not preclude negotiations over economic issues.[13]

Cosatu's call for a macroeconomic negotiating forum and the suggestion that a number of working forums on housing, education, health, technology, investment policy and industrial restructuring[14] be established to include 'broad constituencies that represent the people',[15] seems to reflect the earlier call for a 'reconstruction accord'. However, this proposal goes beyond the earlier proposal of negotiations within the democratic movement and toward a notion of a wider social contract on which to base the democratic transition. It is this principle of direct participation by civil society-based associations in policy formulation and decision-making that highlights the associational aspects of these developments.[16]

Committing themselves to addressing issues of economic growth, social equity and democratic participation in decision-making, labor, business and government launched the National Economic Forum on 29 October 1992. In their statement of intent the parties 'noted the severe inequality in incomes, skills, economic power and ownership in South Africa and agreed to establish a "consensus geared co-operative body to deal with economic and related socioeconomic issues and the economic challenges facing the country".'[17] Although these specific developments do not exclude the possibility of pursuing different strategies in the future, they may have negative implications for the possibility of democratic participation. While most now agree that the trade unions should maintain their independence in post-apartheid South Africa, the trilateralism implicit in the formation of a macro-economic negotiating forum presents a danger that the trade unions and other democratic formations may become tied into a trilateral negotiating system at the national level, becoming bureaucratized over time and thus weakening or excluding local participation.[18]

Community organizations too are beginning to assert an independent role for themselves. Despite a lack of national leverage, civic associations have demonstrated, through consumer boycotts and other actions, that they have the capacity to mobilize communities at the local level. There is, however, no clear consensus about the long-term role of the civics. Some activists argue for an independent 'watchdog' role over a new government, while others argue that they should take a more proactive stance and become directly engaged in the development process.[19]

Although community organizations played a major role in the democratic movement during the 1980s, they were severely weakened by state repression. Their relative weakness was evident in their inability to make an impact on the constitution-making process – for example, the failure to protect or promote civic organization in the ANC's proposed Bill of Rights. After the lifting of the State of Emergency, however, civic associations re-emerged and began to unite in regional bodies, such as the Civic Association of the Southern Transvaal (CAST). In 1991 the UDF was formally disbanded and its resources devoted to the establishment of a national civic coordination body which was transformed into the South African National Civic Organization (Sanco), seen by some as setting itself up as a 'watchdog' over the ANC. Another significant initiative was the establishment of a National Development Forum which, although initiated by the ANC, aimed to pull together regional and local development actors to discuss a national development policy for adoption by the ANC. In addition, the development forums were conceived as mechanisms through which to promote participation and to direct resources to locally determined needs and projects. Although the ANC adopted a national Reconstruction and Development Program, which has become the formal policy of President Mandela's government, it was shaped more by internal ANC policy procedures – including a series of conferences culminating in a national policy conference in December 1993 – than by the National Development Forum.

Representing the black townships whose formal authorities were swept away by anti-apartheid resistance, civic associations became deeply involved in negotiations at local and metropolitan levels for the establishment of transitional local government forums with a view to beginning the task of integrating the administrative and resource bases of former apartheid cities and towns. What remains uncertain is the future of civic associations once local government structures are democratized and local government elections held. Some activists argue that civics should remain autonomous of local government which will be contested on a party political basis. Instead, they argue, the civics should retain an independent role as 'secondary' associations raising community issues. Whether this will allow civics to continue to play an active role in local development forums, and what their relationship will be to democratically elected local government remains unclear. It is in this arena in particular that the debate over the role of secondary associations and associational democracy is most pertinent to the events presently unfolding in South Africa.

Debating Civil Society

Despite the new constitution's commitment to judicial review, the separation of powers and other tenants of constitutionalism, activists in the democratic movement continue to debate socialism, participatory democracy and the role of civil society. Concerned to 'prevent the consolidation of democracy destroying the popular organizations that were the protagonists of the struggle' and which have the greatest potential of contributing 'to establishing the consensual basis and values upon which democracy could be built',[20] these debates within the democratic movement focus on alternative ways of promoting democratic participation, of building civil society or increasing the roles of existing popular organizations such as the trade unions and civic organizations in public policy formulation and implementation. On the one hand, there has been increasing debate on the nature of civil society[21] and its role in what one commentator termed 'building "voice" at grassroots level'.[22] On the other hand, existing social formations such as the trade unions and civic associations have begun articulating new roles for themselves as participants in the democratic process.

The South African debate[23] reveals a degree of confusion over the nature of civil society and the resultant conceptions of associational democracy and democratic socialism. Although it was recognized that civil society tends to be dominated by private capital, one writer argues that it is possible to define 'civil society' so as to exclude private economic power; thus

> a true 'civil society' is one where ordinary everyday citizens, who do not control the levers of political and economic power, have access to locally-constituted voluntary associations that have the capacity, know-how and resources to influence and even determine the structure of power and the allocation of material resources.[24]

Associationalism is thus conceived as an essentially local-level system of voluntary associations which have greater political access to local government than does the central state.[25]

Criticizing this approach as a definition which allows 'civil society' to become 'all things to all people',[26] another contributor to the debate adopts a broad definition of civil society as a contested terrain which is 'located between the public sphere of the state and the private sphere of the individual'.[27] The significance of this critique is its insistence that it is not possible merely to declare certain organized interests to be in or out of civil society and its recognition that unequal power relations will continue to dominate this arena. Instead, it is argued that the vitality of civil society cannot be determined by the number of voluntary associations, but should rather be assessed in terms of a number of factors, including 'the extent to which they are politically dominated, whether they can balance their own interests against broader political imperatives, whether they have organized democratic expression, and whether interest groups can be sufficiently non-sectarian'.[28]

The implications of this analysis for the South African debate, particularly with respect to notions of associational democracy, lies in its recognition that given the large economic monopolies that dominate South African society and the resources at their disposal to 'influence, coerce and shape institutions and individuals',[29] other organizations, including voluntary associations, will remain marginalized. In this context, the state is not only a means to 'mediate between the interests of capital and others',[30] but the fundamental arena within which struggles over the 'structure of power and the allocation of material resources'[31] will continue to be determined. This perspective both recognizes the reality of the growth of the modern state and breaks with the notion that, despite the growing complexity of delivering such services as health care and education in the late twentieth century, the state should wither away.

A possibly more productive line of enquiry would be to concentrate on developing a notion of participatory democracy or associationalism which is premissed on the need to democratize the state.[32] This change in emphasis would enhance the possibility of constructing a notion of associational democracy based on privileging certain institutions or voluntary associations in an effort to influence allocation decisions within the state, whether at the national, regional or local level. Not only may secondary organizations be allocated local state functions and resources for distribution, but a matrix of organizational supports and mechanisms could both encourage the development of secondary organizations in the society and inhibit the ability of any particular interest to gain permanent control over such bodies.

However, this raises the problem of recognition. Who is to determine whether a particular organization or institution should qualify for privileged access or be entrusted with state functions and resources? It has been suggested that the determining factor would be the democratic character of the organization or association; this would be based on regular elections to determine participation in its decision-making bodies and an open membership, or at least a membership defined in a manner reasonably related to its function or purported representativeness. Although this may be a reasonable determinant of whether a local government structure is democratic, how are we to decide between any two voluntary associations which lay claim to the same functions? This may not be an uncommon scenario in circumstances where different political factions are active in the community and feel uncomfortable working in a situation where their policy options are unacceptable to a slight majority of the organization who may be politically aligned to an opposing political formation. One solution is to grant a right of access to all voluntary groups that are able to demonstrate their adherence to democratic processes. However, this is only possible when it comes to access to information or to policy discussions or hearings; it would be more difficult with respect to the distribution of governmental functions or resources.

This approach, however, fails to confront the problem of the continuing power of private economic interests in the society as a whole. Even if denied privileged access to the state, private corporations are able to assert their economic power in their interactions with individuals and communities through their general legal status. This is particularly evident in situations where social and production costs in the form of unemployment or air pollution are borne by the community, to retain the competitiveness of the local economy, while corporations are able to assert rights of autonomy in the distribution of their resources. But this balance of forces may be dramatically altered if we question the privileged legal status of private business corporations, as being equal to natural persons. To do this a distinction may be made between autonomy rights – which are inherent to individual human beings, singularly or collectively – and utilitarian considerations, which are the basis of an organization's assertions of right.[33] Once such a distinction is made, it is possible to conceive of the corporation-individual as a

> clash between utility and autonomy, in which the individual will insist on the supremacy of autonomy rights, whereas the organization will point out the magnitude of the social interest that its claims represent.[34]

In such a clash, the constitutionally protected autonomy rights of the human being deserve the greatest consideration, while the private corporation will, by virtue of its utilitarian basis, be given a separate and weaker constitutional and legal status. Thus although still active in the contestation of civil society, private centers of interest, particularly those whose purpose is profit and not the specific assertion of the rights of human collectivities, will receive weaker constitutional protection and be able to assert fewer social and legal rights.

In contradistinction to this vision and the continuing struggles to broaden democratic participation, the National Party is determined to build a constitutional 'firebreak' between the state and 'civil society'. Emphasizing the public/private distinction, the National Party is determined to insulate private power from state intervention. To this end a provision in an early draft of the interim constitution making the chapter on fundamental human rights binding 'where just and equitable' on non-state action was struck out and replaced with a separate clause prohibiting only unfair discrimination by private bodies and persons. Although the government seems to have adopted the fundamental premiss of the ANC's constitutionalist approach – the constitutional protection of individual rights – they continue to differ on the content of this alternative.

Having retreated from the advocacy of racially defined 'group rights', the National Party seems to have latched on to a notion of individual rights which places the protection of individual property rights at the very heart of the constitutional order. However, unlike the founders of the US Constitution who were only concerned to 'protect property rights against the depredations of the demos',[35] the National

Party's notion of property rights and local autonomy would ensure that the owners of property are constitutionally empowered to extend their right of property into a right of spatial control. This notion of property centered individual rights – reflected too in the constitutional protection of a right to engage in economic activity – would work to ensure the perpetuation of the benefits of apartheid in which owner-ship of property automatically translates into power over the lives of others – employees, tenants and others without property.

Aimed at the protection of existing rights and privileges this approach may prove to be fatally flawed. On the one hand, unless the new constitutional order is able to gain public support and confidence a government frustrated by judicial review in its attempts to address inequality will be sorely tempted to begin amending the constitution. The tendency in such cases is to devalue the whole notion of con-stitutional democracy and soon the rights of personal freedom and security will suffer a similar fate. On the other, failure to address the colonial legacy of poverty and inequality leaves the constitution and new state politically vulnerable. Even a prolonged battle in the courts, in which property-owners are able to invoke the constitution to prevent redistribution, will endanger the new order. Eventually, as in other post-colonial situations, the constitutional constraints placed on the new state last only as long as it takes for a new officer class to emerge in the military and in the name of national salvation and development to suspend the constitution.

Associational Democracy in the New Order?

Describing the ANC's Reconstruction and Development Program (RDP) as a site of struggle, the ANC Member of Parliament and former general secretary of the National Education, Health and Allied Workers Union, Phillip Dexter, argues that the RDP 'presents an opportunity to set our struggle for socialism back on its feet again'.[36] His claim that the RDP offers an 'opportunity to establish a new, progressive hegemony that embraces the values and principles to which the mass democratic forces have committed themselves' is based on the RDP's explicit commitment to democratizing the state and society. Stating that 'democracy for ordinary citizens must not end with formal rights and periodic one-person, one-vote elections', the RDP envisions a democratic order which fosters a 'wide range of institutions of participatory democracy in partnership with civil society'.[37]

The RDP, which is now government policy and subject to constant reinterpretation by the bureaucracy, envisions two distinct forms of associational participation in governance. First, it foresees a role for democratic associations in the policy-making process.[38] In this context the RDP calls for a continued role for various sectoral forums such as the National Economic Forum and for the establishment of more multipartite policy forums at the national, regional and local level 'to promote efficient and effective participation of civil society in decision-making'.[39] Second, the RDP argues that organizations within civil society 'will be encouraged by an ANC government to be active in and responsible for the effective implementation of the RDP'.[40] It is in this context that the RDP calls on the trade unions, sectoral social movements and community-based organizations – particularly the civic associations – to 'develop RDP programmes of action and campaigns within their own sectors and communities',[41] and for their active involvement in 'democratic public policy-making'.[42]

While the RDP is in the hands of minister without portfolio, Jay Naidoo, its implementation – although guided by a national framework – will be dependent on the functioning of local and regional government through which communities and community-based organizations are to access the program. Aside from the difficulties of establishing nine new regional governments and resolving the division of powers between the national and regional levels, the transitional arrangements for local government impose potentially serious limitations on democratic participation.

Although the RDP calls on democratic associations to establish their own RDP programs in their communities the transitional arrangements for local government lock community-based associations into a continuing process of negotiations with institutionalized remnants of the old order. The 1993 Constitution provides for the phasing in of local government through interim procedures detailed in the Local Government Transition Act.[43] Once these measures have restructured local government, 'democratic' local governments are to be established, based on a mixture of proportional and ward representation[44] designed to ensure a disproportionate representation of the formally non-African sections of town and city. The first phase of this process toward the restructuring of local government is to be achieved by the establishment of a Provincial Committee for Local Government in each of the Provinces, which will be empowered to recognize negotiating forums responsible for negotiating the terms for establishing transitional local or metropolitan councils in the particular areas.[45] Section 11 of the Local Government Transition Act also establishes provincial Local Government Demarcation Boards which may be directed to delimit local government areas and electoral wards within such areas. Once the exact structure and geographical jurisdiction of local and metropolitan governments have been negotiated, local government elections will be held on a day set by the Minister of Local Government for the election of transitional councils – probably in late 1995 or 1996.

Autonomous local government is guaranteed in terms of section 174 of the 1993 Constitution. This guarantee carries with it a constitutional obligation on the part of a local government to 'make provision for access by all persons residing within its area of jurisdiction to water, sanitation, transportation facilities, electricity, primary health services, education, housing and security within a safe and healthy environment'.[46] Although this provision recognizes the socioeconomic rights demanded by the ANC's constituency, it is immediately constrained by the proviso that 'such services and amenities can be rendered in a sustainable manner and are financially and physically practicable'.[47] This attempt to place obligations on government to provide basic services in relation to the government's capacity to deliver these services bears resemblance to the framework for the advancement of socioeconomic rights established under the International Covenant on Economic, Social and Cultural Rights of 1966, but fails to establish any link with the RDP's commitment to empowering community based democratic associations.

Although section 179(1) of the 1993 Constitution requires local governments to be democratically elected, the electoral system for local government established by this section has the effect of establishing a consociational system of local government. Based on a combination of proportional and ward representation, with wards distributed according to old apartheid boundaries rather than in proportion to the number of voters in any particular area, the electoral system ensures that the realities of apartheid geography will provide a veto power over budget allocations at local government level.[48] This will perpetuate a degree of racial representation in local government until either the form of representation is changed or communities become effectively integrated. Whether these provisions granting unequal weight to individual votes will survive a constitutional challenge or whether they will have to wait to be swept aside by the constitutional assembly is not yet clear. However, they will certainly become the focus of political conflict as local sections of the democratic movement attempt to engage the RDP only to find themselves faced with the local embodiment of the government of national unity and the commitment to national reconciliation which made the transition possible.

Constitutionalizing Participatory Democracy

Cosatu's debate on a Workers' Charter revealed a growing concern in civil society – particularly those sections dominated by the democratic movement – that the election of a non-racial government not bring the process of democratization to an end. In addition to ensuring the protection of workers' and union rights in the new constitution the Workers' Charter discussion stressed that the trade union movement consider how other constitutional proposals may help to secure democratic government in the future. Some of the issues discussed were proposals for citizens' initiatives or petition rights which would require the state to submit the challenged issue or law to a national referendum; a limit on the number of terms of office the head of the executive branch may serve; and support for a separate Constitutional Court with powers of judicial review.[49]

Although it can be argued that the constitutional guarantees of freedom of association, assembly, expression and information included in the ANC's proposed Bill of Rights are adequate in that they are at least equal if not more protective than constitutional guarantees in most democratic societies, it must also be acknowledged that even these provisions do not explicitly guarantee the degree of access or participation which would encourage the emergence of participatory democracy. Suggestions that citizens be given the right to petition against particular laws and to demand that referendums be held, or even have the ability to place propositions on the ballot – such as the initiative system in California – go some way toward encouraging participation but still maintain a strict barrier between formal processes or 'the state' and popular participation or 'civil society'. Furthermore, as the initiative system in California has demonstrated, these provisions fail to distinguish between democratic participation and the ability of powerful private interests – particularly large corporations – to use their resources to dominate the debate around an issue placed before the public in a referendum or regular ballot.

However, if increased participation is a means to address the interaction of democracy and diversity it becomes important to clarify exactly what is understood by citizenship and the 'civil society' into which a diversity of citizens will enter in order to coexist peacefully. If we accept that a single notion of the substantive common good will at all times be inadequate to address the dynamics of democratic participation and diversity, then we can begin to understand citizenship not simply as a legal status but rather as a form of political identity.[50] This approach implies an understanding of citizenship which sees a collective identification with a radical democratic interpretation of the principles of liberty and equality – 'understood in a way that takes account of the different social relations and subject positions in which they are relevant: gender, class, race, ethnicity, sexual orientation etc.'[51] This conception of citizenship is furthermore consistent with a notion of civil society that rejects any single notion of the good life and instead posits the associational life of civil society as the ground upon which social beings – as citizens, producers, consumers, members of the nation, and much more – continually work out and test their versions of the good. In the end, the 'quality of our political and economic activity and of our national culture is intimately connected to the strength and vitality of our associations.'[52]

Next, it is necessary to ask whether there are any specific constitutional issues which may be identified as pivotal to the emergence and strengthening of participatory democracy in its various forms, including associational democracy. If such issues are identified, it will become possible to consider whether there is any way to guarantee their promotion or protection in South Africa's new constitution. There are a number of prerequisites to increased participation which we can identify. First, there is the need to enhance the society's organizational capacity, both in terms of the ability of different interests to organize themselves and to engage in democratic governance by gaining access to policy-making and decision-making processes; second, there is the need to gain access to information in order to participate fully in policy debate; and third, there must be the ability both to hold the government accountable and to organize against the government's decisions and actions.

Participation could be encouraged in several ways, both constitutional and institutional.[53] These could include first, the explicit protection of rights and granting of privileges of association and participation to specific organizational forms such as trade unions, civic associations, student organizations and nonprofit, non-government organizations. Instead of relying on the courts and their future interpretation of a broad guarantee of freedom of association, there could be, for example, explicit guarantees of trade unions' right to organize in factories and government institutions and student organizations' right to access to classrooms to organize without fear of expulsion from the school system. The state may also be constitutionally mandated to encourage the formation of voluntary associations through institutions such as a department of community organization through which resources and services could be obtained by communities or associations, in addition to guaranteed free access to public buildings for meetings.

Given the centrality of the legal process under a justiciable Bill of Rights, the state may be constitutionally mandated to facilitate the access of voluntary associations to the legal arena. This would need to go beyond the government's creation of a human rights commission or public protector (ombudsoffice) as are provided for in the ANC draft Bill of Rights[54] and the interim Constitution,[55] but may require a department of public advocacy to include not only public defenders and public advocates, but also a program of direct support to an independent public interest law sector.

Participation is dependent on access to information and to government officials. The provision in the interim Constitution guaranteeing citizens access to 'information ... in so far as such information is required for the exercise or protection of any of his or her right'[56] is inadequate in that it places no explicit limit on the state's right to regulate 'required' information on the grounds of national security, nor does it explicitly establish the right of interested organizations such as trade unions or even environmental groups to gain access to private corporate financial records or documents.

A necessary corollary to the need for information is the ability to gain access to government officials and others involved in policy debates. In the case of proposed legislation this is normally achieved by holding public hearings; but members of the legislature or the government normally decide whether public hearings will be held. Instead, we may include a constitutional guarantee requiring the establishment of a system through which secondary organizations are entitled to notification of proposed legislation or even government regulations and may demand hearings before the bill goes before the legislature or regulations promulgated.[57]

Creating the necessary information on which to make informed decisions is a fundamental aspect of participation. A constitutional mandate that all proposed legislation or government regulation be preceded by a 'social impact study' to determine what impact the legislation is expected to have on the poor, rural and other undeveloped areas of the country or even constitutionally mandated affirmative action programs would require government or the advocates of new legislation to produce research detailing the impact they expect their proposal to have. In response, voluntary organizations active in the particular arena may enter policy debates by evaluating this research or providing counter-information on the expected impact of the new law or policy.

Finally, it is necessary explicitly to protect the right to oppose government action. Not only must there be a right to protest, but there should also be a right to demand and receive a public accounting of actions and decisions taken by government officials; to gain access to public places and buildings to hold meetings; and for voluntary organizations to present and defend their views in the mass media, particularly government-controlled radio and television.

Conclusion

Out of the experience of mass action and popular organization during the anti-apartheid struggle there has come increasing debate and demands for popular participation in the new order in South Africa. As the transition continues there will be a growing debate on the specifics of the future constitution. It is in this context that I have attempted in this paper to outline the problems confronting those who are seeking ways of increasing popular participation in the future and sought to identify specific means through which this process may be encouraged. More specifically, I have attempted to identify a number of constitutional provisions that should either be strengthened or introduced in order to facilitate participation by voluntary associations, including the idea of a social impact statement as a means of focusing debate and public attention on the expected consequences of government action or legislation.

Notes

1. Although the Constitutional Assembly is bound, in drawing up the new constitution, by the constitutional principles included in Schedule IV of the 1993 Constitution, there is in fact a great deal of latitude within these constitutional principles to define the exact content of the new constitutional order. The most important influence on these processes will be the degree and source of political pressure on the various parties to ensure a two-thirds majority for passage of the new constitution.

2. E. Marais and J. Rauch, 'Policing the Accord', 78 *Work In Progress* (henceforth *WIP*) 14 (Oct./Nov. 1991), p. 14, col. 1.

3. Ibid., p. 15, cols 2–3. See also C. Shearing, 'Police and Government: The Quest for Impartial Policing', 78 *WIP* 17 (Oct./Nov. 1991), pp. 17–19.

4. Marais and Rauch, 'Policing the Accord', p. 16, col. 3.

5. G. Daniels, 'Beyond Protest Politics', 76 *WIP* 13 (July/Aug. 1991), p. 13, col. 1.

6. Interview with J. Naidoo, 'National General Strike: "It's more than VAT, it's the entire economy"', 16 (2) *South African Labour Bulletin* (henceforth *SALB*) 13 (Oct./Nov. 1991), p. 13, cols 1–2.

7. G. Daniels, 'The Great VAT Strike', 79 *WIP* 18 (Dec. 1991), p. 19, col. 1.

8. Saccola is the South African Employers Consultative Committee on Labour Affairs; NACTU is the National Council of Trade Unions.

9. See 'Special Focus: The Reconstruction of South Africa' 15 (6) *SALB* 14 (March 1991), pp. 14–33.

234   ASSOCIATIONS AND DEMOCRACY

10. See K. van Holdt, 'Towards Transforming SA Industry: A "Reconstruction Accord" between Unions and the ANC?' 15 (6) *SALB* 17, p. 17.

11. J. Copelyn, 'Collective Bargaining: A Base for Transforming Industry', 15 (6) *SALB* 26 (March 1991), p. 26.

12. K. von Holdt, 'From Resistance to Reconstruction: The Changing Role of Trade Unions', 15 (6) *SALB* 14, p. 16, col. 1.

13. Labor Bulletin, interview with Naidoo, p. 14, cols 1–2.

14. Ibid., p. 14, col. 3.

15. Ibid.

16. See D. Nkosi, 'Building Civil Society for Reconstruction', *The Shopsteward*, vol. 2 (3), June/July 1993, pp. 4–6.

17. Ebrahim Patel, 'New Institutions of Decision-making: The Case of the National Economic Forum', in *Engine of Development?: South Africa's National Economic Forum*, ed. E. Patel, Kenwyn, South Africa: Juta & Co. Ltd 1993, p. 6.

18. See C. Ryan, 'NEF: Likely Results', *People Dynamics*, vol. 11, no. 11, Sept. 1993, pp. 8–12.

19. An example of such engagement in the development process was the agreement between Sanco, Cosatu and the civil engineering industry, which provided a framework for labor-intensive public works projects while averting conflict between the labor movement and unemployed communities. See K. Cullinan, 'Union-Community Clash Avoided', in *WIP* 91 (Aug./Sept. 1993), supplement no. 12, Aug.

20. A. J. Manuel Parraguez, 'The Privatization of the State and Community Legal Strategies in the Democratization of Local Power in Chile', 1 *Social and Legal Studies* 229 (1992), p. 232.

21. The South African debate on the nature of civil society reflects a conflict between the two sources of the concept identified by Cohen and Arato – 'conceptual history and the self-understanding of social movements'. J. Cohen and A. Arato, 'Politics and the Reconstruction of the Concept of Civil Society', in *Cultural-Political Interventions in the Unfinished Project of the Enlightenment*, ed. A. Honneth, T. McCarthy, C. Offe and A. Wellmer, Cambridge, MA: MIT Press 1992, p. 121. See also J. Cohen and A. Arato, *Civil Society and Political Theory*, Cambridge, MA: MIT Press 1992. This conflict is especially evident in the debates between Friedman and Swilling in *Theoria* vol. 79 (May 1992).

22. M. Swilling, 'The Case for Associational Socialism: Socialism, Democracy and Civil Society', 76 *WIP* 20 (July/Aug. 1991), p. 22, col. 1.

23. As reflected in *Work in Progress*, an independent left magazine, and the academic journals *Theoria* and *Transformation*. See D. Nina, 'Beyond the Frontier: Civil Society Revisited', *Transformation* 17 (1992), pp. 61–73.

24. M. Swilling, 'The Case for Associational Socialism: Socialism, Democracy and Civil Society', 76 *WIP* 20 (July/Aug. 1991), p. 22, col. 1.

25. Ibid., p. 23, col. 2.

26. M. Narsoo, 'Civil Society – A Contested Terrain', 76 *WIP* 24 (July/Aug. 1991), p. 24, col. 2.

27. Ibid., p. 25, col. 3.

28. Ibid., p. 27, col. 3.

29. Ibid.

30. Ibid.

31. M. Swilling, 'The Case for Associational Socialism: Socialism, Democracy and Civil Society', 76 *WIP* 20 (July/Aug. 1991), p. 22, col. 1.

32. See P. Q. Hirst, *Law, Socialism and Democracy* (1986), pp. 108–23; and P. Hirst, *Associative Democracy: New Forms of Economic and Social Governance*, London: Allen & Unwin 1994.

33. See M. Dan-Cohen, *Rights, Persons, and Organizations: A Legal Theory for Bureaucratic Society*, Chicago: University of Chicago Press 1986, pp. 55–119.

34. Ibid., p. 83.

35. William W. Fisher III, 'Making Sense of Madison: Nedelsky on Private

Property', 18 (3) *Law and Social Inquiry* 547 (1993), p. 548; *American Constitutionalism: The Madisonian Framework and its Legacy*, Chicago, IL: University of Chicago Press 1990; James W. Ely Jr, *The Guardian of Every Other Right: A Constitutional History of Property Rights*, New York: Oxford University Press 1992.
  36. P. Dexter, 'Make the RDP make the Left', *Work in Progress* 95, Feb./Mar. 1994, p. 30.
  37. ANC, *Reconstruction and Development Programme* (1994), para. 5.2.6, pp. 120–21.
  38. See M. Hlangeni, 'Implementing the RDP', *Mayibuye* 4 (5), May/June 1994, p. 23, col. 2.
  39. *RDP*, para. 5.13.7, p. 132.
  40. *RDP*, para. 1.1.5, p. 1.
  41. *RDP*, para. 5.13.2, p. 131.
  42. *RDP*, para. 5.13.3, p. 131.
  43. Act 209 of 1993.
  44. Ibid., section 179.
  45. Ibid., section 3.
  46. 1993 Constitution, s. 175(3).
  47. Ibid.
  48. 1993 Constitution, s. 176(a).
  49. Copelyn, 'Collective Bargaining', p. 29, col. 3.
  50. Chantal Mouffe, 'Democratic Citizenship and Political Community', in *Dimensions of Radical Democracy*, ed. C. Mouffe, London: Verso 1992, p. 235.
  51. Ibid., p. 236.
  52. Michael Walzer, 'The Civil Society Argument', in Mouffe, *Dimensions of Radical Democracy*, p. 98.
  53. See R. B. Seidman, 'On the Legal Structure of a Vigorous Civil Society: A Research Agenda', unpublished, July 1991.
  54. See ANC Constitutional Committee, *A Bill of Rights for a New South Africa*, Art. 16, paras 6–14 (1990).
  55. *Constitution of the Republic of South Africa*, Act 200 of 1993, Articles 110–18.
  56. Ibid., Article 23.
  57. See H. Klug, D. Davis and E. Mureinik, Submission to the Rules Committee of the Pretoria-Witwatersrand-Vereeniging Provincial Legislature, June 1994.

13

Solidarity, Democracy, Association

Joshua Cohen and Joel Rogers

We are grateful for the comments our paper has provoked – both those published here and those provided in other venues. Spurred in part by them, we have refined our original views in several ways. These refinements include an even starker view of the ways in which current social and economic change limit the appeal of traditional social democratic strategies of democratic revival, and greater clarity on the conditions under which associative artifaction is appropriate. More positively, they include as well arguments for the moral and functional appeal of the 'weaker' organizations, and more transient arenas of democratic deliberation, such artifaction would facilitate.

More clearly than in the original paper, we also see the question of whether associative democracy is a new form of constitutional order or merely a new strategy within the current one to be an empirical one; its answer goes less to the basic conception than to the extent of its adoption. With matters of kind thus reduced to matters of degree, we also permit ourselves a more optimistic view on problems in state capacity – both regarding extant demands on the state and those that artifaction of the associative environment would place. Again more clearly than in the original paper, we now see those problems dynamically related to, and in part solved by, the gradual and structured promotion of associative solutions to social problems we more generally recommend. Such promotion would expand the range of areas in which popular democratic sovereignty could be effected (if not directly by the state itself), and gradually redefine the state's role from 'first problem-solver' to 'first organizer of social capacities for their solution' – a role less taxing than the one it inadequately performs at present. The result of these refinements, finally, *is* a matter of kind – a view of associative democracy less as an amendment to traditional social democratic strategies than as a synthesis of social democracy and radical democracy.

The fact of some change in our own views, along with limitations of space and the diffuse and wide-ranging character of the comments published here, dictates our strategy of response to those comments. Rather than respond to them one by one, or attempt an exhaustive canvass of the varied issues they raise, we intend simply to state our current thinking about associative democracy. As we do so, however, we shall emphasize three points that distinguish our current thinking from that reflected in the original essay and that correspond to three concerns raised in the replies in this volume.

One concern is that our conception of democracy is too 'rich' and expansive. That conception self-consciously incorporates sub-stantively egalitarian and procedurally democratic elements. While each is attractive as a component of a political philosophy, many commentators noted that the components may not be compatible in practice. The first section (Egalitarianism and Democracy) speaks to this concern, both by redescribing our normative ambitions and by indicating their relationship to the notion of associative democracy we advance. More than in our original paper, again, we emphasize the roots of the associative democratic conception in both egalitarian and radical democratic political traditions. We also argue that the current troubles of social democracy may create an especially promising opportunity for unifying those traditions. Far from rendering them practically incompatible, present circumstance suggests that they may be mutually supporting – in particular, that equality may depend on deepening democracy.

A second concern is the relationship of associative democracy to corporatism. With an enthusiasm or alarm that we find equally mis-guided, many commentators read our paper as proposing 'corporatism for America'. Somewhat more plausibly, others understand us to be advancing a postmodern corporatism expanded to include bargaining partners beyond the traditional social partners of labor and capital, and policy arenas beyond the economy. In the next two sections ('Social Democracy and its Discontents' and 'What is to be Done?'), we seek to distinguish associative democracy from these corporatist interpretations. 'Social Democracy and its Discontents' offers a diag-nosis of the crisis of social democracy, and in so doing explains why any simple rejuvenation or inclusion-minded reform of corporatism is not a promising political project. Moreover, in restating the associative democratic project, 'What is to be Done?' emphasizes elements of that project that do not fit the renewed corporatism picture – in particular the idea of *deliberative arenas* for politics that do not privilege the given preferences of actors or their current organization.

A third issue concerns our conception of associations. In a nutshell, many contributors are skeptical about the plausibility of using the powers of the state to alter the associative environment in ways that benefit democratic governance. One particular concern focuses on the functional capacity, or social basis, of the partially 'artificial' associations we recommend. To play a constructive role in an egalitarian-democratic order, many commentators assert, associations must be rooted in common pre-political identities which our 'artificial' associations by definition lack. We address this concern in 'Why Associative Democracy?' Filling a gap in the original presentation, we argue to the contrary that a world with less organically conceived associations and deliberative arenas might have real advantages, both moral and functional, over a world in which groups have more particularistic identities.

Egalitarianism and Democracy

The egalitarian-democratic political project aims at 'a reconciliation of liberty with equality'.[1] Committed to a framework of universal civil and political liberties, it seeks to advance an ideal of *substantive political equality*, ensuring that citizens' political influence is not determined by their economic position, a requirement of *real equality of opportunity*, condemning inequalities in advantage tracing to differences in social background,[2] and a conception of the general welfare giving *priority to the least well-off*.[3]

Until the second half of the twentieth century, such a reconciliation was only a theoretical possibility.[4] But the rise and postwar consolidation of social democracy and its central creation, the modern welfare state, gave the egalitarian-democratic project practical force. Social democracy was always criticized by some egalitarians for accommodating capitalism and by others for excessive statism. Still, it achieved considerable success both in protecting basic liberties and severing the fate of equal citizens from their unequal advantages in the labor market.

Today, however, the characteristic ideology and political practice of social democracy, including the welfare state as a form of social administration and guarantor of equality,[5] are in considerable disarray.[6] With the decline of the social democratic model – at once a *particular* model of egalitarian-democratic governance and the only one to have enjoyed much success – genuine doubts have re-emerged about the prospects for a happy marriage of liberty and equality.

We assume that current difficulties in egalitarian-democratic practice owe less to changes in human nature or aspiration than to what may be broadly classed as 'organizational' problems – specifically, to a mismatch between the characteristic organizing and governance practices of social democracy and changed material conditions. Our question is how this mismatch might be remedied. Given changed circumstances, what institutional model might again advance egalitarian-democratic ideals?

The gist of our view is that advancing egalitarian-democratic ideals requires a social base of support for those ideals; that realizing such a social base requires deliberate attention to its creation; that the appropriate form of attention includes the devolution of certain characteristically state responsibilities to associative arenas of civil society; that such devolution has been made plausible by the same forces that account for the evident disarray in traditional social democratic politics; and that associations with devolved responsibility might help to support democratic political consensus and increase social learning capacities – both essential to stable egalitarian order, and currently in short supply.

As its emphasis on devolution might suggest, associative democracy aims to carry social democracy's egalitarian ideals forward through a more *radical democratization* of traditional egalitarian practice. In so doing, it seeks a *reconciliation* of the radical democratic and egalitarian traditions while moving beyond them both. We offer a word at the outset on the terms of that reconciliation.

The central ideal of radical democracy is to root the exercise of public power in practices of free discussion among equal citizens, with the understanding that the relevant conditions of discussion cannot be confined to formal political arenas.[7] Proceeding from this concern for participation and discussion, radical democrats have expressed persistent disquiet with the *statism* of the egalitarian tradition and of social democracy in particular. They criticize statist versions of egalitarianism for undervaluing the benefits of decentralized authority for citizen education and self-government; for exaggerating commonalities of citizens at the expense of their heterogeneity, and thus promoting an assimilationist conception of social unity; and for advancing a distributive conception of politics that inevitably promotes the administration of passive, consumption-oriented clients rather than self-rule by active citizens.

Telling as these criticisms may be, the *constructive* content of a radical-democratic institutional model has long been obscure.[8] According to some critics of radical democracy, this obscurity should come as no surprise, as it reflects the political irrelevance in a mass democracy of the radical democratic ideal of discussion among equal citizens.[9] The alleged irrelevance has two principal sources. First, mass democracy's characteristic pluralism implies that political discussion cannot assume a unitary community with a shared conception of the good; the absence of such a community raises doubts about the ideal of discussion aimed at consensus. Second, in large societies with complex divisions of social labor, democratic discussion cannot simply replace such conventional mechanisms of social coordination as markets, administrative hierarchies and group bargaining; this throws into question the practical interest of discussion as an organizing principle.[10]

Our proposed reunion of radical democratic and egalitarian traditions seeks to accommodate their mutual criticisms. We think that the radical democrat has identified important limits of statist egalitarianism, and that these limits are now evident in social democratic difficulties. At the same time, in the design of a constructive institutional model, we premiss pluralism and concomitant limits on consensus;[11] we also assume the need for markets, hierarchies and bargaining, and accept the bar their existence imposes on over-ambitious versions of the radical democratic project.

On these terms, how far might reconciliation proceed? We do not know, and the answer makes a difference to how associative democracy is understood. Conceived minimally, associative democracy offers a *strategy* to relieve some of the difficulties of social democracy by harnessing associative energies more deliberately – it provides a tool that can, for example, aid in the performance of regulatory tasks lying beyond the competence of the state. At the (untested) maximum, it suggests a new form of *political-constitutional order*. Characterized simultaneously by greater reliance on non-state institutions to define and resolve social problems, the application of more exacting standards of universalism on those institutions and more deliberate efforts to construct requisite social solidarities, this order would comprise a rival to the traditional social democratic welfare state.

Social Democracy and its Discontents

How did social democracy work in its heyday, and why has that day passed?

First and last a working-class political project, social democracy offered 'soft' redistribution[12] toward workers and limited power-sharing, in both the firm and the state, between workers and capitalists. Social democratic economic policy relied on Keynesian alchemy to transform the particular interests of workers to general social interests. Wage increases or state-led redistribution toward labor increased effective demand, which was captured by domestic firms supplying employment; stabilization of markets encouraged investment, which increased productivity, which lowered the real costs of consumption goods, which, along with wage increases, spurred further consumption and rising living standards for all. In everyday politics and governance, strong industrial union movements made deals with 'monopoly' capital directly – in centralized systems of wage-bargaining – or through the state – classically, exchanging wage moderation for commitments to increased social welfare spending and guarantees of full employment.[13] By relieving some of the competition among capitalists, these deals facilitated cooperation between the classes in meeting the more stringent standards on capitalist performance they also imposed.

What undid social democracy most basically was the collapse of a series of key background conditions that supported the advances just described. Most prominently these included:[14]

1. A *nation-state* capable of directive control of the economic environment within its territory. This control assumed a national economy sufficiently insulated from foreign competitors that the benefits of demand-stimulus could be reliably captured within its borders, and a monetary policy apparatus sufficiently insulated from world-wide financial flows to permit unilateral correctives to recession. Of particular relevance to social cohesion, the sheer competence of the state in managing the macroeconomy – Keynes's central discovery – provided compelling material reasons for participation in national political discourse.

2. The organization of capital into a system of *mass production*[15] and an economy dominated by large, lead, stable firms in different key industry clusters. Such firms provided ready targets for worker organization and levers in extending the benefits of organization throughout the economy they dominated. In the mass production setting, firm stability – underwritten by demand stabilization policies – also meant career stability for the workers within them. Stability of mass producers and careers in turn facilitated the evolution of the 'industrial' model of union organization, centered on centralized bargaining and joint administration of the internal labor market.

3. The overwhelming dominance of *class concerns* in the politics

of equality. The dominance owed to the existence of a more or less determinate working class, the strength and superiority of whose organization dwarfed other secular, non-business organizations and concerns. Aided by pre-existing 'organic' solidarities and all manner of social restrictions, the distinctiveness and integrity of this class was assured by the leveling tendencies of mass production. These both limited the force of traditional craft divisions and, on the assembly line, forcefully clarified the distinctive interests of labor and capital.

These premises, both institutional and social, can no longer be taken with confidence. Instead, current circumstances include:

1. More sharply delineated *limits on and of the state*. Increased internationalization of product and capital markets has qualified the old Keynesian alchemy. Simple unilateral reflations can no longer proceed in confidence that increased demand will be met by domestic firms. The same factors have enlarged domestic capital's possibilities of exit from progressive national tax regimes. In addition to new limits on the state, moreover, changes in the sorts of problem the state is asked to address or in the background conditions under which it does so have highlighted longstanding incapacities of state institutions.[16]

In economic policy, for example, concern has in some measure shifted from macroeconomic demand stabilization to the intricacies of moving individual firms or industries toward higher and more socially satisfying levels of performance. This has underscored the limits of 'strong thumbs' and the need for local cooperation and 'nimble fingers' of the sort the state commonly cannot provide or secure. In social policy, the hollowing out of communities and other sources of informal self-regulation, along with irreversible increases in female labor market participation, have encouraged the state to take on functions previously discharged by families or communities with sensibilities and local knowledge unavailable to it. The increase in generic regulation of capital – in, for example, the areas of environmental regulation or occupational and safety and health – has underscored the difficulty of applying general standards to dispersed, heterogeneous sites, or imposing a particular solution prior to negotiation among affected actors. And the concatenation of these problems with a widening range of citizen demands[17] has underscored the degree to which successful governance strategies require coordination and negotiation across traditional policy domains or organized interests, and then often in areas so murky or turbulent as to defy any single correct or stable solution. From this, all manner of problems with legitimation and administration follow.[18]

The unsurprising result of these changing problems and background conditions is that the state is commonly, and in considerable measure properly, perceived as incompetent. It lacks the monitoring and enforcement capacity to make rules stick; it is inefficient in its required compliance strategies; it is incapable on its own of solving any truly complicated social problem.[19]

2. The collapse of traditional mass production, and with that collapse, *increased social heterogeneity*. Competition among firms has vastly increased and in response the organization of production has changed. Whatever the final result of the ongoing battle among different strategies of response – from simple sweating of labor to lean production to the many variants of high-skill strategies geared to product distinctiveness – virtually all appear to disrupt the commonalities of experience that provided the foundation of traditional industrial unionism. There is greater firm decentralization and, within more decentralized units as well as across them, greater variation in the terms and conditions of work, the structures of career paths and rewards, the marketability of heterogeneous skills. Even before it is enlarged by variations across worksites, moreover, workforce heterogeneity is underscored by increased mobility of workers across firms, the casualization of much employment and the increased distance of worksites from homes.

In addition to immensely complicating the development of general standards on economic performance and wage and benefit equality, increased workforce heterogeneity disrupts the possible agent of such equalization. It goes without saying that any political project needs a social base which supports that project against opposition. Given possibilities of defection from general social norms – possibilities enlarged by the existence of markets – egalitarian-democratic alternatives must be especially attentive to the need for social integration and solidarity. Again, social democracy found that base in a working class partly 'made' under conditions of mass production.[20] But the world of relatively stable employment for workers performing relatively common tasks in relatively stable firms has widely disappeared, 'unmaking' the working class as a mass agent. Moreover, because the articulation of work and family within the welfare state meant that conceptions of class were gendered, the increases of women's labor market participation have had similar effects. In brief, workforce heterogeneity now approximates the heterogeneity of the broader society, qualifying the working class as a determinate agent of that society's transformation.[21]

3. Increased *political heterogeneity* within the broader class of

citizens who might support egalitarian ideals. In addition to social solidarity, any political project needs agreement among its agents on the terms of that project, and that agreement must be sufficiently encompassing to provide the fuel for mass action. Social democracy dealt with the problem essentially by declaring class interests to be – in a way braved rhetorically since Marx but demonstrated materially only after Keynes – universal. Assuming the primacy of the class cleavage, it solved a problem for capitalism – and so for everyone – by redistributing to workers.

Today, however, not just this particular universal class, but the idea of universalism itself, is in disrepair. As an organizational matter, no single set of institutions – save perhaps, business firms – is sufficiently powerful to *impose* its interest as the general interest. And as a matter of ideology, none but the sectarian are prepared to elevate any particular interest – whether class or gender or race or the environment or sexual toleration – to that exalted status. Even where, as is less and less the case, political party organization remains a site of broader convergence, that convergence suffers from its distance from the most vital organizations and practices within this divided field. The convergence is less passionate than that found in old social democratic parties fueled by an insurgent labor movement. Nor is there any obvious basis in everyday life and culture for some other-regarding universalism of new citizen subjects. If anything, indeed, the relentless commodification and privatization of civic culture, combined with a general failure to refashion eighteenth-century political rights in light of late twentieth-century conditions, makes the informed, active, other-regarding citizen increasingly fugitive.

With its means of administration widely regarded as incompetent or worse, its social base decomposing and its political cohesion come unstuck, little wonder that social democracy has fallen on hard times. For those committed to egalitarian-democratic ideals, these troubles underscore the need to look for an alternative institutional model. But such a model cannot simply derive new institutions and policies from attractive principles of justice. It must also take the sources of disruption of social democracy seriously. And that means presenting an institutional model that successfully addresses or avoids these problems in constructing a social base for that alternative.

What is to be Done?

The problems of social democracy have generated considerable disarray among people sympathetic to its egalitarian aims. Here we sketch three lines of response, distinguishing them by the implications they draw from the declining social base of social democracy.

Lowered Expectations

One characteristic response to social democratic difficulties is to lower expectations – to take the decline of social democracy as signalling the impossibility of realizing the procedural and substantive political values that define the egalitarian-democratic project.

A popular version of this response begins by noting the new heterogeneity of politically relevant identities – the dominance of an 'identity politics' – and concluding that the more encompassing solidarities required to advance any egalitarian project have irreparably collapsed. In a social world densely populated by hyphenated, particularistic identities, citizens will not be prepared to 'regard the distribution of natural talents as a common asset and to share in the benefits of this distribution whatever it turns out to be' or to 'share one another's fate'.[22] Without the relevant solidarities, the fact that some people have 'drawn blanks rather than prizes in the lottery of life'[23] may be mourned but it cannot be remedied. The best political hope is a commitment to fair procedures for collective decision-making among unequals.

Considered on its own terms, such a chastened aspiration to a merely procedural justice risks incoherence. It assumes, implausibly, the robustness of fair procedures independent of substantive agreement. Associated with that, it draws an overly sharp distinction between the solidarities required to sustain fair procedures, which it assumes to be relatively thin, and the attachments required to sustain substantive fairness, which it supposes to be relatively thick.[24] Moreover, it presumes an implausible fixity of current, fissiparous political identities.

Intellectual coherence aside, among those committed to egalitarian-democratic ideals the position should only be considered in default. Premissed on the unavailability of something better, lowered expectations should only be accepted after that premiss is truly tested.

Redefined Property Rights

Social democracy sought to meliorate the consequences of the exercise of capitalist property rights through popular organization and political power. Leaving the basic assignment of those rights undisturbed, it countered them with unions, political parties and the welfare state. With problems having emerged for these organizational forms, one egalitarian strategy is to alter that basic property rights assignment – to redistribute initial property rights – and to construct new sorts of markets for their exercise. In essence, the strategy is to accommodate the decline in social democracy's organizational basis by focusing attention on reordering economic background conditions.

John Roemer's recent market socialist scheme is an example of such a strategy.[25] Premissing the importance of markets as sources of dynamic efficiency, Roemer's proposal would promote greater equality by distributing the profits of firms to citizens – giving citizens shares that can be traded on a stock market, that cannot be cashed in and that revert to the state on the holder's death. Samuel Bowles and Herbert Gintis have suggested a similar 'asset-based redistribution' approach.[26] They propose to remove productivity-suppressing wealth inequalities while enabling average citizens to vote with their feet (vouchers, etc.) in the accountability of public institutions, and to protect citizens from the vicissitudes of the market by constitutionalizing certain citizen property rights – for example, to benefits in the areas of health, education, training and disability insurance.

Should egalitarian democrats endorse such strategies? Certainly, any fairer distribution of property rights is to be welcomed. And certainly, properly designed markets can provide powerful accountability mechanisms on runaway or incompetent government. On these terms, then, at this level of abstraction, the answer is 'absolutely'.

But any endorsement should stop short of agreement that the organizational issue can be fully ignored or treated as a sociological supplement to an already well-defined and robust new property rights regime. To be sure, the property rights variant of egalitarianism makes an important point: realist assumptions of market governance under capitalism and of pluralism and dissensus within politics, along with attention to the decline in 'organic' solidarities of all kinds, recommend economizing on the scarce motives of trust and solidarity. Still, *some* such motives are necessary. And that means that some strategy for achieving them – if need be, through deliberate encouragement and construction – must also be at the core of any new egalitarian model.

Trust and solidarity are important because no social design is strategy-proof. No matter how careful its initial setup[27] or ingenious its incentives to equality-enhancing behavior, those motivated only by self-interest or narrow group concerns will find a way to spoil it. And once they do, even those earlier prepared to be bound by minimal solidaristic norms will depart from them; to be solidaristic is not, after all, to be a dupe. The stability of any egalitarian scheme depends, then, on a social basis of support more robust than the qualified support among the self-interested, who might be offered a generally attractive property rights regime. To maintain equality, it needs an egalitarian political culture and a 'civic consciousness' in its participants congruent with egalitarian ends.[28]

Such consciousness cannot, moreover, depend exclusively for its institutional support on the fact that individuals enjoy the status of equal citizenship. Assuming democratic conditions and rights of association, organized groups will emerge which provide potentially competing bases of political identity, with dispersed 'veto powers' to block alternatives that do not conform to their particular ends. So, a political culture sympathetic to equality requires support in those groups themselves. Such organizations must be sufficiently rooted in the particularity of individual experience to be regarded by members as compelling expressions of their identity and instruments of their interests. At the same time, they need to be congruent with a general interest in equality – else the constitutionally equalizing property regime falls prey to the same group rent-seeking and particularism that now plagues all pluralist democracies.

In short, there is no way round the problem of ensuring a social base for egalitarian governance. If existing institutions do not provide it, new ones must be built. And the need to build them must inform the overall conception of an egalitarian political project.

Reconstruction

Without gainsaying the importance of procedural fairness or, certainly, a fairer or smarter distribution of initial property rights, strategies of reconstruction aim more directly at the problem of the missing social base.

Most such strategies are pursued within an explicitly social democratic frame – to 'reinvent' social democratic parties as appealing to a collection of particular interests beyond those of labor, or 'reinvent' labor unions as something more than collective bargaining institutions (or at least as bargaining institutions concerned with more than wages and working conditions). They propose, however, no fundamental alteration of the traditional social democratic model now in difficulty. If our diagnosis of social democracy's problems is right, those problems lie deeper than such conventional strategies of reconstruction suggest. Whatever their immediate importance, then, for our purposes such conventional strategies are not very interesting.

We come, then, to our own associative strategy. We begin with a now familiar premiss: any working egalitarian-democratic order requires an organized social base. We assume that what was true of the social democratic model is true of any egalitarian model operating under mass democratic conditions with rights of association: secondary associations are needed to represent otherwise under-represented interests (e.g. trade unions supporting redistributive policies) and to add to state competence in administration (e.g. trade unions and employer associations negotiating standards on training). We observe the obvious: that the right kinds of association do not naturally arise in either the representative or more functional spheres. Pathologies of inequality and particularism abound in representation, while the range of areas where associative sorts of governance or assistance is imaginable in theory but not available in practice is vast – and, we believe, expanding.

Putting the need for a favorable associative environment together with the fact that such an environment is not naturally provided, we propose a deliberate use of public powers to promote the organiza-tional bases needed for egalitarian regimes – to encourage the development of the right kinds of secondary association. Where manifest inequalities in political representation exist, we recommend promoting the organized representation of presently excluded interests. Where group particu-larism undermines democratic deliberation or popular sovereignty, we recommend efforts to encourage the organized to be more other-regarding in their actions. Where associations have greater competence than public authorities for achieving democratic ends, or where their participation could more effectively promote political values, we recommend encouraging a more direct and formal governance role for groups.

We concentrate here on this last recommendation – the more deliberate use of associations in regulation – both because of its relative concreteness and because it, perhaps more clearly than the other recommendations, suggests both the minimum and maximum possi-bilities of associative democracy: its appeal as a strategy and as an alternative order.[29]

In our earlier discussion of the limits of the state, we sketched the background problem of state regulation in general terms.[30] For reasons ranging from a wider array of social concerns to the decline of tradi-tionally 'self-regulating' institutions, the state is called on to declare and enforce standards of performance in a vast range of areas. In some areas, such declaration and enforcement is fairly straightforward. Broad purposes are clear or readily discernible through legislative debate; centralized mechanisms of monitoring and enforcement – supplemented by civil liability schemes or field inspectorates – suffice to generate compliance; ongoing negotiation of terms is unnecessary or even unwelcome.

But in four broad classes of cases – each densely populated with issues of social concern on which state action is sought – things are not so straightforward:

1. Where government has the competence to set specific regulatory terms, but the objects of regulation are sufficiently numerous, dispersed or diverse to preclude serious government *monitoring* of compliance. Many workplace regulations – on appropriate wages and hours, compensation and especially the appropriate organization of work, pertaining for example to occupational health and safety – provide instances of this monitoring problem.

2. Where government has the competence to set general standards of performance, but the objects of regulation are sufficiently diverse or unstable to preclude government specification of the most appropriate *means* of achieving them at particular regulated sites. Much environmental regulation is of this kind. Although the state is competent to declare general air quality standards and end-of-pipe abatement goals or standards of toxic source reduction, divergent and changing technologies or production patterns constantly shift the efficient strategies for achieving these goals; and what is most efficient or appropriate is known only by those with local knowledge of heterogeneous circumstances.

3. Where government may (or may not) be able to enforce standards once set, but cannot set appropriate *ends* itself.[31] Often, an appropriate standard can only be determined by those with local knowledge not readily available to government, or can only be specified as the outcome or in the context of prolonged cooperation among non-government actors. Industry standards on product or process uniformity and performance are often of this kind. So too are education and especially training standards. The appropriate norm shifts constantly; the content of the norm derives from cooperation in the process of its establishment.[32]

4. Where problems are substantially the product of multiple causes and connected with other problems, crossing conventional policy domains and processes. In such cases, the appropriate strategy requires *coordination* across those domains as well as cooperation from private actors within them. Urban poverty, local economic development and effective social service delivery are among the familiar problems that

occupy this class. None can be solved without cooperation across quite different institutions and groups – lending institutions, healthcare providers, technology diffusers, education and training establishments, housing authorities, community development corporations, neighborhood associations – operating wholly or substantially outside the state itself. These and other 'stakeholders' in the problem and its proposed solution, however, typically have distinct if not competing agendas, and different identities and interests.

When these sorts of problems are encountered – and as described they are more or less coextensive with modern regulation – our associative approach recommends explicit harnessing of the distinctive capacity of associations to gather local information, monitor compliance and promote cooperation among private actors by reducing its costs and building the trust on which it typically depends. In those areas where the problems are more or less *functionally specific*[33] – where ends are set but monitoring capacities need to be enhanced, or means or ends are uncertain but the area of concern is narrowly cabined – European social democracy is rife with examples of just such associative governance. As a general matter, they are most developed in the areas of workplace regulation and training, and rely on institutions controlled by the traditional 'social partners' of labor and capital. The use of plant committees to enforce occupational safety and health regulations, for example, or groupings of trade unions and employers to facilitate technology diffusion, or employer and union associations to set standards on training, are all familiar.

We have suggested that the lessons of practice in these areas be more explicitly generalized to include non-traditional stakeholders, and that where necessary appropriate supports for that generalization be deliberately constructed. Moreover, as the scope of associative efforts moves beyond functionally specific problems to issues that are decidedly more sprawling and open-ended – as in the urban poverty or regional economic development examples – the associative strategy recommends the construction of new arenas for public deliberation that lie outside conventional political arenas,[34] and whose ambit is not exhausted by any particular interest solidarity at all.

Notice, however, that both the inclusion of non-traditional stakeholders and the decline of functional specificity suggest a new possibility: that the bases of social solidarity may partially shift from 'found' commonalities rooted *outside* the process of defining and addressing common concerns – and relating to those concerns only incidentally or in ways not transparent to those doing the relating – to commonalities that are, and are understood to be, constructed *through* that process. It is one thing for a well-funded union to be asked to participate in the design of training standards of obvious concern to it as well as the broader society. It is quite another for an underfunded community environmental organization to gain significant resources (and thus greater organizational life) on condition of its assistance in the design of an environmental 'early warning' system, and for those recruited to that project to be recruited essentially on the basis of public service, or for a neighborhood association and economic development corporation in a poor community to receive assistance conditional on their jointly organizing a training program for parents and a childcare program for trainees as part of a broader job-training effort.

Such solidarities will, of course, differ from those rooted in common culture and life circumstance. They will be the bonds of people with common concerns – say, a concern to address persistent urban poverty – treating one another as equal partners in the resolution of those shared concerns.[35] But the bonds arising from participation in such arenas, in the solution of large and commonly recognized problems, need not be trivial or weak; and they could be strengthened by the repeated experience of cooperation itself. There is, after all, no limit to the number of arenas that might thus be constructed, then folded on the completion of the task; no restriction on the number of times individuals or groups might have the experience of such joint problem-solving under conditions that are defined only by their intended facilitation of that problem-solving.

The role of deliberative arenas in the associative conception is perhaps the sharpest expression of its radical democratic inspiration. To highlight the importance of such arenas, it may help to conclude this sketch by distinguishing associative democracy from another project of radical democratic inspiration: the project of building economic democracy around worker cooperatives or self-management at the level of individual firms.

Increased workplace democracy would be an important social improvement, and we certainly believe that associational rights within the workplace should be strengthened to that end. But we are much less confident than traditional workplace democracy advocates that the firm provides an appropriate unit of organizational analysis in the construction of a democratic society.

The reason why goes back to the stylized facts of social democratic decline offered above. In a world of high mobility across firms and heterogeneity of interests within them, the individual firm per se is diminished as a locus for the aggregation of interests and formation of solidarities. While the degree to which the real economy approximates a 'virtual' one – with Moebius-like boundaries between carnivalesque firms and plastic identities of workers within them – is commonly exaggerated, we take it now to be beyond question that an exclusively firm-based system of economic democracy no longer fits the actual economy.[36] In addition to institutions within firms, then, we need mechanisms of economic democracy articulated on a supra-firm basis. Moreover, the fact of political heterogeneity indicates a need for different mechanisms to address different dimensions of concern; for example, wages, education and training, environment, health and safety. We need, in short, more broadly defined deliberative arenas than those suggested by workplace democracy.

If the social solidarity arising from practice within such deliberative arenas were not trivial, it would comprise a sort of *tertium quid*: a form of solidarity operative in civil society, transparently not 'natural' or 'found' or particularistic, not based in direct participation in the national project of citizenship, but definitely founded on participation in deliberative arenas designed with a cosmopolitan intent.

An ample supply of this new kind of solidarity, finally, at least hints at a way through the present morass of social democratic distemper and increasingly barren exchanges between radical, participatory democrats and statist egalitarians. At once more efficient in administration and more directive of secondary association, more encompassing in its ambitions and less indicative on all but the terms of civil deliberation, more attentive to the construction of solidarity but less patient with its found forms, here associative democracy the *strategy* might become associative democracy the different *order*.

Why Associative Democracy?

For some, this associative democratic project may appear fanciful, or worse. Objections to it might be summarized as charges of undesirability, impossibility and futility – respectively, that the associative strategy will give rise to new and dangerous forms of group abuse of organized power; that it cannot get started because patterns of group organization and behavior lie beyond deliberate politics; that it will not work because the associations it fosters lack the very characteristics that make associative solutions attractive.

Because we have addressed the undesirability and impossibility objections at length elsewhere,[37] we give them short shrift here. Suffice it to say that the undesirability objection understates the extent to which the current group system infirms egalitarian-democratic order, while the impossibility argument exaggerates the fixity of associations, beginning with the assumption that secondary associations are a product of nature, or culture, or some other unalterable substrate of a country's political life.[38]

Concentrating, then, on the futility objection, the issue is this. Assume that the impossibility objection is wrong and that the structure of the secondary associative environment is indeed subject to influence and artifaction. Still, such artifaction may come at the expense of the very features that make secondary associations attractive. These features derive principally from the ability of associations to elicit cooperation and trust among otherwise disconnected subjects. But this ability depends, the objection goes, on the experience of associations as organized expressions of a pre-political identity. As the politics of associations grows increasingly deliberate and intentional, then, associations will lose their distinctive ability and thus add less to more remote forms of governance. The more social solidarities are not simply found but fabricated, the less useful they are in addressing real problems.

Our response to this objection accepts its premiss about the change in character of associations that follows from artifaction, but draws more optimistic conclusions about the implications of that change. That is, we agree that the solidarities engendered in our proposed practice would be different from 'natural' solidarities – different, at a minimum, because they would not be experienced as natural and would lack the dense cultural texture associated with things so experienced. But rather than treating these differences as deficiencies, we think they are *desirable*, given the changes in the world that provide our point of departure.

How could this possibly be? How could more cosmopolitan but thinner solidarities be exactly what is needed now? The answer has both moral and functional elements. It concerns both the fit of such new solidarities with the need for democratic consensus and the contribution such new solidarities might make to social learning.

New Solidarities and Morals[39]

To see the case on the moral side, recall the social and political heterogeneity we take to be standing features of the world. Such heterogeneity makes it difficult to achieve consensus on a political conception of justice, including the conception summarized by egalitarian democracy. This is a problem. Consensus on political fundamentals is desirable for any conception of justice, and is particularly important for an egalitarian conception operating under the realist constraints – capitalism, markets, strategic behavior – we elsewhere accept.

For any conception of justice, consensus increases the likelihood that the order will stably conform to the conception. Moreover, consensus directly promotes a variety of more specific values – social trust and harmony, social peace, simplified decision-making, reduced monitoring and enforcement costs, and (assuming the consensus is reflected in public debate and decisions) reduced citizen alienation from public choices. Furthermore, it helps reconcile the ideal of an association whose members are politically independent and self-governing with the fact that social and political arrangements shape the self-conceptions of members and limit their choices.[40] Consensus also encourages mutual respect among citizens – with political argument offered in the form of considerations that others are willing to accept and state action justified and cabined by the same considerations.

Reaching such consensus under democratic pluralist conditions, however, is difficult. The reason is that a political consensus that reflects values of self-government and mutual respect must be arrived at under free conditions, including the protection of basic expressive and associative liberties. And under such conditions citizens will be drawn to competing comprehensive moral, religious and philosophical outlooks – with some founding their political values on an Aristotelian ideal of human flourishing or a Kantian morality of autonomy or conscientious religious conviction and others endorsing pluralistic moralities which combine relatively autonomous political and personal values. A political consensus suited to such conditions, then, cannot rest on any particular comprehensive outlook.

But a consensus on a *political* conception of justice can perhaps survive such *moral* pluralism. Citizens endorsing conflicting moral, religious and philosophical convictions may still enjoy an 'overlapping consensus' on a political conception that includes principles of justice, political values such as fairness and toleration, and a conception of the person identifying relevant features of citizens from a political point of view.[41] Citizens might endorse the same political *theorems*, as it were, even as they derived those theorems from different moral, religious and philosophical *axioms*. What is essential is that the value of fair cooperation among equals finds support within each of their respective sets of axioms (as it does within the comprehensive views offered in illustration above).

Political consensus is possible, then, under conditions of pluralism. But possibility is one thing and real practicality is another. Practicality depends, at a minimum, on the availability of institutional mechanisms that might promote an overlapping consensus. Are there any such mechanisms?

One ready answer is that consensus is advanced by political discussion within a stable democratic process. Assuming consensus on constitutional democracy, the fact that individuals and parties need to win support for their views and projects puts pressure on their views to accommodate the deeper idea of citizens as equal persons, both reconfirming the constitutional consensus and at the same time deepening and extending it.[42]

Consider, for example, the evolution of the political rhetoric and project of socialist parties in this century.[43] They begin the century with a class project, presenting themselves as agents of the industrial working class; they expect the maturation of capitalism to turn the working class into a majority of the population; and they understand that they can only sustain their claim to serve as an agent of the working class if they participate in democratic politics, winning near-term gains by winning elections. But the identification of the industrial working class with the majority is increasingly baffled by its numerical minority status in the population. Hence their electoral dilemma. To serve that class through elections they need to win elections, but winning elections means extending their political appeal beyond the working class itself. The result is that socialist parties – at least those that preserve electoral commitments – universalize their appeal and address themselves to all citizens, as equals. As Przeworksi observes:

> Differentiation of the class appeal ... reinstates a classless vision of politics. When social democratic parties become parties of 'the entire nation,' they reinforce the vision of politics as a process of defining the collective welfare of 'all members of the society.' Politics once again is defined on the dimension individual-nation, not in terms of class.[44]

But while political argument under democratic conditions can deepen consensus by encouraging commitments to the idea of citizens as equals, formal political arenas are unlikely to foster widespread commitment to the value of fair cooperation among equals if that commitment is too sharply at odds with convictions formed outside the public political arena. Consider a state whose citizens are divided into two religious groups with strong religious identities, whose members live entirely separate lives, never associating with members of the other group. In such a world there are no social pressures for religious convictions themselves to accommodate the idea of citizens as moral equals. Apart from the epiphanies of national politics there is no experience that supports that idea – no regular practices of discussion in which each group is called upon to find terms that the others can accept.

And so we ask: are there practices *outside* the formal political arena that are educative in the ways of overlapping consensus – schools of overlapping consensus that encourage non-particularistic forms of solidarity? We would argue that the experience of cooperation within specifically artifactual arenas of deliberation appears to provide just such encouragement.

Such arenas are 'schools of democracy' in a special way. Apart from generating enlarged sensibilities and encouraging a sense of competence and self-confidence, they foster solidarities congruent with the mutual respect among citizens that lies at the heart of overlapping consensus. This is especially so when coordination is not functionally specific. Deliberative arenas established for such coordination bring together people with very different identities. Successful cooperation within them should encourage willingness to treat others with respect as equals, precisely because discussion in these arenas requires fashioning arguments acceptable to those others. In this respect a social world in which solidarities are formed in deliberative arenas is distinct from a social world in which arenas (other than the state itself) have more particularistic cast, perhaps encouraging comprehensive views to which values of fair cooperation among equals are foreign. Organic solidarities stand in a more tenuous relationship to the equal citizenship than do artifactual solidarities built on a background of common purposes and discussion.

To emphasize, associations and deliberative arenas are not and are not intended to be alternative loci of solidarity as classically understood. Nor is the intent to supplant existing comprehensive moral or religious views with new ones. The idea is that the bonds they foster are more like the solidarities of citizenship. They develop shared ground among people with different identities and views, thus encouraging the elaboration of comprehensive views in ways that are congruent with values of fair cooperation among equals. The effort might be thought of as one of 'decolonizing the life world' – of establishing arenas of discussion that lie outside the formal political system and are not mediated by money and power. What we claim is that just such an effort is what is needed today to establish an overlapping consensus on an egalitarian-democratic conception of justice.

New Solidarities and Functions

What we have just argued as a moral matter may also be argued functionally, with the virtues of looser solidarities now translated into practical benefits in matters of governance.[45]

For functionally specific sorts of problems, the case for the benefits of integrating secondary association in regulative governance is made easily enough. Often, to recur to our ideal-typical classes of regulatory problems, the *monitoring* of compliance with clear norms across numerous or dispersed sites overtaxes the capacities of state inspectorates; and often, within well-defined problem areas, specific *means* to the achievement of compliance with agreed standards are best left to the discretion of local actors. In such circumstances, the recruitment or encouragement of extra-state popular capacities in the achievement of regulatory goals is often recommended, and secondary associations are a natural target of recruitment. Always, of course, there are problems in identifying the appropriate groups in civil society and in guaranteeing against their domination in local sites or their abuse of the public powers effectively devolved to them. But none of these problems seems intractable. If workers in firms are assigned monitoring and enforcement powers in occupational safety and health, they clearly need training in the exercise of those powers and to be linked back into the wider system of state enforcement. If neighborhood groups are permitted to negotiate local compliance strategies with area polluters, the deals they arrive at must themselves be reviewed in the light of broad statutory purposes. Throughout, however, the specificity and clarity of those purposes provides a legitimating framework for devolution.

As functional specificity declines, however, things become more interesting. We begin to approach such areas when the precise *ends* of policy are unclear, even if there is broad background agreement on the purposes against which those ends are measured.

Consider again the example of training. The precise breadth and depth of skill standards in what is *already understood* as an occupationally-based human capital system is usefully subject to local negotiation. Such negotiation can also be mandated and encouraged by the state with some confidence that the range of outcomes is more or less cabined and the relevant players in the discussion are more or less known and not subject to challenge. But changes in firm production strategies owing to changes in the external terms of competition, and spillovers from human capital decisions to other areas of social concern (e.g. gender equity) may begin to disrupt such confidence, throwing the routines of policy formation into question.

Generally stated, as the range of social concerns implicated in any given problem area shifts or expands, or as the interdependence of solution strategies in different areas becomes more obvious or fluid, we can expect administrative or legitimation difficulties. In such cases, social problems typically do not correspond to the competences of *any* particular state agency or any particular found group or interest. In consequence, addressing such problems requires coordination within the state across its formal decision-making or administrative machinery in different policy domains, and agreement on that coordination with the relevant – and mutually distant – private actors affected by each. To solve such problems, routinely what is needed within the state, but *especially* among scattered private actors, is some institutionalized learning capacity – a capacity specifically to identify new problems and experiment with solutions that disrespect existing organizational boundaries and competences.

But this learning capacity will not be forthcoming in the absence of discussion and negotiation across such bounded interests and organizations. And that discussion and negotiation, for familiar reasons, is unlikely to happen at all, let alone routinely, without encouragement. What is needed is the deliberate construction of arenas for such deliberation, and deliberate inducements to enter them.

That the state could engage in such construction and inducement we take to be just short of uncontroversial. Typically in any given problem area, the range of affected interests is known to the state, even if it is not organized. And certainly, the promise of a solution to the relevant problem itself provides inducement to discussion. So too would be signals from the state that its policies and future distribution of sanctions and supports would be shaped by that discussion – for example, through offers of state support to selected projects generated out of arenas in which stakeholders address common concerns. Indeed, the demarcation of such deliberative arenas that bring together organizations concerned to address commonly recognized social problems is *easier* for the state than direct efforts to revive solidarity. Easier, that is, than imposing its view of civic vitality on a neighborhood, or attempting to specify the new terms of worker culture, or founding a new religion, or in some other improbable way seeking literally to construct the sorts of deeper and more particularistic solidarities that have been eroded.

The only relevant questions about such an exercise concern purpose and effect. Are problems of this kind widespread enough to warrant deliberate attention? And would the construction of new deliberative arenas not based on strong prior solidarities – initially, not based on anything stronger than a common commitment to addressing an issue of serious social concern – plausibly generate the desired learning capacities?

Our short answer to the first question is yes – just such problems now occupy a growing, dominant share of commonly recognized problems. That they do explains many of the governance problems of the modern administrative state. The legitimacy and effectiveness that under classical liberal legal regimes was secured by enforcing abstract rules on the terms of individual contracting, and in more innocent times in the welfare state secured by discrete interventions in cabined problem areas of visible concern only to major actors in those areas,[46] is today denied a state asked to accommodate a wider range of substantive concerns but lacking the capacity to coordinate across them. Holding social organization fixed, problems are thus increasingly defined in ways that point up the impossibility of their solution. On the one hand, most important problems require the cooperation of a wide range of 'stakeholders'. On the other, the lack of vehicles for the coordination of those stakeholders – accepted as a tragic fact or as a residue of senseless modernization or the politics of the 'claimant state' – precludes that cooperation. From this perspective, then, the construction of arenas of deliberation attractive to such stakeholders is of *surpassing* importance.

Should the effort be successful, notice at once its legitimacy effects for the state itself. Instead of being held responsible for its failure to solve problems that all recognize it cannot solve on its own, the state could throw back to civil society a large share of responsibility in devising and implementing their solution. It would say: 'In this area we all know, however rarely we admit it, that the following interests are at stake; if you get in a room together and, under reasonable conditions of deliberation, come up with a plan, the government will help you implement it.' The role of government in such a scheme would in effect be to help staff the deliberation, to set the broad requirements of participant inclusion, to ensure the integrity of the process and, finally, to authorize the strategy conceived. It would devolve power to the civil society, but under universal terms not now embraced by its members. It would retain its own capacities for final authorization, but with the confidence that decisions made would enjoy, from the moment of their enunciation, organized social support. It would, in short, establish a more coherent, and acceptable, definition of its role in social governance.

But is there much reason to expect success? To answer this question, consider first the effects such a process, such a style of governance, might plausibly have on the participants in it.

Assuming fair conditions of discussion and an expectation that the results of deliberation will regulate subsequent action, the participants would tend to be more *other-regarding* in their political practice than they would otherwise be inclined to be. Just as constitutionalized respect for democratic practice affects formal political strategies, so it would affect informal ones. The structure of discussion – the requirement of finding terms that others can agree to – would plausibly drive argument and proposed action in directions that respect and advance more general interests. Moreover, pursuing discussion in the context of enduring differences among participants would incline parties to be more *reflective* in their definition of problems and proposed strategies for solution; it would tend to free discussion from the preconceptions that commonly limit the consideration of options within more narrowly defined, stand-alone groups. Furthermore, *mutual monitoring* in the implementation of agreements would be a natural byproduct of ongoing discussion.[47] And, assuming progress toward solution, we would also see growing confidence in the possibility of future *cooperation*.

If these claims about effects on participants are right, then the functional benefits of deliberative arenas are clear. For example, other-regardingness would encourage a more complete revelation of private information. This information would permit sharper definition of problems and solutions, straightforwardly adding learning capacity. At the same time, reflectiveness would, by suspending conventional preconceptions, lead to a more complete definition and imaginative exploration of problems and solutions. Combined with such informed and inclusive definition, mutual monitoring would heighten the willingness to experiment in solution strategies, itself bringing additional learning effects. Cooperation in those strategies would permit an expansion of the capacities they could draw on, making success more likely.

In all these ways, then, deliberation about common problems with diverse participants might thus reasonably be thought to enhance social learning and problem-solving capacity. The relative 'thinness' of the common identity as participants – both entering the process of deliberation and leaving it – here begins to look like a real benefit.

Moreover, as this strategy was pursued more routinely, as the deliberate construction of deliberative arenas across groups became more or less standard operating procedure, and as group experience of it was repeated in partially overlapping arenas and problem clusters, we could expect the character of groups to change. At the margin, they would shift toward practices more geared to multivalence, open-endedness and learning. The unsubtle mechanism of this expected effect is twofold. On the one hand, the new character becomes more available, settled and familiar through repetition itself. On the other, the fact that this character is sought and rewarded in governance induces its consolidation.

Greater openness and experimentation would, in turn, alter our expectations about what it means to be an effective association or interest group. Some forms of joint firm-community management of environmental problems, or joint labor-feminist-environmental-health-education community-led strategies of economic development in major cities, or multi-firm and multi-union efforts to establish regional wage or product quality norms already suggest that participation changes the internal institutional character and behavior of their participants in the ways we have described.[48] Just as labor-management cooperation in one area commonly has the side-effect of promoting cooperation in others, with cumulative effects eventually affecting global strategies and expectations of their respective members, so too cross-group discussion and exploration of joint strategies alters internal group governance and membership expectation. Under such conditions, the conception of effective representation itself shifts. Instead of meaning that the representing group expresses a particular core demand of its members, it comes to mean that the group acts with a more comprehensive understanding of the good of its members and is more open to addressing that good cooperatively.

Given the changes in the economy and society inventoried above, such internal institutional reform and behavioral change is precisely what is needed in administration and governance *generally*. As the organization of production changes, as new demands are put on human capital systems, as career paths become less certain, as the boundaries of firms become less definite, as the reconciliation of diverse social interests stands ever more clearly as a precondition for the solution of common problems, as found solidarities disappear . . . what could be more helpful in social management than the promotion of solidarities of deliberative learning, mutual respect in navigating change, openness to new institutional forms, provisional commitments to supporting those forms given like commitment by others – all developed under terms of universalism, with a practical intent?

Conclusion

We have been arguing that the sorts of new solidarity engendered by an associative democratic strategy – more provisional and open-ended than the found solidarities of particularism, with benefits for learning capacity and pragmatic functionality, more cosmopolitan not just in their framing but in their own content – are well suited to a pluralist democracy going through rapid change and needful of new forms of governance both more socially rooted and more adaptive than the state or fierce particularism can provide.

But are these 'new' solidarities redundant? More cosmopolitan groups, with learning capacities, deliberating about public ends . . . isn't that what the state and citizenship are supposed to be about? Perhaps associative governance makes sense when it comes to monitoring occupational safety and health laws or devising a new training regime – functionally-specific duties that have in the past been devolved to groups. But particularly in functionally nonspecific areas, isn't this a very long way around to an active citizenry? Isn't one state enough?

Our response here is roughly that the objection names our project correctly, but draws the wrong conclusion. It is true that we are promoting what once marched under the banner of 'citizenship'. But the fact that it no longer marches indicates the utility of the project. Once more, our starting point is the decline of a base of active and informed citizens supportive of egalitarian democracy. If such a base can be engendered by the more explicit engagement of citizens in social problem-solving, under universalist terms of deliberation, then value is indeed added.

Assuming some such addition, moreover, the broader point is this. Statist forms of egalitarianism have fallen on hard times because they premissed natural solidarities which have now eroded; given that erosion, the state itself appears distant from, hostile to or incapable of the solution to real-world social problems. Radical democracy has long called for the effective liquidation of the state into more socially rooted popular governance; but it must now confront not just the need for the universal ordering that can be provided only by the state but as well the dissolution of the social base on which it presumptively relies. Threading between these failures while drawing lessons from both, we have here suggested a different route for egalitarian governance: use the state in part to construct solidarities; pursue that construction by focusing on recognized problems, with partial agreement at least on their existence and need for solution; and set the deliberative arenas within a democratic state that imposes universalist constraints on the processes and content of their solutions. The result of this is that practices within civil society come to look more like the state, even as they are given more autonomy from the state and assigned a proportionately greater role in governance. Radical democracy and egalitarianism are joined through a state that stakes deeper social roots in a more cosmopolitan civil society.

Whether such reunion will ever be achieved is one more thing we simply do not know. And how the order it implies – in which the state-society distinction is blunted by the existence of a plurality of deliberative arenas standing in uncertain relations to conventional political ones – might be constitutionally regulated is something on which we do not wish to speculate here. What we are persuaded of, however, is that something like this sort of order is in fact possible and desirable. It can be imagined, there are intimations of it all around us and it may well be necessary to the advance of egalitarian-democratic ideals.

Acknowledgment

An earlier version of this paper appeared in Wolfgang Streeck, ed., *Staat und Verbände. Sonderheft der Politischen Vierteljahresschrift*, Wiesbaden: Westdeutscher Verlag 1994. Along with the contributors in this volume, thanks to Charles Sabel for countless discussions of this subject.

Notes

1. As cited in John Rawls, *A Theory of Justice*, Cambridge, MA: Harvard University Press 1971, p. 204.

2. Ronald Dworkin ('What Is Equality? Part Two: Equality of Resources', *Philosophy and Public Affairs* 10 [Fall 1981], pp. 309–11) calls this a conception of 'starting gate equality'.

3. This priority need not be absolute, but it does imply that greater gains among the more advantaged get less weight than improvements among people who are less well-off. For the classic argument for priority, see Rawls, *A Theory of Justice*; also Thomas Nagel, *Equality and Partiality*, New York: Oxford University Press 1991.

4. At least since John Stuart Mill, some political theorists have held out the prospect of reconciling broad rights of suffrage, protections of basic individual liberties and greater distributive equality. See, for example, Keynes's remarks on 'social philosophy' in *The General Theory of Employment, Interest and Money*, New York: Harcourt Brace 1964, ch. 24. Not until the 1950s, however, did we have an up-and-running, practical model of such reconciliation.

5. There is no consensus on the degree to which the modern equality-promoting welfare state can survive without explicit organizational commitments to an ideal of egalitarian democracy. Some seem to believe that individual citizen commitments to the welfare state make it robust even in the absence of such organization. With the possible exception of very general insurance programs (in particular, health and old

age insurance), we doubt it. This is only one instance of our general doubts about stand-alone, 'asset-based redistribution' models, discussed above.

6. We take this claim to be uncontroversial. For a review of some of the electoral evidence, see (ignoring his bizarre commentary on the US case) Seymour Martin Lipset, 'No Third Way: A Comparative Perspective on the Left', in Daniel Chirot, ed., *The Crisis of Leninism and the Decline of the Left: The Revolutions of 1989*, Seattle: University of Washington Press 1991, pp. 183–232; or, taking account of recent gains, 'The Left in Western Europe: Rose-tinted Visions', *Economist* 331 (11–17 June 1994), pp. 17–19. The *Economist* discussion sharply underscores our point about the need for a constructive model.

7. The ideal, as Jürgen Habermas ('Further Reflections on the Public Sphere', in Craig Calhoun, ed., *Habermas and the Public Sphere*, Cambridge, MA: MIT Press 1992, p. 446) puts it, is to establish 'all those conditions of communication under which there can come into being a discursive formation of will and opinion on the part of a public composed of the citizens of a state' (see also Joshua Cohen, 'Deliberation and Democratic Legitimacy', in Alan Hamlin and Phillip Petit, eds, *The Good Polity*, Oxford: Blackwell 1989, pp. 17–34). Habermas's own version of this ideal also emphasizes the restricted scope of discussion: discourses 'generate a communicative power that cannot take the place of administration but can only influence it. This influence is limited to the procurement and withdrawal of legitimation. Communicative power cannot supply a substitute for the systematic inner logic, of public bureaucracies. Rather, it achieves an impact on this logic "in a siege-like manner"' (Habermas, 'Further Reflections on the Public Sphere', p. 452). Our conception of associative democracy is more ambitious, perhaps because we are less struck by the 'systematic inner logic of public bureaucracies'. In any case, we do have 'communicative power' picking up some of the work of the administrative state, not simply imposing a siege upon it.

8. For one effort to remedy that obscurity, see Roberto Unger, *False Necessity*, Cambridge: Cambridge University Press 1987, pp. 441–539.

9. As Carl Schmitt (*The Crisis of Parliamentary Democracy*, Cambridge, MA: MIT Press 1985, p. 6) stated this view, without nuance: 'the development of modern mass democracy has made argumentative public discussion a mere formality'. See also Max Weber, *Economy and Society*, vol. 3, Guenther Roth and Claus Widditch, eds, New York: Bedminster Press 1968, pp. 1381–469; and Joseph Schumpeter, *Capitalism, Socialism and Democracy*, New York: Harper & Row 1942, chs 21–2.

10. On the contrast between discussion and these other means of coordination, see Jon Elster, 'The Market and the Forum: Three Varieties of Political Theory', in Jon Elster and Aanund Hylland, eds, *Foundations of Social Choice Theory*, Cambridge: Cambridge University Press 1986, pp. 103–32; and Cohen, 'Deliberation and Democratic Legitimacy'.

11. Though we do not agree that pluralism excludes consensus. See above, pp. 253–6.

12. The term comes from Samuel Bowles and Herbert Gintis, 'An Economic Strategy for Democracy and Equality', unpublished mimeo, 1993. Redistribution was 'soft' in the sense that it proceeded in a context providing increased living standards for all, even if the disproportionate share of that increase was captured by the less well-off.

13. The expansion of the welfare state – both in expenditures and formal guarantees – was, of course, intimately tied to the maintenance of effectively full employment. The latter provided the tax base for expenditures, while reducing the rate at which safety-net protections were invoked. The social democratic welfare state was always a high-employment welfare state.

14. While the story has been told many times, the next three paragraphs draw from Joel Rogers and Wolfgang Streeck, 'Productive Solidarities: Economic Strategy and Left Politics', in David Miliband, ed., *Reinventing the Left*, London: Polity Press 1994, pp. 128–45.

15. We recognize that not all production was 'mass' in the relevant sense – that craft was not obliterated – and that there was considerable variation in the forms of mass production, but still find this generalization useful.

16. To be more precise, these incapacities are not just 'longstanding', but more or less definitive of modern state governance.

17. See the discussion of political heterogeneity above, pp. 243–4.

18. For details, see above, pp. 257–9.

19. Understandable, then, the declaration of the Partito Democratico della Sinistra, in *L'Italia verso il 2000: Analisi e proposte per un programma di legislatura*, Rome: Editori Riuniti 1992, p. 136: 'We have abandoned every preconceived sympathy for the public sector ... because it is not justifiable in light of the principles which our party supports: the satisfaction of needs, and therefore efficiency in the supply of goods and services, equality, solidarity, and democracy.' Cited in Bowles and Gintis, 'An Economic Strategy for Democracy and Equality'.

20. On the evolution of social democracy as a working-class project, see Adam Przeworski, *Capitalism and Social Democracy*, Cambridge: Cambridge University Press 1985, pp. 7–46.

21. Of course, working-class solidarity also drew from sources outside the firm – from working-class neighborhoods, for example, or shared cultures outside work. But the news gets no better here. Neighborhood life today, which is both more planned (by a distant state) and anarchic (made so by a faceless capital) than in the past, is less visibly authored by residents. Culture is deeply commodified and privatized (shopping and watching TV consume most leisure time, usually pursued alone). The decline in such community life threatens even the most limited of egalitarian practices by making the organization of people, on whom any such practice depends, more costly. But a more ambitious egalitarianism, rooted in more encompassing understandings of self than those defined by narrow communities, is also threatened with their disruption. Commodification and the extension of administrative power have not only eroded the agency of particular communities. In doing so they have undermined the socialization practices that, while particular, sustained citizens in the exercise of a more universal and other-regarding public reason. As Habermas ('Further Reflections on the Public Sphere', p. 453) observes: 'A public sphere that functions politically requires more than the institutional guarantees of the constitutional state; it also needs the supportive spirit of cultural traditions and patterns of socialization, of the political culture, of a populace accustomed to freedom.'

22. Rawls, *A Theory of Justice*, pp. 101, 102.

23. Milton Friedman, *Capitalism and Freedom*, Chicago: University of Chicago Press 1962, p. 163.

24. See Joshua Cohen, 'Pluralism and Proceduralism', *Chicago–Kent Law Review* 69, 3 (1994), pp. 589–618 for an attack on the importance of this distinction in political argument.

25. John Roemer, *A Future for Socialism*, Cambridge, MA: Harvard University Press 1994.

26. Bowles and Gintis, 'An Economic Strategy for Democracy and Equality'.

27. And under realistic conditions, just how careful could it possibly be?

28. We would say the same of suggestions – for example, that made by Philippe C. Schmitter, in 'Corporative Democracy: Oxymoronic? Just Plain Moronic? Or a Promising Way out of the Present Impasse', unpublished mimeo, Stanford University 1988, and this volume, Chapter 7 – that aim directly at opening the market on representative institutions themselves, in part by subsidizing citizen support of them. While we are all for such opening and subsidy (in campaign finance, consumer affairs, worker organizing, environmental concerns, etc.) we do not see them as a panacea for current imperfections in pluralist representation. Pathologies of particularism will abound even if those of inequality are partly remedied; and remedies on the inequality front will need to be continually revisited for correction, which will not be successful unless it can draw on social support for equality itself. Nor does the effort do much (or, in fairness,

claim to do much) to solve the problems of popular regulatory capacity – as against representative equality – that also concern us.

29. As the text suggests, our emphasis on regulation is not only a matter of convenience. We think associative democracy is most plausibly first advanced in areas where there is clear need of additional popular regulatory capacity. Without making too much of the point, this emphasis on an associative politics of regulation, as against simply representation, is one difference with Schmitter (see note 28), Iris Marion Young (*Justice and the Politics of Difference*, Princeton, NJ: Princeton University Press 1990, and this volume, Chapter 11) and others focused more exclusively on problems in representation.

30. See above, pp. 242–3.

31. Or it can set them only in very abstract terms, for example, as requirements of 'reasonableness' or 'due care'.

32. The problem is complicated by the fact that the standards of business performance themselves – quite apart from more particular standards on products or processes – are continually shifting, especially in this age of 'continuous upgrading' as the accepted goal for advanced firms. See Charles Sabel, 'A Measure of Federalism: Assessing Manufacturing Technology Centers', *Research Policy*, forthcoming, for useful discussion. Taking this point seriously elides the distinction between this category of regulation and that considered immediately below.

33. Corresponding more or less to the first three classes of cases described above.

34. Though to the extent that they receive public support, they are to be subject to constitutional constraints, in particular guarantees of equal protection.

35. This claim depends, of course, on the background assumption of a democratic state protecting basic liberties and ensuring equal protection.

36. The carnival metaphor comes from Tom Peters, *Liberation Management*, New York: Fawcett Ballantine 1992, pp. 15–17.

37. In addition to the earlier essay printed here, see Joshua Cohen and Joel Rogers, 'Democracy and Associations', *Social Philosophy and Policy* 10 (Summer 1993), pp. 282–312; Joshua Cohen and Joel Rogers, 'Associative Democracy', in Pranab Bardhan and John Roemer, eds, *Market Socialism: The Current Debate*, New York: Oxford University Press 1993, pp. 236–52; and Joshua Cohen and Joel Rogers, 'My Utopia or Yours? Comments on *A Future for Socialism*', *Politics & Society*, 1994.

38. Robert Putnam (*Democracy and the Civic Community: Tradition and Change in an Italian Experiment*, Princeton, NJ: Princeton University Press 1992) seems to have this view: if your associative environment is not good, your only option is to 'get a history'.

39. The discussion that follows draws on John Rawls, *Political Liberalism*, New York: Columbia University Press 1993, lectures 1 and 4; Cohen, 'Pluralism and Proceduralism'; and Joshua Cohen, 'A More Democratic Liberalism', *Michigan Law Review* 92, 6 (1994), pp. 1503–46.

40. When a consensus on norms and values underlies and explains collective decisions, citizens whose lives are governed by those decisions may still be said to be independent and self-governing. Each citizen endorses the considerations that produce the decisions as genuinely moral reasons and affirms their implementation.

41. On the ideas of overlapping consensus and political conception of justice, see Rawls, *Political Liberalism*, lecture 1.

42. Robert Dahl (*Democracy and its Critics*, New Haven, CT: Yale University Press 1989) suggests this. He discerns a 'rough pattern' in the idea of the intrinsic equality of human beings 'has steadily gained strength as an element in the constitutional consensus and political culture' (ibid., p. 187) along with the associated requirement of giving equal consideration to the interests of citizens. Dahl urges that stable democracy requires constitutional consensus – a widespread belief in the value of democratic process and 'habits, practices, and culture' (ibid., p. 172) suited to that belief. But he suggests as well that constitutional consensus tends to a deeper, overlapping consensus

extending beyond democratic process to 'an ever more inclusive commitment to ideas like intrinsic equality and equal consideration' (ibid., p. 179).

43. Przeworski, *Capitalism and Social Democracy*, pp. 7–46.

44. Ibid., p. 28.

45. Our case bears a certain affinity to Unger's 'negative capability' argument about the practical benefits that flow from less fixed forms of identity and less entrenched social practices, to Habermas's suggestions about a connection between social learning and more reflective forms of identity, and to Sabel's 'learning by monitoring'. See Unger, *False Necessity*, pp. 277–312; Jürgen Habermas, *Communication and the Theory of Society*, Boston: Beacon Press 1979, pp. 130–77; and Charles Sabel, 'Learning by Monitoring: The Institutions of Economic Development', in Neil J. Smelser and Richard Swedberg, eds, *The Handbook of Economic Sociology*, Princeton, NJ: Princeton University Press 1994, pp. 137–65.

46. Consider here most industry-specific regulation, which described an 'interest group' politics, intent on rent-seeking, widely taken to be definitive of modern regulatory efforts.

47. See Sabel, 'Learning by Monitoring'.

48. For evidence from cases directly known to us, see Joel Rogers, 'The Wisconsin Regional Training Partnership: A National Model for Regional Modernization Efforts?', in *Proceedings of the 46th Annual Meeting of the Industrial Relations Research Association*, Madison: Industrial Relations Research Association 1994, pp. 403–11; and Joel Rogers, 'Sustainable Milwaukee: A Community Plan for Metropolitan Economic Development', unpublished mimeo 1994.